IRREVERENT

guide to

New Orleans

Frommer's

IRREVERENT guide to New Orleans

5th Edition

By
Malia Boyd

Wiley Publishing, Inc.

other titles in the

IRREVERENT GUIDE

series

Irreverent Amsterdam
Irreverent Boston
Irreverent Chicago
Irreverent Las Vegas
Irreverent London
Irreverent Los Angeles
Irreverent Manhattan
Irreverent Paris
Irreverent San Francisco
Irreverent Seattle & Portland
Irreverent Vancouver
Irreverent Walt Disney World®
Irreverent Washington, D.C.

About the Author

A New Orleans resident since 1995, **Malia Boyd** has written about the city for *Travel & Leisure, Food & Wine, Child, Fortune,* and *Frommer's Budget Travel Magazine,* among other publications. She also co-authored the *Compass American Guide to the Gulf South.*

Published by:
Wiley Publishing, Inc.

111 River St.
Hoboken, NJ 07030-5774

ISBN 0-7645-7147-8

Interior design contributed to by Marie Kristine Parial-Leonardo

Editor: Stephen Bassman
Production Editor: Tammy Ahrens
Cartographer: Nick Trotter
Photo Editor: Richard Fox
Production by Wiley Indianapolis Composition Services

For information on our other products and services or to obtain technical support, please contact our Customer Care Department within the U.S. at 800/762-2974, outside the U.S. at 317/572-3993 or fax 317/572-4002.

Wiley also publishes its books in a variety of electronic formats. Some content that appears in print may not be available in electronic formats.

Manufactured in the United States of America

5 4 3 2 1

Acknowledgments

Thanks to Stewart Yerton and Aliina Penn for their invaluable assistance on this project.

A Disclaimer

Prices fluctuate in the course of time, and travel information changes under the impact of the varied and volatile factors that influence the travel industry. We therefore suggest that you write or call ahead for confirmation when making your travel plans. Every effort has been made to ensure the accuracy of information throughout this book and the contents of this publication are believed correct at the time of printing. Nevertheless, the publishers cannot accept responsibility for errors or omissions or for changes in details given in this guide or for the consequences of any reliance on the information provided by the same. Assessments of attractions and so forth are based upon the author's own experience and therefore, descriptions given in this guide necessarily contain an element of opinion, which may not reflect the publisher's opinion or dictate a reader's own experience on another occasion. Readers are invited to write to the publisher with ideas, comments, and suggestions for future editions.

Your safety is important to us, however, so we encourage you to stay alert and be aware of your surroundings. Keep a close eye on cameras, purses, and wallets, all favorite targets of thieves and pickpockets.

CONTENTS

INTRODUCTION

They're building a Wal-Mart in the Lower Garden District. Mississippi has knocked Louisiana off as the most politically corrupt place in the country. And New Orleans has plummeted from number 1 to number 22 on the America's Fattest Cities list. In any other part of the world, citizens would see these developments as great leaps forward. Positive evolution. Progress.

Not here.

Along with the deaths of Ernie K-Doe and Tuba Fats, the decamping of Vampire novelist Anne Rice to the countryside, and the committal of Ruthie the Duck Lady to an old folks' home, they are seen by many as blows—big ones—to the singular character of New Orleans. Next thing you know they'll be canceling Mardi Gras and inviting Yanni to play at the Jazz Fest. In a city that's been around for 300 years and resisted floods, pestilence, and the Protestant work ethic, change of any kind is typically about as welcome as a West Nile–infected mosquito. Heck, our biggest claim to fame, the French Quarter, is nothing more than a 300-year-old termite cafeteria being held together by fancy wrought iron and a few tenacious bricks.

Yes, these broken-down shotgun houses of ours, these old-timey, Frenchified street names, these scratchy jazz tunes from the beginning of the previous century, these are the things, the ancient, immutable things, we value most. So fearful of change are some folks here that every time something does morph—the big ugly casino building that went up at the foot of Canal Street,

Map 1: New Orleans Neighborhoods

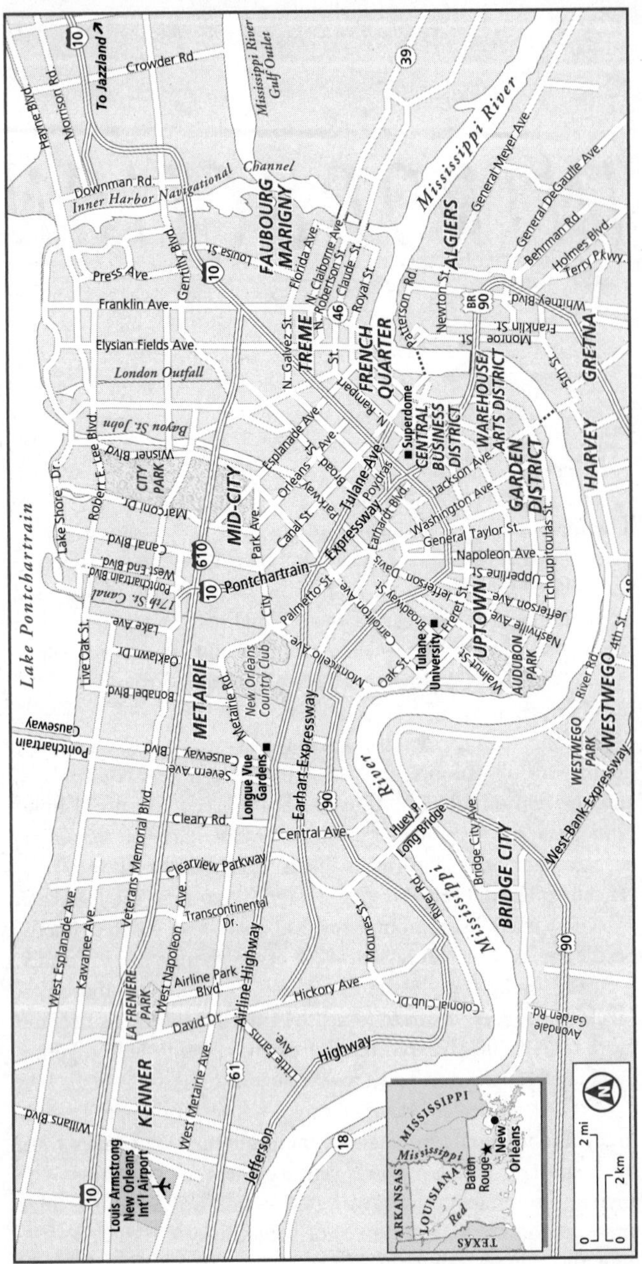

the much-loved department store that was turned into a Ritz-Carlton, the integration of the Old Line Mardi Gras krewes—they get their panties all up in a wad and proclaim it a harbinger of doom. "We are losing our uniqueness! Pretty soon New Orleans'll be indistinguishable from any other city in the South!" Well, guess what? No matter how many Wal-Marts, Gaps, and Starbucks open up here, New Orleans is never going to become "Anytown, USA," and here's why:

1. **History.** We've got a centuries-long past peopled by scoundrels and eccentrics. What happened back then is done, etched into our books, and no one can take that away from us. It informs everything that we are. For instance, some of our first European inhabitants were French convicts who were given a choice by the crown of rotting in jail or resettling in Louisiana. Colorful people? You bet. The next big immigration wave was a huge group of folks tricked into coming by a crooked Scot running a rotten real estate scam. Those two points alone speak volumes about our gene pool. And it sure goes a long way in explaining why corruption is endemic here at all levels. After all, our forebears were all cons and rubes.
2. **Jefferson Parish.** Luckily for us we've already got anonymous, characterless suburban wastelands on all sides. Why try to reinvent the wheel in Orleans Parish when you can just go to Metairie or the West Bank?
3. **The people.** Where else will you find a city that has a district attorney with a lounge act? A city coroner who moonlights as a jazz trumpeter? The ex-lover of a former president of the United States singing torch songs? Only in New Orleans will a nasty feud between the Chicken King (Al Copeland, the founder of Popeye's Fried Chicken) and the Vampire Queen (author Anne Rice) make front-page news. Only in a one-of-a-kind city could it be considered the pinnacle of high-society success to wear a blond pageboy wig, rhinestones, and tights as the King of Carnival does. Nowhere else do you get the Mardi Gras Indians, who spend an entire year creating elaborate costumes of feathers and beads so they can parade around the city staging mock battles with other tribes. Even the people who are gone stay with us: Perri the Hobo, the drunken street clown who made balloon sculptures for kids

while regaling their parents with dirty jokes; Ernie K-Doe, the self-proclaimed Emperor of the Universe who tramped around town in a cape and crown singing his inimitable tunes; Ruthie the Duck Lady, dressed in a bridal gown, sometimes on roller skates, always followed by a line of waddling ducks. Sure, every city has its collection of freaks and fruit loops. But in New Orleans, we celebrate and venerate ours. Big Easy eccentrics aren't limited to the lowest rungs of society, either. Here, we'll even vote 'em into office.

4. **The traditions.** We've got too many of them and we take them all *very* seriously. For instance, did you know that even though it is *not* a federal holiday, there is no mail delivery in New Orleans on Mardi Gras day? That's right, those mail carriers'll go through rain, sleet, or snow, but they won't miss a parade. Jazz Fest? Locals routinely get mysterious illnesses on that Fest Thursday and find that the best way to recover is to take a sick day and get some music therapy. And let's not forget our laissez-faire attitude towards drinking. Passengers can legally drink liquor in cars around many of these parts; we have drive-thru daiquiri shops; and we were the *last* state in the union to cave in to a 21-year-old drinking age, which is still only vaguely enforced. And if walking around with a go-cup sounds like something people only do on a drunken night on Bourbon Street, think again. Every year at the very pious Holy Name of Jesus School fair (set in a polished Uptown neighborhood), along with kiddie rides, bake sales, and midway games, they also hawk beer, Bloody Marys, and margaritas for those parents who can't wait 'til after noon for their tequila. Oh yeah, and one more tradition that really sets us apart: shooting guns into the air on New Year's Eve. That's right, despite the fact that people have been hit and killed by the falling bullets and there's a major police effort to quell offenders, every year you hear it—our citizens acting like a bunch of Pashtoun tribesmen firing their AK-47s and Glocks into the night sky to mark a new beginning.
5. **The *joie de vivre*.** There's a certain upbeat feeling here, a relaxed attitude. In our swampy, pungent world, every day has the lightness and anticipation of a Friday. It's

> why we dance at funerals. It's why we talk longingly of our next meal while we still are voraciously consuming our first. It's why some of our men are the most beautiful women you've ever seen.
>
> Perhaps this attitude goes all the way back to the city founders, who looked at this mushy land where nothing grew but alligators and mosquitoes and breezily said, "Yeah, we can build a really cool city here."

Certain alarmists may fear the imminent demise of New Orleans every time a building is repainted or an entertainer dies or another Applebee's throws open its doors. But they'd be wasting some perfectly good angst. It's taken us 300 years to get where we are. The city is not going to wash away overnight. Okay, well, actually, it could. But it won't be Wal-Mart or virtuous politicians or stricter liquor laws that do it. It'll be that Category 4 hurricane that comes into the Gulf from the southeast and blows up just to the west of the river. On its way in it'll bust the riverside levees, and on its way out it'll flood the lake, burying the entire city under 20 feet of water. Now *that* may well be enough to put the kibosh on the Big Easy for good.

But more than likely, survivors would grab their mama's cookbooks, their saxophones, their go-cups, and their guns and wait for the waters to go down so they could start rebuilding—just as they have so many times before.

YOU PROBABLY DIDN'T KNOW

What is the French Quarter, and why is it so famous?... Today this part of town is a far cry from the canebrakes and squishy swamplands the French fashioned into a colony back in 1718. Locals call it "the Quarter," but the exit sign off I-10 reads VIEUX CARRE—"Old Square," *en français*. The Quarter is home to about 4,000 Orleanians, but it's also the city's biggest tourist draw. For a whole slew of visitors, the Quarter means only one thing: Bourbon Street, named for the 18th-century French royals and not, as it may seem, from its scent and reputation for the adult beverage. Locals know that Bourbon is hardly the be-all of the Quarter. For them, the Quarter means breakfasting on croissants and café au lait at Croissant d'Or and lunching at Galatoire's; grocery shopping at the Royal Street A&P or Matassa's; picking over fresh produce at the Old Farmers' Market; tending to the profusion of subtropical plants in their courtyards; browsing through the musty old books at the Librairie or Beckham's; having a gin-based Pimm's Cup cocktail at the Napoleon House; and trying to maintain as much privacy as possible in a major tourist center. The Quarter wears its age (about 300 years) well, all done up with narrow streets overhung with lacy, wrought-iron balconies; little 18th- and 19th-century buildings and cottages with gables, dormers, French windows, and shutters; and hidden courtyards bursting with banana trees and subtropical blooms. Skyrocketing rents—perhaps due to an influx of glitzy Hollywood types—in the Vieux Carré are already beginning to force some longtime residents out. Perhaps it's true that all good things must come to an end.

Who lives in the French Quarter?... Behind those batten or louvered shutters, Quarterites are happily at home in various sleek condos, creaky attics, chic town houses, and quaint gingerbread cottages. The live-and-let-live ambience of the neighborhood attracts not only a sizable and visible gay community, but also celebrities who are able to live in relative peace and quiet. Homeowners include Lenny Kravitz, Francis Ford Coppola, and Taylor Hackford. Lindy Boggs, ambassador to the Vatican, has a lovely home in the Quarter on Bourbon Street. There are also local artists and musicians; a slew of writers; waiters; doctors; and lawyers—probably even a few candlemakers.

Is New Orleans a city of aristocrats or lowlifes?... It's both. Uptown, the Garden District (including St. Charles Ave.), and parts of the lakefront area are all bastions of old-line, old-money Orleanians. It is those folks who turn up, for the most part, on the society pages of the *Times-Picayune* and who uphold the rituals of the city's most revered blowout. During Mardi Gras, flags of various kings and queens of Carnival are displayed on palatial mansions along St. Charles Avenue, symbols of the "royalty" that reside within. It is these clubby, staid, and stolid business professionals who don sequins, plumes, capes, and masks in order to toss trinkets and bikinis from three-story-high floats lurching along Canal Street. The Quarter is a whole different story, a mixed bag of politicians, professionals, ordinary folk, and sundry street people who make the word "diversity" seem stilted.

How do locals pronounce the name of the city?... That's hard to say. Literally. The average Joe New Orleanian pronounces it something like "New *Or*-luns." Certain city folk (who we can't help but think are trying to put on airs) have taken to calling it "New *Or*-lee-uns," like some kind of Frenchified throwback. True old-timers of a certain social standing call it—this is especially hard to capture in print—"New Oyuns." And though the town is papered with various promos, ads, and such in which the word "N'Awlins" appears, there are not many people who actually drop the "New" that emphatically. Feel self-conscious with any of these pronunciations? Well, if you say "Noo Or-*leens,*" you may as well have a large, red letter Y branded on your forehead, you Yankee. And just to further complicate things for outsiders, Orleans Street and Orleans Parish are both pronounced Or-*leens.* Not fair, is it? Incidentally, don't expect anyone in the Big Easy to have a stereotypical Southern accent—for reasons of immigration patterns, they sound much more like they came down recently from Brooklyn. And note that locals tend not to use the terms "Crescent City," "Big Easy," and certainly not "The City That Care Forgot," though you'll hear the media use those nicknames.

What does "Creole" actually mean?... Like the French Quarter population itself, the definition for the word "Creole" has evolved over the years. Back in the Quarter's colonial days, a Creole referred to anyone of French descent born in la Nouvelle Orleans. Once the Spanish took over for their brief stint at running the show, the definition expanded to include their descendants as well. In the meantime, as the slave trade picked up, more and more people of African heritage came to call the place home. Slaves, as in many places across the country, had little to no rights or standing. But there was a class of blacks called *gens de couleur libre* (free men of color) who populated the city and were also called Creoles. Nowadays you hear the term much more often attached to styles of architecture, like a Creole cottage, or produce, like a Creole tomato. Or, of course, the delicious Creole cuisine, which tends to blend aspects of each of the aforementioned cultures, plus Italian for good measure.

What's the scoop on voodoo? Real? Or a sham to take in tourists?... Voodoo, as promoted by the Historic Voodoo Museum on Dumaine Street, is a prime tourist attraction, but you'd be hard-pressed to find true voodoo when you visit. It's estimated there may be some 20,000 believers in voodoo in the New Orleans area, the overwhelming majority of them African Americans, but the uninitiated are never privy to secret rites. The believers do consider voodoo a religion, and those who practice it take it very seriously. Originating centuries ago in the West African province of Dahomey (now the Republic of Benin), voodoo was transported to these shores by slaves in the late 18th and early 19th centuries. Following the slave uprisings in Saint-Domingue (now Haiti) at the turn of the 19th century, voodooists flooded New Orleans and south Louisiana, their pulsating drumbeats, blood sacrifices, snakes, and frenetic dancing instilling terror in the hearts of whites. There are some shops that sell potions, oils, and the voodoo charms called gris-gris (pronounced *gree-gree*), which you can find in the Shopping chapter. But don't expect to see anything very authentic.

Where can you rent decent Mardi Gras costumes?... For the New Orleanians who stay in town, Carnival is a family event. They'll spend weeks, if not months, making costumes for all the kids and cousins, then get all dolled up and take picnics to the parade routes. While most self-respecting folks here make their own, there are always the uninspired souls who'd rather rent. Thus, if you want to rent a costume, you should call as far in advance of Fat Tuesday as possible. If you want to get properly (or improperly) costumed in a rental for Fat Tuesday, board the St. Charles streetcar and in 5 minutes you'll arrive at **MGM Costume Rentals** (tel 504/581-3999; 1617 St. Charles Ave.), which has thousands of costumes from the old MGM studio in Hollywood. In the unlikely event you can't satisfy that suppressed desire there, you can search for your boas, beads, and Big Birds at **Broadway Bound** (tel 504/821-1000; 2737 Canal St.), which sells as well as rents costumes (see p. 184). Way Uptown, and thus a haunt of many locals and college students, is **Uptown Costume and Dancewear** (tel 504/895-7969; 4326 Magazine St.). They rent a lot of cossies, but they also have excellent wigs, masks, makeup, accessories, and costumes to buy. If you're really creative—and here you will have stiff local competition—sign up for the **Mardi Gras Mask-A-Thon.** The annual locally televised contest takes place on

Fat Tuesday morn, with various dancing raisins and walking crawfish sashaying across a stage on Canal Street. (If all you want is a bit of face paint, stop by the French Market, where several street artists set up shop.)

What's so jazzy about Jazz Fest, and how do you get the most out of it?... First of all, put a sponge on your head—no kidding, soak a big, fat sponge in cold water and plop it on your head to keep you cool. Sun-shielding headgear is highly important at this annual music blowout, as is sunscreen. By the last weekend in April, when the fest kicks off, it's sizzling hot in the city, and the temperature is only going to climb during the 10-day bash. For local music lovers, and a large number of international visitors, **Jazz Fest** is the event of the entire year. During its two weekends, the main venue is the infield of the Fair Grounds, where tents and stages are set up and some 70,000 fans per day swarm over the grounds, juking, jiving, and second-lining to the likes of the Neville Brothers, Chuck Berry, Dr. John, Wynton and Branford Marsalis, Wilson Pickett, Gladys Knight, and a few hundred other top-name entertainers. Be in the gospel tent on the final Sunday night, when Aaron Neville traditionally chimes in with the Famous Zion Harmonizers in a soulful show that brings down the tent (figuratively speaking). Officially called the **New Orleans Jazz and Heritage Festival,** the shebang features not only music but also crafts and, of course, food—this is, after all, New Orleans. (See p. 110 for more.)

Learn the Lingo

Where y'at? *is the Ninth Warders' favorite greeting. It means "Hey, how're ya doin'?" If it can be said that there's an indigenous New Orleans accent, the natives of this sprawling working-class neighborhood speak it. The accent is a softer, slightly slurred version of Brooklynese—the "dese," "dat," and "dose" are the same, only less harsh. The Ninth Ward is* ***who dat*** *country, as in "Who dat say dey gonna beat dem Saints?" Ninth Warders tend to be rabid Saints fans, locally nicknamed* ***Yats,*** *derived from "Where y'at?"*

What is zydeco, and who cares?... New Orleanians love Cajun music and its red-hot cousin, zydeco, which you may have been turned on to by the soundtracks of movies such as *The Big Easy* and *Passion Fish.* Zydeco takes Cajun and adds some African blues and R&B to it. The word derives from the French word for snap beans: say *les haricots* fast and it comes out, roughly, "zydeco." According to lore, some folks snapped beans on country back porches while other folks played on their fiddles and *frottoirs* (washtubs).

Are all Louisiana pols crooked?... Louisiana seems to breed, and often elect to high office, wheelers and dealers of all, shall we say, stripes. New Orleans, in particular, seems to have more than its share of shady characters. Perhaps it shouldn't be surprising, given that the founding of New Orleans can be traced to a crook—a man named John Law. Pierre LeMoyne, Sieur d'Iberville, who was a naval hero, was the founder of Louisiana. His brother, Jean-Baptiste, Sieur de Bienville, also a hero, was the esteemed founder of New Orleans, but he acted on orders from John Law. Law was the protagonist of a plot that came to be called the Mississippi Bubble, a major land speculation scam in which he exploited the Louisiana Territory and eventually threw France into bankruptcy. It was he who named New Orleans (after his pal, Philippe, duc d'Orleans), and he who persuaded scores of gullible Europeans to emigrate to a no-man's land mired in swamps, tortured by hurricanes, and infested with alligators and malarial mosquitoes. Bienville and his hardy French henchmen get all the credit for pulling things together, and Law has been swept under the carpet. Don't look for any monuments dedicated to him.

Where are the hippest art galleries?... Royal Street is famous for its century-old antiques shops and snazzy art galleries, but local aficionados haunt the contemporary galleries in the renovated warehouses of the Warehouse/Arts District. Most of the galleries there are on Julia Street, though there are a fair few that populate its cross streets. The Contemporary Arts Center on Camp Street is the mother of all such galleries, and the scene of the big blowout that concludes fall's Art for Art's Sake openings. But the Warehouse is starting to get some major competition from Magazine Street, where contemporary art and antiques shops are popping up seemingly by the day. The benefit of the Warehouse/Arts District is its concentration of businesses. You can easily take in the area on foot in a day. Magazine Street, stretching as it does from the CBD all the way to the Riverbend, is far more spread out, requiring a car and probably 2 or 3 days to do it justice.

What's the best way to get around town?... The areas you'll probably spend most of your time in—the Quarter, the CBD, and the Garden District—are all best seen on foot. To reach the Garden District from the Quarter and the CBD, where most visitors stay, take the St. Charles streetcar, which will also deliver you to Audubon Park and the zoo. You can roll up to the New Orleans Museum of Art in City Park on the Esplanade bus. Beyond these areas, New Orleans sprawls all over the place, and even locals get confused about which ways north, south, east, and west are. At night it's best to leave the walking behind and step into a cab. As in any big city, the creeps come out after dark and you don't need to run into them on foot.

Where does novelist Anne Rice live?... Well, no one really knows anymore. The author of the wildly popular *Vampire Chronicles*, not to mention other novels like *Exit to Eden* (under the pen name Anne Rampling) and porn novels like *The Claiming of Sleeping Beauty* (under the name A. N. Roquelaure), used to live at 1239 First St. in the Garden District, a ritzy residential section upriver of the French Quarter. But after losing her husband, artist Stan Rice, in 2002, Anne went into major Life Change mode. First, she put St. Elizabeth's on the market. An orphanage for 118 years, the Napoleon Avenue property housed Anne's collection of dolls (which she also put up for sale) and wedding dresses and a gallery of Stan's artworks, and it used to be open for tours. The 55,000-square-foot mansion spans virtually a whole block, and is a good place for a photo op, even from the street. After that, Rice was said to have lost 100 pounds, some say thanks to a stomach staple. Then in her final act of shedding the past, Rice delivered news that thrilled foes (a strong personality, she had a vocal cadre of local detractors) and crushed fans: She was selling her remaining two Garden District properties and decamping to the "country." Rice has pointedly declined to say where her new retreat is. It seems she is ready to live more privately than she did here, where she frequently had fans camped outside her home waiting for a glimpse and where she also had a phone number they could call to leave her messages and hear a recording from her. If you're burning to get more on Anne, you can visit several Rice websites, including "The Official Anne Rice Page," www.annerice.com, which has a wealth of Rice-related information. For fans, it has recent missives written by Anne that catch you up on her latest thoughts, plans, and opinions.

Where does Fats Domino live?... The R&B icon lives in the big pink and yellow house at **5525 Marais St.,** on the corner of Marais and Caffin Avenue in the working-class Ninth Ward, downriver of the French Quarter. It's his private home and can be ogled only from the street.

What's a po'boy?... A po'boy, if you really don't know, is one of the area's indigenous sandwiches. The other's a muffuletta, but we'll get to that in a minute. Served on feather-light French bread, the po'boy can contain anything from fried oysters to ham and cheese to french fries. (Yes, a french-fry sandwich.) You can get a po'boy, "dressed" with lettuce, tomato, pickles, and mayo; "dressed dry" without the mayo; or "plain" sans everything but the main filling. The best kind to get while you're here—the ones that locals really excel at making—is, of course, one filled with fried seafood. Really, what's a stay in the Big Easy without a shrimp po'boy, overflowing with crispy little critters and wrapped up in white paper with the grease seeping through? By the way, they travel very well. We recommend ordering one on the way to the airport and unwrapping it just as the airplane food/beverage cart lurches unappetizingly into the aisle. Boy, won't you feel superior. Also, do not feel self conscious about calling it a "po'boy." That's its name. Not "poor boy." Speaking of hard-to-pronounce sandwich names, the muffuletta (muh-fuh-*lah*-duh) is the other breathtakingly fabulous local sandwich. Set on a massive round sesame-studded semolina roll, it contains mortadella, salami, provolone, and this tangy/garlicky green olive salad that'll make your tongue twirl. Some folks also like to throw a little prosciutto in there, as if there's not enough cured meat stuffed in it already. Here's what you need to know about a muffuletta: Half of one is a portion for a normal person, you'll definitely need a napkin, it's best accompanied by a root beer, and the most amazing one is served at **Central Grocery** (see p. 84) in the French Quarter.

Why do they talk funny here?... Like folks everywhere, we New Orleanians have our little local affectations and pronunciations. We just seem to have more than most. And since the city gets so many tourists, there are naturally more people around to mock and marvel at them. For instance, the freeway exit sign for the French Quarter says VIEUX CARRE. Most people here don't call it that anyway. But they *really* won't know what on earth you are talking about if you try to say it like a Frenchman would—which sounds a bit like you've just eaten something distasteful and that is impossible to spell phonetically. Here they just say "voo" and that's that. Next, once you get into and around the Quarter you will run into streets like Chartres (we say *Char*-ters), Conti (we say *Con*-tie), Burgundy (we say bur-*gun*-dee), and Calliope (we say *Cal*-lee-ope). You might also happen across Esplanade Avenue, which we pronounce like "lemonade." A good rule of thumb in these parts is to think of the most outlandishly twisted pronunciation you can muster and then say it. You'll probably nail it.

Is Mardi Gras just a sex fest?... Well, yes and no. If you go down to the Quarter on Fat Tuesday, all the things you've seen on the "Girls Gone Wild" videos and Fox News will greet you in stark naked living color. Lots of bare breasts, many thongs (on men and women), more and more male full-frontals—and yes, even sex acts if you're really looking hard (though the cops have tried to crack down). ***So beware:*** If you are not prepared for this type of mayhem, do not go to the Quarter on Mardi Gras day. If you've never been to Carnival, then you may wonder what else there is to do, and the answer is a resounding "Plenty!" Every single one of the 20-plus parades that roll in the 2 weeks preceding Mardi Gras day originate in good old New Orleans neighborhoods, replete with grandmas, moms, and thousands of children. There are no boobs and butts Uptown, you can be sure. Besides the parades, there's the Lundi Gras celebration by the river the day before Mardi Gras, and countless special events throughout the 2-week extravaganza that have nothing to do with naked folks. So don't hesitate to bring the kids, but choose your events wisely.

What are the ethnic groups in New Orleans?... The original inhabitants of New Orleans were the mosquitoes and alligators who called the swamps home before the city was built atop it. While their descendants are still here, they share the city with the descendants of a variety of humans. The French came first in the 1600 and 1700s, followed soon by the Spanish, and then the Acadians (eventually called Cajuns) who'd recently been expelled from Canada (though most of them settled west of the city). Next, the French and Spanish began importing slaves from both Africa and the Caribbean. The early- to mid-1800s saw a flood of Americans, Italians, Irish, and Germans. This ethnic mix held more or less steady until the late 1900s, when an influx of Latin Americans from Mexico and Honduras (among other countries) arrived to feed the economy, along with a sizeable number of Vietnamese fleeing the war at the invitation of the Catholic Church. Today there are enclaves of almost every ethnicity in New Orleans thanks to its many service jobs, its universities, and its small number of internationally headquartered businesses.

In a city that's so laid-back about everything else, why are they so uptight about parking?... When it comes to collecting money, the city and its workers display a remarkable level of industriousness. Enforcing parking rules is a relatively easy way to rake it in. God save the poor soul who tries to make sense of the parking signs and rules in the Quarter. We recommend just biting the bullet and parking in lots. One of the main things you do *not* want to do during your stay is go down to the car pound on Claiborne Avenue and cough up untold amounts of cash to retrieve your (probably) battered rental car. If you do try street parking in the Quarter and there is any question as to whether your spot is legal, always err on the conservative side. There are many meters around town. Feed them. If the signs near them say 2-hour parking, do not park for more than 2 hours. You *will* get ticketed. You might get towed. And remember this: Towing and ticketing efficiency turns to unabashed ruthlessness during Mardi Gras and Jazz Fest. Perhaps you should just skip the car altogether and stick to cabs....

ACCOMM

ODATIONS

1

Map 2: New Orleans Accommodations Orientation

To METAIRIE

UPTOWN

BROADMOOR

GARDEN DISTRICT

LOWER GARDEN DISTRICT

See "Map 4: Central Business District Accommodations"

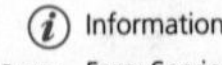
Information

Ferry Service to Algiers Point

Riverwalk streetcar route/stops

St. Charles streetcar route/stops

Canal streetcar route/stops

Vieux Carre loop route/stops

B & W Courtyards **14**
Beau Sejour **2**
Claiborne Mansion **15**
Garden Guest House **1**
Holiday Inn Select New Orleans —Convention Center **10**
Hostelling International—Marquette House New Orleans **4**
House on Bayou Road **16**
Josephine Guest House **6**

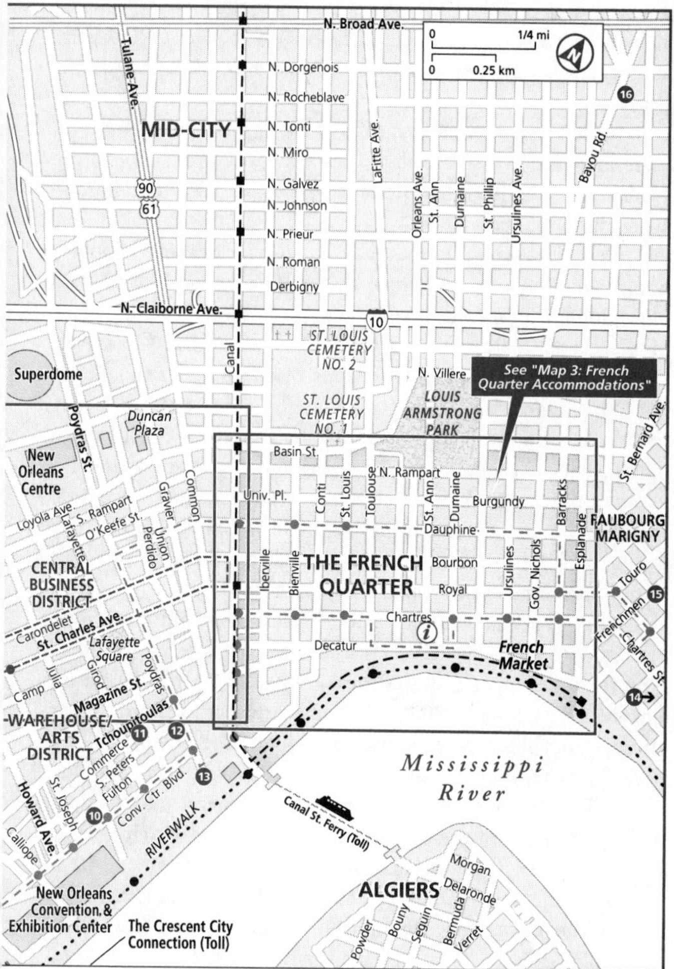

Loews Hotel **12**
McKendrick-Breaux House **9**
Moreau Townhouse **8**
New Orleans Hilton Riverside **13**
Pontchartrain Hotel **5**
Renaissance Arts **11**
St. Charles Guest House **7**
Sully Mansion **3**
Woods Hole Inn **1**

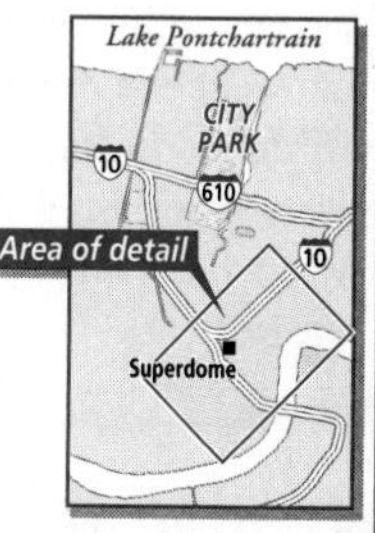

Basic Stuff

The first rule of New Orleans hotels is that there are no rules—at least when it comes to room rates. Many places are decent and organized enough to have a high and a low season. Not the Big Easy. For instance, time was, most hotels in town would practically *give* you a room during the long, hot summer. Summers are no cooler these days, but you can't even depend on Hades-like weather conditions anymore to keep the hordes away and hotel rates low.

New Orleans's "high season," when rates can double, occurs anytime a lot of people are looking for a place to stay. The euphemism for this phenomenon is "a special event." Some of the events truly are special: Sugar Bowl, Mardi Gras, Jazz Fest. But sometimes a big convention also falls under this heading. Now, unless you are a person having a heart attack, when was the last time you considered a gathering of 20,000 cardiologists a special event? But the docs have the cash and that's the name of the game when you're trying to squeeze revenue out of your hotel rooms. And as if paying more weren't enough, often during such "special events," many hotels require a 3- to 5-day minimum; some even want full payment up front.

Plus, many hotels don't publish rack rates and won't give you a quote until you tell them the exact dates you're coming. And then they charge whatever the traffic will bear. A few years ago the City Council made a laughable attempt to control price gouging, but the ordinance was virtually ignored. Most people have forgotten it ever existed.

Whatever your bill, the bottom line will increase to the tune of 11%, courtesy of the city and state—plus another city tax of $1 to $3 per night, depending upon the size of the hotel (this from the same City Council that worries about price gouging).

One more basic tip: Be mindful of Mardi Gras. Thousands of people come to New Orleans for the big blowout—a term used advisedly—with the great hordes usually pouring in for the final weekend of Carnival. People tend to, shall we say, let their hair down during the wind-up, and behavior is often absolutely outrageous. Hotel staffs do a heroic job just staying open in the face of the onslaught, but nothing runs quite smoothly during Carnival time. If you're looking for a romantic getaway, stay away from New Orleans during this season.

Winning the Reservations Game

When you call to reserve, ask about package deals and corporate or any other special rates. For example, during December's monthlong "Christmas in New Orleans," most hotels offer special Papa Noel rates, discounted by about 30%. Summertime rates can traditionally be über-low, but it depends on the influx of conventioneers. (This is something you can check by calling the New Orleans Metropolitan Convention and Visitors Bureau.) Almost all major hotels (but few guesthouses) offer some sort of deal when business is on the slow side. Packages usually include, say, a 2- to 4-night deal with some meals thrown in, plus perhaps a breakfast at Brennan's, a carriage ride, a night on the town, or a sightseeing outing on a riverboat, at the aquarium, or at the zoo. New Orleans's tour operators that package Mardi Gras, Sugar Bowl, Superbowl, and Jazz Fest include **Hotard Vacations** (tel 504/942-5708 or 800/535-2732; www.hotard.com; 2838 Touro St., New Orleans, LA 70122) and **Travel New Orleans** (tel 504/561-8747 or 800/535-8747; www.travelneworleans.com; 400 Poydras St., Suite 1720, New Orleans, LA 70130). If you can't find a room on your own, call **Turbotrip.com** (tel 800/473-STAY; www.turbotrip.com). With their blocks of rooms, this outfit can usually find a place even when the hotels say they're full.

Is There a Right Neighborhood?

For many people, the **French Quarter** is the only place to stay. That's where most visitors spend their time anyway, exploring and overeating. There's lodging for almost every taste there, from large luxury hotels awash with restaurants, bars, and music clubs, to little family-run guesthouses with minimal extras. The **Central Business District (CBD)** is adjacent to the French Quarter, on the Uptown side of Canal Street and within an easy stroll of the Quarter's amusements. In addition to a whole slew of high-rise hotels, the CBD is home to the Superdome, the Convention Center, upscale shopping malls, and Spanish Plaza, where sightseeing riverboats dock and the big free Lundi Gras bash is held the day before Fat Tuesday. Most of the CBD hotels are boxlike modern high-rises, many of them are chains, and they tend to attract convention and tour-group business.

Staying anywhere else in town means some travel time. **The Garden District** or **Uptown** along a bend in the river is only about 5 to 25 minutes by streetcar depending on what part of it you're in. If you have family or business reasons for staying in a hotel or motel in east New Orleans, on the **West Bank,** or in **Metairie,** you'll be a 20- to 30-minute drive (depending on traffic) from the French Quarter action. And there are plenty of affordable motels scattered all over town—in the Quarter, in the

CBD, on the West Bank, near the airport—that are not much different from those anywhere else in the country if that's your need or style. If you like an idyllic country setting—tall pine trees, rolling hills, ponds, and peace and quiet—there are some charming bed-and-breakfasts on the **north shore of Lake Pontchartrain,** but you'll have to cross the 24-mile-long causeway to reach them. They're anywhere from 45 minutes to an hour from downtown and the French Quarter. On the plus side, they're handy to the Global Wildlife Center, a place for the kiddies to pet live giraffes and other exotic wildlife. Plus there's some mighty fine eating out thataway. If you opt for **Kenner,** you'll be near the airport and the Treasure Chest casino. And for certain types, that's enough.

The Lowdown

Pools with a view... New Orleans's hot and humid weather is nothing if not conducive to poolside lounging. In the CBD, the **Wyndham New Orleans** has a 29th-floor rooftop outdoor pool with a panoramic view of the river and the city. The 16-story **Hotel Monteleone,** the tallest building in the Quarter, has a pool on its roof, too; from it you can see the river three blocks away, the CBD two blocks away, and the Quarter, which sprawls down below. The **Omni Royal Orleans,** known to locals as the Royal O., smack in the middle of the French Quarter, has the rooftop La Riviera Club, with a pool and snack bar; though it's only six stories high, it allows a closer-up view of the Quarter's shingles and dormers. The **W Hotel** in the CBD on Poydras has a predictably chic fourth-floor pool that gives you an uncharacteristically urban view of the Crescent City.

Sleeping in the warehouse... In the Warehouse District, several upmarket hotels are convenient to Gallery Row, the National D-Day Museum, the Ernest N. Morial Convention Center, and the CBD, which the Warehouse District adjoins. The sleek **Holiday Inn Select** is right across the street from the convention center, and the **Ambassador Hotel** is just two blocks away. All three are housed in former 19th-century warehouses. On St. Charles Avenue is the **Lafayette Hotel,** a little hotel with a French flavor. The recently opened **Renaissance Arts Hotel** pays homage to its arty surroundings with a ground-floor gallery chock-full o' original art. Even the rooms are decked with contributions by local *artistes,* as well as boldly colored and printed linens. Over on Lee Circle, the **Hotel Le Cirque** also has artistic aspirations: an original Herb Ritts in the lobby, sparely designed rooms in shades of taupe with pistachio accents—and Robert E. Lee (or his statue) peeking into many of the street-side rooms.

Glam crash pads... Hotel Monaco, a quirkily ornate boutique hotel in an old Masonic Temple, is one of the few pet-friendly hotels around. If you're traveling petless, they'll bring you a goldfish companion. A high-concept boutique hotel in the Warehouse District, **Loft 523** attempts to bring SoHo to NOLA. Rooms are spare (some might say bare) affairs kitted out with Fortuny lamps, Agape "Spoon" tubs, Sony Dream systems, Frette linens, and Modern Fan Company's "Whirlybird" ceiling fans. Rooms also come with a personal assistant. Hmmmm. The Loft's sister hotel, the **International House,** is equally focused on style but much more attentive to place, with Louisiana wildflowers in the rooms along with black-and-white photos of local jazz greats. It's also in a swish old Beaux Arts building with a happenin' bar called loa. The city's two **W Hotels**—one in the CBD and one in the Quarter—are twin bastions of cool, epitomized, perhaps, by the button on all their in-room phones which reads: "whatever, whenever." Besides this enlightened attitude toward service, both hotels have Aveda bath products, pillowtop mattresses, sleek decor, and voodoo dolls for sale in their minibar. But only the W French Quarter has in-room gumball machines. On Canal Street, the **Ritz-Carlton** and its even ritzier sister the **Maison Orleans** have also been hotbeds for hotties, with their high service and swanky rooms. But one of the biggest hotties at either actually works there—Jeremy Davenport, named one of *People* magazine's top 50 bachelors in 2001, plays trumpet and sings every Thursday, Friday, and Saturday at the hopping French Quarter Bar. If you're a celeb and you want to kick it old school, then your only real choice is the posh **Windsor Court Hotel,** where people ranging from leaders of heavy metal bands to leaders of the free world routinely hang their guitars/Hermès ties.

Super Dome-ains... The **Hyatt Regency Hotel** zooms and sprawls over a considerable portion of the Superdome area in the CBD: It isn't possible to sleep any closer to the Superdome unless you pitch a tent on the turf. Built around the chain's signature atrium, in this case lit by sky-high, steel-frame windows, the Hyatt is a part of the Poydras Plaza and New Orleans Center complex, with a glass-enclosed walkway connecting the hotel and the sports arena. Less pricey, less luxurious digs are in the **Holiday Inn Downtown-Superdome,** an aptly named motel with Holiday Inn–type rooms. There is only the one restaurant, but the parking is on-site. Gracious **Le Pavillon**—a very good CBD buy—is also close to the Superdome.

If you're a little bit country... You need wheels and a certain amount of flexibility if you opt for the **House on Bayou Road,** but this is one of the city's best B&Bs. You'll only be about a 10-minute cab ride from the Quarter, but don't expect to stroll out the front door and be in the middle of anything except a residential neighborhood. A 19th-century house on a historic portage road, it has five guest rooms, two suites, plus a private cottage, and you'll swear you're waking up somewhere in the peaceful Louisiana countryside. Way farther afield, **Woods Hole Inn,** on the north shore of Lake Pontchartrain (anywhere from a 45-minute to an hour's drive from the city), is hidden amid tall trees and lush foliage. Two private cottages and a rustic cabin are discreetly far from the proprietors' house; you could lay in a supply of food and hole up for days on end. Also on the North Shore, the **Garden Guest House** is a similar retreat, with handsomely decorated suites in a house that sits on 10 wooded acres, lavishly landscaped with tall trees, bromeliads, orchids, and a 1,800-square-foot greenhouse.

Chain, chain, chain... New Orleans assiduously courts the convention trade, and offers big hotels to service it. The granddaddy of them all is the **New Orleans Hilton Riverside,** one of the Gulf South's biggest hotels. It's absolutely loaded with restaurants, cafes, bars, lounges, and nightclubs. There's a quarter-mile jogging track on the roof, as well as tennis courts, a golf clinic, and a health club. Only somewhat smaller are the **New Orleans Marriott** and the

Sheraton New Orleans, which face each other across Canal Street. Both offer the whole laundry list of amenities—pool, health club, restaurants, lounges, and big lobbies. Despite its size, the **Sheraton** manages a somewhat warmer, cozier ambience than the **Marriott,** and the service is pretty good for New Orleans. Not nearly as big as these modern chain hotels, but still big and splashy in a 19th-century way, is the **Chateau Sonesta,** which opened in 1995 as sister to the Quarter's **Royal Sonesta;** its handsome building was once the D. H. Holmes department store, one of the Gulf South's finest. Finally, the **Astor Crowne Plaza** and **Loews Hotel** are two new chains to grace the city. The Astor has the advantage of being right on the Quarter's border, but the Loews is convenient to the Convention Center and offers an excellent level of service.

Dignified grande dames... The **Monteleone Hotel** has been one of the top French Quarter hotels almost since it opened in 1886, and the old girl continues to maintain her charms. Blimp-sized chandeliers hang from a sky-high ceiling and shine over a large, bustling lobby where liveried staff roll carts piled high with tour groups' luggage. The **Carousel Bar**—one of several bars and restaurants just off the lobby—is done up like an old-fashioned merry-go-round (though there are bar chairs instead of horses), and slo-o-wly revolves while you imbibe. Descendants of Antonio Monteleone, the Sicilian cobbler who founded it, still own and operate the hotel. Her CBD counterpart is the **Fairmont Hotel,** a grand old hotel, circa 1893, which many locals still call the Roosevelt. Fairmont rooms are oversized, beds have two down pillows apiece, and bathrooms have electric shoe polishers, and—a wicked twist for this hard-eating town—bathroom scales. The Fairmont's **Sazerac Bar & Grill** serves the kind of rich food a classic hotel dining room ought to serve, but has slid woefully over the years. The Garden District entry is the estimable **Pontchartrain Hotel,** a comparative youngster—it opened in 1927 as a posh residential hotel—notable for its celebrity-named suites. A high-vaulted ceiling soars over the Pontchartrain's smallish marbled lobby, with its Oriental carpets and potted palms. Just off the lobby, the **Pontchartrain Café** is a favorite Sunday breakfast spot for uptowners, and the **Bayou Bar** (where the Saints signed their NFL contract in 1975) is a cozy piano bar. One last note to visiting claustrophobics: Inquire about room size before you book.

Great eats downstairs... Your average picky gourmet generally turns a nose up at hotel dining rooms, but every kitchen in New Orleans is up against stiff competition. Locals rub shoulders with the tourists and visiting swells in the **Windsor Court's** recently renamed **New Orleans Grill.** Guests at the **W New Orleans–French Quarter** hotel have the advantage of gussied-up pizzas from **Bacco,** Ralph and Cindy Brennan's little Italian restaurant. The hotel's sister property in the CBD, the **W New Orleans,** is the proud home of **Zoë Bistrot,** a high-end eatery patterned after a Parisian brasserie. Rooms in the **Saint Louis Hotel,** built in the 1960s, fail to deliver on the promise of beauty held out by the glorious courtyard, but its **Louis XVI** is a fine French restaurant, and breakfast is served there around the glamorous stone fountain. Want even more Frenchified food? The two newish Renaissance hotels, the **Pere Marquette** in the CBD and the **Renaissance Arts** in the Warehouse District, offer **Rene Bistrot** and **la Cote Brasserie,** respectively, with former Windsor Courtier and affable Frenchman Rene Bajeux at the helms of both. In the CBD, **Hotel Monaco**'s blue-hued **Cobalt** dishes up tasty new Southern fare to the sounds of live jazz (on weekends).

(Supposedly) haunted houses... Paranormalists and ghost hunters of all shades and degrees of intelligence inhabit New Orleans, and they're quick to point out the town's haunted venues. (Fact checkers, beware! We do not stand by the veracity of any of this.) Many of the gossiped-about hotels are French Quarter guesthouses. Housekeepers at the **Lafitte Guest House** think the ghost who, um, lives in room 40 was probably the lady of the house when it was built as a home in 1849. The parlor is Victorian right down to the fringed lampshades, and guest rooms are done up with testers, half-testers, and marbletop tables. At the **Olivier House Hotel,** several guests have been startled by the appearance in their rooms of a peripatetic pair—a woman in antebellum garb chatting up a Confederate soldier. The 42-room guesthouse, built in 1836 as a town house for the widow of a Creole planter, rambles around two courtyards and has a mix of antiques, reproductions, and contemporary furnishings. Don't expect biscuits at the **Biscuit Palace;** the name comes from the advertisement for Uneeda Biscuits painted in huge letters on the high gable. This was an 1820s private residence, now offering modestly furnished apartments around a flowery courtyard; it has its original spiral staircase and, possibly, an original tenant—a pale, petite female apparition who the staff considers benevolent, albeit transparent.

Several hotels have ghost gossip, too: A stressed out teenage girl reportedly smacked and killed by a carriage lives in the CBD's **Le Pavillon.** You'll share **cottage no. 4 at the Maison de Ville** with an old soldier with an apparent affinity for country music. **The Provincial** was allegedly a place where Civil War soldiers were treated. At night it is said you can still hear the wounded soldiers moaning in agony. (We think it's just the Bourbon Street drunks.) And lastly, the old **Hotel de la Poste**—which is now the **W French Quarter**—hosted a bevy of apparitions. No word on whether they were forced to move when the hipsters remodeled and took over.

Suite deals... Those who need more space than a mere room provides can strew their things about in one of the all-suite hotels. Top of the line in that category is the **Windsor Court**—the luxury hotel in the city, loaded with artwork, liveried staff, and enough flowers to stock a fair-sized florist shop. Most of its rooms are posh suites, done up with wet bars, phones in each room (including, of course, the oversized marble bathrooms), canopied or four-poster beds, and cushy furnishings. Ingenue to the Windsor Court's Grande Dame is the **Iberville Suites.** Alluring with antiques and generously sized rooms, it shares a building with the Ritz-Carlton, so Iberville Suiters get perks like access to the R-C's sumptuous spa and charging privileges at the hotel's bars and restaurant. Plus, unlike the Windsor Court, the Iberville Suites is in the Quarter. Farther afield, the **Moreau Townhouse** is an oasis in the still somewhat grungy Lower Garden District. Studio and 1- and 2-bedroom suites in the 1830s town house have polished hardwood floors, soaring ceilings (some with a skylight), and full kitchens, as well as necessities such as a private phone line, answering machine, and microwave.

And at the low end, **Comfort Suites** is a good buy for budget travelers. It's in a restored 1904 CBD office building whose lobby is minimalist, to say the most. Nothing at all fancy, but the price is excellent for the CBD and they do have a sauna and Jacuzzi.

Inn the mood... Quiet seclusion in glamorous surroundings has lured a variety of celebs to the **Claiborne Mansion,** a bed-and-breakfast on the outskirts of the French Quarter. The spacious rooms are light-filled, with gleaming hardwood floors and high ceilings; furnishings and beds boast top-quality fabrics in rich colors and designs. Rooms and suites are in the main house and in the rear carriage house, just off the lavish garden and heated pool. There's no restaurant, but the Frenchmen Street and the French Quarter restaurants are nearby. Actually within the Quarter, the **Soniat House** is a complex of 19th-century town houses furnished with a vast and staggeringly gorgeous collection of Louisiana and European antiques. It is truly a gem and worth the relatively high rates for its thrilling combination of location, beauty, and service. Meanwhile, the **Hotel Maison de Ville** strives for the ambience of a French country inn and would succeed were it not for its unfortunate proximity to three noisy after-hours clubs. *However,* two blocks away on Dauphine Street lie the Maison's sister property, the **Audubon Cottages,** divine mini-houses surrounded by banana trees clustered round a little swimming pool. If you can book one of these tiny treats, you may never leave.

Mi casa es su casa... Tucked behind a plain facade deep in the Faubourg Marigny is **B&W Courtyards,** a collection of six guest rooms clustered around three courtyards, each blessed with a burbling fountain. Over breakfast each day you can debrief with your hosts Rob Boyd and Kevin Wong, two colorful characters always willing to steer you toward the best meals and clubs. Room decor ranges from the sublime to the outrageous—kinda like Boyd and Wong. Upriver in the French Quarter, directly across the street from the Croissant d'Or patisserie, the **Hotel Villa Convento** is a modest place operated by the friendly Campo family, who readily confess that the furnishings are reproductions. It was built in 1848 for a Spaniard named

Fernandez, and local carriage drivers perpetuate the myth that this was the fabled House of the Rising Sun (the Campos haven't a clue how that rumor got started), famous in local legend as the house to which young men in the olden days were supposedly taken by their fathers to, um, become men. Toward Mid-City at the **House on Bayou Road,** which sits on 2 acres of lawns and gardens, you have the option of staying in one of the antiques-filled rooms in the big West Indies–style house, or you can take one of the dreamily appointed cottages. Breakfast each morning on the veranda or out by the pool is a toothsome affair with freshly made everything, from *pain perdu* to OJ. The Garden District offers several beguiling mansion-away-from-home choices. **McKendrick-Breaux House** is a misnomer of sorts, as the place is actually two fabulously restored 1865 Greek Revival homes that share a yard between them. The nine rooms bear unrestrained touches like floor-to-15-foot-high-ceilinged silk dupioni drapes, fresh cut flowers, and en suite bathrooms nearly as big as the rooms themselves. And if you need a free moment just to sit and contemplate, the Mc-B House has one of the most comfy covered porches in town. A big Italianate manse, replete with white columns, is home to the **Josephine Guest House.** Elaborate European antiques—called by owners Dan and Mary Ann Fuselier "Creole Baroque"—include a really awesome bed, black as night and inlaid with bone and ivory. And your fresh breads for breakfast, homemade by Mary Ann, come to you on Wedgwood china. If you've always wanted to live in a glamorous Queen Anne manor, head for the **Sully Mansion.** It's one of the few houses in that posh residential district that visitors can actually enter. The house, with its turret, veranda, and gingerbread froufrou, is tucked away behind an iron fence and shaded by big trees. Designed and built in the 1890s by 19th-century New Orleans architect Thomas Sully, it has 12-foot cove ceilings, original stained glass, and a grand piano in the foyer. Continental breakfast, included in the rate, is served informally in a formal dining room. You can't call the **St. Charles Guest House** a mansion, but it is a simple, unpretentious place, with serve-yourself breakfast and a copy of the owners' own "survival manual" provided for navigating the wilds of New Orleans. Waaay Uptown and conveniently located on a Mardi Gras parade route (if you happen to be there then), **Beau Sejour** is a convivial six-guest-room Italianate on wide and leafy Napoleon Avenue. It has simple but attractive and comfortable rooms, and outside there is a patio with a grill and a small pool. It's very laid-back, due in large part to its owners Kim and Gil Gagnon, the consummate warm, relaxed hosts.

Most French Quarterly of hotels outside the French Quarter... Every hotel in town attempts to convince guests that it's actually in the Quarter, or at least "within minutes" of the main tourist attraction. But some hotels that claim to be within the Quarter actually are not, given that the Vieux Carré Commission technically has jurisdiction only over the section bordered by Iberville Street (not Canal St.), the river side of Rampart Street, the upriver border of Esplanade Avenue, and Decatur Street. Sure, the restrictions are rigid, but then the Vieux Carré Commission is not locally noted for flexibility. Given those parameters, the **French Quarter Courtyard**—which sits on the lake side of Rampart Street—gets the nod. Like many of the French Quarter guesthouses, it's a big 19th-century abode (painted pink in this case), with green shutters, a rear courtyard, and polished wood floors. Also technically outside the Quarter, the Italianate **Lanaux Mansion** has a front balcony (which belongs to the owner's room) overlooking the big leafy trees on Esplanade Avenue and another one in the rear, with an almost bucolic view of the courtyard.

A room with a view... The romantic appeal of the Mississippi has not been lost on local hotel developers. In the CBD, a brace of high-rise hotels boast spectacular views of Old Man River. Top honors go to the **Wyndham New Orleans,** whose large Carrara marble lobby on the 11th floor of the Canal Place mall has two-story arched windows that frame the great bend in the Mississippi and the rooftops of the Quarter. Every guest room has a view either of the river or of the cityscape; go for the spectacular river vistas over the others, which are marred by the sprawling parking lot. Glass elevators purr upward above the mall's splashing fountain. Rooms in the **New Orleans Hilton Riverside** also offer unobstructed Mississippi views. Above the 10th floor, riverside rooms of the **Windsor Court, Le Meridien,** the **DoubleTree,** the **New Orleans Marriott,**

and the **Sheraton New Orleans** also offer great Mississippi panoramas. The 200 or so shops and restaurants in the Riverwalk mall are within spitting distance, so to speak, from all of these hotels.

Gym dandies... Most people do not come to the Big Easy to worry about things like nutrition and fitness. However, if you actually think you're going to work out while you're here (pardon us while we stifle a scoff), some cribs have the equipment you're looking for. The **New Orleans Hilton Riverside**'s rooftop Rivercenter Racquet and Health Club has a masseur and whirlpool to soothe you after workouts on the tennis, racquetball, squash, and basketball courts; laps in the pool; aerobics and exercise; and jogging on the quarter-mile path. **Sheraton New Orleans, Hyatt Regency, New Orleans Marriott,** and **Le Meridien** hotels all have the usual complement of facilities you'd expect from a large chain hotel. If you'd rather stay in a charming place in the Quarter, though, try the **Dauphine Orleans** for its small exercise room off a rear courtyard.

Taking care of business... Business is business, and the main business of the CBD hotels is convention and business travelers. It's a highly competitive trade, with the **Hyatt Regency Hotel,** the **Hotel InterContinental,** the **Wyndham New Orleans**—in fact, all of the chain high-rises—vying to see which can install more modems. In any suite of the **Windsor Court,** you're never more than a few inches from a phone or a few feet from a two-line phone with computer hookups, and all of the suites in the **Fairmont Hotel** have their own fax machines. In the late 1990s, two hotels opened whose names confuse everyone (with the possible exception of the respective staffs): The **Omni Royal Crescent** (a smaller kid sister to the **Omni Royal Orleans** in the Quarter) and the **Queen & Crescent Hotel,** both carved out of former office buildings and both with the requisite high-tech stuff. Business is no less dull in the French Quarter, with top honors going to the **Royal Sonesta Hotel,** the **Omni Royal Orleans,** and the **Monteleone Hotel.** However, if you'd rather combine business with small-hotel charm, check out the **Soniat House,** which has 21st-century services in a 19th-century setting, including a 24-hour concierge to take care of nuisances like faxing and photocopying.

Bang for the buck... Finding affordable digs in the Quarter can be a challenge no matter what time of year you come to the city. But there are two perennially underrated spots that really can deliver. On the plus side, **Le Richelieu** sports all the amenities you'd want in a hotel, including a great location on the quiet side of the Quarter. It also offers a pool, a restaurant/lounge, and ample parking, which is like gold in the car-hostile Vieux Carré. But, to put it gently, Le Richelieu has lived a full life. Her worn carpets, musty smell, faux and dusty lobby flowers, and funky tiled bathrooms all indicate a blossom past her high bloom. In fact, she really peaked in the mid-seventies when Paul and Linda McCartney lived on the top floor for 2 months while he made an album at a local recording studio. So stay at Le Richelieu, but love her for who she is. Just up the road a patch is the **Hotel Provincial,** a kindred spirit with Le Rich. The Provincial is a series of buildings that date back to the early 1800s, and each of the 93 rooms has a different layout. Some rooms are better than others, but all feature slightly worn reproductions. You sure won't think you've died and woken up in hotel heaven here. On the plus side, you'll find a pool, lots of parking, and a friendly staff, and the price for French Quarter quarters is reasonable.

Even cheaper sleepers... The **Hostelling International-Marquette House New Orleans,** one of the nation's biggest youth hostels, has the usual bunk beds associated with such places, but also several apartments and a few private rooms with bathrooms. It's very popular, and reservations are essential. The **Depot House at Madame Julia's Boarding House** is better located—near the Warehouse District, within walking distance of museums, art galleries, and restaurants. In the Lower Garden District, the **St. Charles Guest House** has long been known as an oasis for budgeteers and backpackers. Rooms are merely functional in decor, but there is a pool and a big sun deck, and your morning coffee, juice, and pastries come with the bargain. The **Hampton Inn** may be in a homely high-rise, but it will look very good to budgeteers in search of a good buy in the CBD.

Map 3: French Quarter Accommodations

Map 4: Central Business District Accommodations

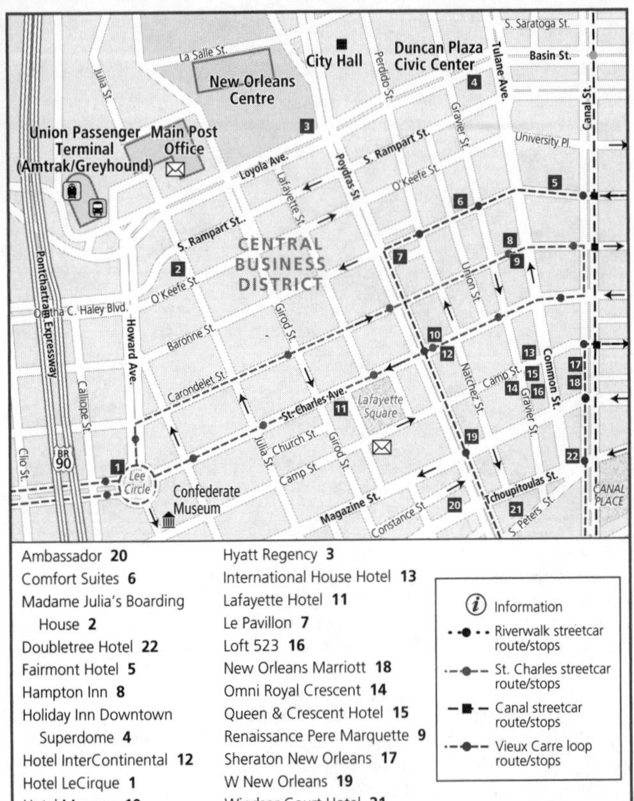

Ambassador **20**	Hyatt Regency **3**
Comfort Suites **6**	International House Hotel **13**
Madame Julia's Boarding House **2**	Lafayette Hotel **11**
Doubletree Hotel **22**	Le Pavillon **7**
Fairmont Hotel **5**	Loft 523 **16**
Hampton Inn **8**	New Orleans Marriott **18**
Holiday Inn Downtown Superdome **4**	Omni Royal Crescent **14**
Hotel InterContinental **12**	Queen & Crescent Hotel **15**
Hotel LeCirque **1**	Renaissance Pere Marquette **9**
Hotel Monaco **10**	Sheraton New Orleans **17**
	W New Orleans **19**
	Windsor Court Hotel **21**

Information
Riverwalk streetcar route/stops
St. Charles streetcar route/stops
Canal streetcar route/stops
Vieux Carre loop route/stops

The Index

$$$$$	over $200
$$$$	$125–$200
$$$	$90–$125
$$	$50–$90
$	under $50

Price ratings are based on the lowest price quoted for a standard double room in high season, including taxes and charges. Unless otherwise noted, units have air-conditioning, phones, private bathrooms, and TVs.

The following abbreviations are used for credit cards:

AE	American Express
DC	Diners Club
DISC	Discover
MC	MasterCard
V	Visa

Alexa Hotel/Astor Crowne Plaza (p. 25) FRENCH QUARTER The Alexa and the Astor are adjoining properties. You dial one number for both, but you can request which hotel you prefer. The Alexa usually runs about $10 or so cheaper than the Astor. The Alexa is conveniently located near the Royal Street galleries. Alexa rooms have exposed brick walls and French-style furniture. The Astor is on Canal Street at Bourbon. It's closer to the party and the rooms are comfy. It has the added benefit of a club level where rooms come with extra service and amenities. ***Note:*** The Alexa has rooms only. The pool and gardens, fitness center, restaurant, and concierge are all over at the Astor.... *Numbers for both: Tel 504/962-0600, 888/487-9643. Alexa Hotel: Fax 504/962-0501; www.alexahotel.com; 119 Royal St., 70130; 188 rooms, 2 suites. Astor Crowne Plaza: www.astorcrowneplaza.com; 739 Canal St., 70130; 490 rooms, 29 suites. AE, DC, DISC, MC, V. $$$–$$$$$*

See Map 3 on p. 33.

Ambassador Hotel (p. 22) WAREHOUSE DISTRICT Three renovated 19th-century warehouses were combined to form this sleek entry to the Warehouse District/Convention Center scene. Hardwood floors, high ceilings, exposed old brick and beams, and white porcelain fixtures are reminiscent of bygone days. Furnishings include wrought-iron beds and reproduction 18th-century writing desks. Modern times, however, are reflected in amenities such as voice mail, dataports, in-room safes and coffeemakers, hair dryers, and cable TVs tucked into armoires.... *Tel 504/527-5271, 888/527-5271. Fax 504/527-5270. www.ahno.com. 535 Tchoupitoulas St., 70130. 165 rooms. AE, DC, DISC, MC, V. $$–$$$$$*

See Map 4 on p. 34.

B&W Courtyards (p. 28) FAUBOURG MARGINY Just downriver from the Quarter, this six-room B&B is run by two fabulous guys who know and love the city and are more than willing to help you with reservations and recommendations. Rooms range in size and style from tiger stripes to Balinese, and most of them open to one of three fountained courtyards....*Tel 504/945-9418, 800/585-5731. Fax 504/949-3483. www.bandwcourtyards.com. 2425 Chartres St., 70117. 6 rooms. AE, DISC, MC, V. $$$–$$$$$*

See Map 2 on p. 18.

Beau Sejour (p. 30) UPTOWN Well located on one of the Mardi Gras parade routes and just a few blocks from the St. Charles streetcar, this sunny B&B has six rooms in a 100-year-old Italianate home set high on an avenue canopied by live oaks. The ground-floor suite is the room to book, but the two street-side rooms upstairs have balconies. There's also a pool and a gas grill for the city's plentiful warm nights.... *Tel 504/897-3746, 888/897-9398. Fax 504/891-3340. www.beausejourbandb.com. 1930 Napoleon Ave., 70115. 6 rooms. AE, DISC, MC, V. $$–$$$$*

See Map 2 on p. 18.

Biscuit Palace (p. 27) FRENCH QUARTER Just two blocks off Jackson Square and 50 feet from Bourbon Street, the somewhat rustic apartments of the Biscuit Palace (a fading sign advertising Uneeda Biscuits is painted on the gable) overlook a flowery courtyard. It doesn't have a pool and doesn't need a restaurant because there are dozens of eateries nearby.... *Tel 504/525-9949. Fax 504/525-9949. www.biscuitpalace.com. 730 Dumaine St., 70116. 3 suites, 1 apartment. MC, V. $$–$$$$*

See Map 3 on p. 33.

Chateau Sonesta (p. 25) CBD A large, upscale hotel, the Sonesta is technically in the CBD, but it faces Canal Street and has the French Quarter at its back door. Front rooms have big windows overlooking Canal Street. Rooms are not overly large, but they are designed in interesting configurations, with nooks and crannies, and have minibars and the usual amenities: hair dryers, toiletries, the works. There are courtyards inside and out.... *Tel 504/586-0800. Fax 504/586-1987. www.chateausonesta.com. 800 Iberville St., 70112. 237 rooms, 14 suites. AE, DC, DISC, MC, V. $$$–$$$$$*

See Map 3 on p. 33.

Claiborne Mansion (p. 28) FAUBOURG MARIGNY Continental breakfasts, complimentary cheese and crackers, beverages, in-room phones with voice mail, and TVs with VCRs are but some of the attractions in this luxury bed-and-breakfast. The Greek Revival house in Faubourg Marigny, overlooking Washington Square Park, was built in the 1850s for the son of Louisiana's first American governor, W. C. C. Claiborne. Rooms are huge, ceilings are 14 feet high, and the furnishings are elegant. Rooms and suites are in the main house and in the rear carriage house, overlooking the pool and cabanas. Smoking is not permitted indoors; advance arrangements can be made for small pets.... *Tel 504/949-7327. Fax 504/949-0388. www.claibornemansion.com. 2111 Dauphine St., 70116. 2 rooms, 4 suites. AE, MC, V. $$$–$$$$$*

See Map 2 on p. 18.

Comfort Suites (p. 28) CBD The little suites in this converted CBD office building won't win any decorator awards, but they come with hair dryers, in-room safes, high-tech phones, minifridges, and microwaves. Continental breakfast is included in the rate, and there's even a sauna and Jacuzzi.... *Tel 504/524-1140, 800/524-1140. Fax 504/523-4444. www.comfortsuites.com. 346 Baronne St., 70112. 103 suites. AE, DC, DISC, MC, V. $$–$$$$$*

See Map 4 on p. 34.

Dauphine Orleans (p. 31) FRENCH QUARTER You get a lot for your money here—no restaurant, but continental breakfast (accompanied by the morning paper) is included in the rate, and all rooms have safes, minibars, and hair dryers. The most interesting rooms are those in the rear of the main building, with exposed brick-between-posts walls and Jacuzzi baths. There's a charge for parking, but it's on-site and secure. A small exercise room is just off the rear courtyard.... *Tel 504/586-1800, 800/521-7111. Fax 504/586-1409. www.dauphineorleans.com. 415 Dauphine St., 70116. 111 rooms. AE, DC, DISC, MC, V. $$–$$$$$*

See Map 3 on p. 33.

Depot House at Madame Julia's Boarding House (p. 32) CBD Joanne and Dennis Hilton, of the St. Charles Guest House, also operate this little inn, which they have patterned, in part, after an old-time railroad boarding house. ("In part" because the only meal offered is a "bakery breakfast"—elsewhere known as a continental breakfast.) Rooms are simply decorated but comfortable; all have queen beds. Guests have access to the pool at the St. Charles Guest House. Be prepared to share a bathroom. The hotel is near the Warehouse District, and seven blocks from Canal St..... *Tel 504/529-2952. Fax 504/529-1908. www.mmejuliadepothouse.com. 748 O'Keefe St., 70113. 20 rooms, 6 bathrooms. No credit cards. $$–$$$*

See Map 4 on p. 34.

DoubleTree Hotel (p. 30) CBD If this luxury high-rise, which soars like a stone tree straight up out of the foot of Canal Street, were any closer to Harrah's Canal Street casino, casino guests could play blackjack without getting out of bed. Fresh flowers grace the small marble lobby, along with crowds of chewing and chatting conventioneers. Blond woods and pastel colors make the French country-style rooms seem larger than they actually are. There is a pool, coffee shop, and restaurant; the shops of Riverwalk are a 3-minute stroll away.... *Tel 504/581-1300, 800/222-TREE. Fax 504/522-4100. www.doubletree.com. 300 Canal St., 70130. 367 rooms, 12 suites. AE, DC, DISC, MC, V. $$$-$$$$$*

See Map 4 on p. 34.

Fairmont Hotel (p. 25) CBD A row of crystal chandeliers runs slap through the block-long lobby, shining on gilded pillars, marbled floors, and a motley crew of conventioneers, movie stars, and heads of state. Scenes from both *Blaze* and *The Pelican Brief* were shot in the Sazerac Bar. Rooms are extra large, and suites are sufficient for entertaining a fair-sized dinner party.... *Tel 504/529-7111, 800/527-4727. Fax 504/522-2303. www.fairmont.com. 123 Baronne St., 70130. 701 rooms, 85 suites. AE, DC, DISC, MC, V. $$-$$$$$*

See Map 4 on p. 34.

French Quarter Courtyard (p. 30) FRENCH QUARTER On iffy Rampart Street, but only a couple of blocks from popular niteries Funky Butt and Donna's, this small guesthouse occupies a building with a colorful past. It was built as a private mansion in the mid–19th century—there are high ceilings and polished wood floors throughout. In the late 1980s it was a wildly popular gay bar. No restaurant, but there is a complimentary continental breakfast and a courtyard, as the name promises.... *Tel 504/522-7333, 800/290-4233. Fax 504/522-3908. www.neworleans.com/fqch. 1101 N. Rampart St., 70116. 51 rooms. AE, DC, DISC, MC, V. $$-$$$$$*

See Map 3 on p. 33.

Garden Guest House (p. 24) NORTH SHORE Lazing between two bayous on the North Shore of Lake Pontchartrain, Paul and Bonnie Taliancich's secluded bed-and-breakfast is about an hour's drive from downtown New Orleans. Both Bonnie and Paul are avid gardeners and antiques collectors, and their interests are in evidence both inside and out. Their 1905 home, separate four-bedroom cottage, and three-bedroom Acadian House are decorated with American and European antiques, and sit on 10 acres that are awash with lush flowers and tall trees. The cottage is divided into four private suites, the Acadian House into three suites; guests may opt for a continental breakfast in their rooms or a full breakfast in the main house. Bonnie's homemade breads, muffins, and scones are not to be missed. No pets or kids, and smoking is not permitted.... *Tel 985/641-0335, 888/255-0335. www.gardenbb.com. 34514 Bayou Liberty Rd. (including Slidell),*

70460. 1 4-bedroom cottage, 1 3-bedroom cottage. AE, DC, DISC, MC, V. Traveler's and personal checks accepted. $$$

See Map 2 on p. 18.

Hampton Inn (p. 32) CBD One of the best buys for budgeteers the CBD has to offer, this is only two blocks from Bourbon Street, and a short walk from all the goings-on at the foot of Canal Street. There's also an interior walkway to the shops and fast-food restaurants in Place St. Charles, a high-rise office complex with a ground-floor mall. Rooms are extra large, and each has a hair dryer and amenity packet. Some suites have whirlpools, and there is even an exercise room. Valet parking, free local calls, and a continental breakfast (included in the rate) are other lures for budget-watchers.... *Tel 504/529-9990, 800/292-0653. Fax 504/529-9996. www.neworleans.com/hampton. 226 Carondelet St., 70130. 187 rooms. AE, DC, DISC, MC, V. $$–$$$$$*

See Map 4 on p. 34.

Holiday Inn Downtown–Superdome (p. 24) CBD True to its name, the Holiday Inn Downtown-Superdome is downtown in the CBD, near the overgrown Superdome. There are a rooftop pool and an indoor restaurant and lounge. The rooms offer no surprises, but the price is right, and they offer a free shuttle to the Quarter.... *Tel 504/581-1600, 800/535-7830. Fax 504/586-0833. www.hi-neworleans.com. 330 Loyola Ave., 70112. 290 rooms, 3 suites, 4 minisuites. AE, DC, DISC, MC, V. $$–$$$$$*

See Map 4 on p. 34.

Holiday Inn Select New Orleans–Convention Center (p. 22) WAREHOUSE DISTRICT As spiffy as they come, this upmarket Holiday Inn has a handsome marble lobby and enclosed three-story atrium. Guest rooms are extra-large, and come with a large desk/dining table, three phones, coffeemakers, and full-length mirrors. Suites have a large living room, wet bar, and 25-inch TV. All three meals are served in the atrium dining area, and Ray T's lounge picks up the slack with gourmet coffees and pastries. There's a good workout room, business services center, and coin-operated Laundromat.... *Tel 504/524-1881, 888/524-1881. Fax 504/528-1005. www.hiselect.com. 881 Convention Center Blvd., 70130. 170 rooms, 3 suites. AE, DC, DISC, MC, V. $$–$$$$$*

See Map 2 on p. 18.

Hostelling International–Marquette House New Orleans (p. 32) UPTOWN Strictly for budgeteers, this Uptown youth hostel is one of the nation's largest. Lodging is in dormitory rooms or apartments and there's no restaurant, though there is a community kitchen where you can stash your snacks, and picnic tables in a leafy patio area where you can enjoy them. The price is rock-bottom.... *Tel 504/523-3014. Fax 504/529-5933. 2249*

Carondelet St., 70130. 150 dorm beds, 12 apartments. AE, DC, DISC, MC, V. Member discounts. $

See Map 2 on p. 18.

Hotel InterContinental (p. 31) CBD The local rendition of this upmarket business-traveler chain is in a rose-granite building in which escalators roll up to a second-floor lobby with fresh flowers, recessed lighting, and artwork by local contemporary artists. The surprisingly tasteful sculpture garden on the fifth floor is a pleasant place to read and quietly contemplate your life.... *Tel 504/525-5566, 800/445-6563. Fax 504/523-7310. www.interconti.com. 444 St. Charles Ave., 70130. 482 rooms, 32 suites. AE, DISC, MC, V. $$$$–$$$$$*

See Map 4 on p. 34.

Hotel LeCirque (p. 23) WAREHOUSE DISTRICT Standing 10 stories tall on Lee Circle, this newish hotel is a great choice for people who plan to do a lot of gallery hopping in the neighborhood. The rooms are small and modern, outfitted in a tranquil array of neutrals. There's a pretty good (if pricey) restaurant downstairs, and you also get free access to a nearby gym.... *Tel 504/962-0900, 800/684-9525. Fax 504/962-0901. www.neworleansfinehotels.com. #2 Lee Circle, 70130. 137 rooms, 2 suites. AE, DC, DISC, MC, V. $$–$$$$$*

See Map 4 on p. 34.

Hotel Maison de Ville & Audubon Cottages (p. 27) FRENCH QUARTER One of the city's best-known small hotels, the Maison de Ville has luxurious rooms and suites in the main hotel, as well as in the cottages two blocks away, but those in the main house are really quite small for such a high price. Bathrooms, though outfitted with marble vanities, are just plain tiny. Rooms in the restored slave quarters all open onto the courtyard; to have any privacy, draw the drapes. Best bets are the Audubon Cottages, including a two-story affair with a terra-cotta floor and private patio. The pool is at the cottages, in a peaceful courtyard. Continental breakfast and afternoon port and sherry service are included, and there is an excellent restaurant, the Bistro.... *Tel 504/561-5858, 800/634-1600. Fax 504/528-9939. www.maisondeville.com. 727 Toulouse St., 70130. 14 rooms, 2 suites, 7 cottages. AE, DC, DISC, MC, V. $$$$–$$$$$*

See Map 3 on p. 33.

Hotel Monaco (p. 23) CBD A former Masonic temple has been transformed into a glamorous boutique hotel with plush decor and every amenity you can dream up. They'll even let you bring your pet, and, of course, "turn down" Rover's bed and leave a biscuit on the pillow. The in-house restaurant, Cobalt, was opened by local celebrity chef Susan Spicer.... *Tel 504/561-0010, 866/685-8359. Fax 504/310-2777. www.monaco-neworleans.com. 333 St. Charles Ave., 70130. 250 rooms, 12 suites. AE, DC, DISC, MC, V. $$$–$$$$$*

See Map 4 on p. 34.

Hotel Monteleone (p. 22) FRENCH QUARTER The Quarter's oldest and tallest hotel, the 16-story Monteleone wears her 100-plus years well, though she has had a number of face-lifts. There are three restaurants and a rooftop pool and health club. Each of the rooms and suites is decorated differently, some with handsome antiques or reproductions and four-poster beds.... *Tel 504/523-3341, 800/535-9595. Fax 504/528-1019. www.hotemonteleone.com. 214 Royal St., 70130. 543 rooms, 57 suites. AE, DC, DISC, MC, V. $$$–$$$$$*

See Map 3 on p. 33.

Hotel Provincial (p. 32) FRENCH QUARTER Because it occupies several buildings built in the mid-1800s, each room at this affordable hotel features a unique layout. The antique and reproduction furniture has seen better days, but when you take into account its prices, ample parking, and two pools, it's a great place to call home for your Crescent City vacation.... *Tel 504/581-4995, 800/535-7922. Fax 504/581-1018. www.hotelprovincial.com. 1024 Chartres St., 70116. 94 rooms, 10 suites. AE, DC, DISC, MC, V. $$–$$$$*

See Map 3 on p. 33.

Hotel Villa Convento (p. 28) FRENCH QUARTER In the lower Quarter, near the Old Ursuline Convent, this little family-run guesthouse isn't luxurious, and it doesn't have a pool or a restaurant, but the Campo family makes it terrifically friendly. The four-story hotel, built as a town house in the 19th century, has pale green ironwork and front balconies overlooking Ursuline Street and the nearby Old Ursuline Convent. The average-sized rooms, which could do with some freshening up, are furnished with reproductions of 19th-century antiques. A continental breakfast, served in the shaded courtyard, is included in the rate.... *Tel 504/522-1793, 800/887-2817. Fax 504/524-1902. www.villaconvento.com. 616 Ursulines St., 70116. 25 rooms. AE, DC, DISC, MC, V. $$–$$$$*

See Map 3 on p. 33.

House on Bayou Road (p. 24) MID-CITY When Dan Aykroyd was in town opening the House of Blues, he stayed at this small outlying bed-and-breakfast. Peace, country quiet, rocking chairs, wind chimes, antique four-posters, and a gourmet breakfast give it its charm. The private cottage is splendid, with a skylight, scads of books, and a Jacuzzi. Everyone can dip in the gazebo-covered hot tub (even when it's raining). On weekends a sumptuous champagne brunch is served around the pool; the B&B's adjacent restaurant is called Indigo, in tribute to what once grew on these former plantation's grounds.... *Tel 504/945-0992, 800/882-2968. Fax 504/945-0993. www.houseonbayouroad.com. 2275 Bayou Rd., 70119. 5 rooms, 2 suites, 1 cottage. AE, DC, DISC, MC, V. $$$$–$$$$$*

See Map 2 on p. 18.

Hyatt Regency Hotel (p. 24) CBD Big, splashy, and over-stuffed with creature comforts, the Hyatt is in a complex of massive modern concrete that includes Poydras Plaza, New Orleans Center, and the Superdome, plus there's a shuttle to tool you over to the French Quarter and back. The extra perks—concierge services, private key–access elevator—are in the Regency Club. Otherwise, rooms and suites are scattered in various low- and high-rise sections. The Hyatt is home to the city's only revolving rooftop restaurant; Top of the Dome has a splendid view of the cityscape, and kids go hog-wild over the nightly Chocoholic Bar.... *Tel 504/561-1234, 800/233-1234. Fax 504/587-4141. www.hyatt.com. 500 Poydras Plaza, 70113. 1,184 rooms, 48 suites. AE, DC, DISC, MC, V. $$$–$$$$$*

See Map 4 on p. 34.

The Iberville Suites (p. 27) FRENCH QUARTER Here's the story with the Iberville Suites: They are fairly new, located on a not-so-fabulous block on the very edge of the Quarter, and they offer some of the best lodging value in the city. Each room is relatively spacious and offers distinct living and sleeping areas—perfect for families or businesspeople needing to entertain. You get a free continental breakfast every morning. Its building connects to the Ritz-Carlton, so for $10 you can work out at the Ritz's excellent gym, and you also have charging privileges at all of their bars and restaurants.... *Tel 504/523-2400, 866/229-4351. Fax 504/524-1320. www.ibervillesuites.com. 910 Iberville St., 70112. 490 rooms, 37 suites. AE, DC, DISC, MC, V. $$$–$$$$$*

See Map 3 on p. 33.

International House (p. 23) CBD Located in a beautiful Beaux Arts building near the Quarter, I-House was one of the first locally owned boutique hotels to open in the city. Lobby decor is changed seasonally, so the mood always matches the weather. The rooms are peacefully decked in neutrals, and there are many touches to indicate where you are: original black-and-white photos of local musicians, Louisiana wildflowers, furniture designed by local artisans.... *Tel 504/553-9550, 800/633-5770. Fax 504/553-9560. www.ihhotel.com. 211 Camp St., 70130. 116 rooms, 3 suites. AE, DC, DISC, MC, V. $$–$$$$$*

See Map 4 on p. 34.

Josephine Guest House (p. 29) GARDEN DISTRICT In the Garden District, a block from the streetcar line, the Josephine is an Italianate mansion dating from 1870 and filled with handsome antiques. Continental breakfast is included in the rate. No pool, unfortunately.... *Tel 504/524-6361, 800/779-6361. Fax 504/523-6484. www.josephine.us. 1450 Josephine St., 70130. 6 rooms. AE, DC, DISC, MC, V. $$$–$$$$*

See Map 2 on p. 18.

La Maison Marigny FAUBOURG MARIGNY This comfortable B&B is nicely situated on Bourbon Street, a short stroll from the teeming crowds of drunks and revelers, but far enough away so the unending cacophony doesn't keep you from your beauty rest. One of the proprietors is a former concierge, so he knows where to send you for drinks, dinner, and music. He also knows how to keep guests happy, with well-appointed rooms and hearty, homemade breakfasts. Don't pass up the baked goods.... *Tel 504/948-3638, 800/570-2014. Fax 504/945-5012. www.lamaisonmarigny.com. 1421 Bourbon St., 70116. 4 rooms. AE, DC, DISC, MC, V. $$$*

See Map 3 on p. 33.

Lafayette Hotel (p. 22) CBD The chic little Lafayette tries hard to perpetuate the myth that New Orleans is a French city. The switchboard operator answers with *"Bonjour"* and *"Bon soir."* Rooms and suites have high ceilings, lovely millwork, marble bathrooms with brass fittings and bidets, and cushy easy chairs. It's in the CBD, roughly midway between Lee Circle and Canal Street.... *Tel 504/524-4441, 800/270-7542. Fax 504/523-7327. www.neworleansfinehotels.com. 600 St. Charles Ave., 70130. 24 rooms, 20 suites. AE, DC, DISC, MC, V. $$–$$$$$*

See Map 4 on p. 34.

Lafitte Guest House (p. 26) FRENCH QUARTER One of the most charming of the Quarter's guesthouses, this Victorian-decor spot has no restaurant or pool, but an in-room continental breakfast accompanied with fresh flowers is included in the rate. All rooms have private bathrooms, too. It's on the quiet end of Bourbon Street.... *Tel 504/581-2678, 800/331-7971. www.lafitteguesthouse.com. 1003 Bourbon St., 70116. 14 rooms. AE, DC, DISC, MC, V. $$$$–$$$$$*

See Map 3 on p. 33.

Lanaux Mansion (p. 30) FAUBOURG MARIGNY On the edge of the Quarter, this Italianate mansion near the French Market offers complete privacy in elegant suites and a cottage. No pool or restaurant, but continental breakfast fixings are brought nightly to your room, and you prepare it at your leisure.... *Tel 504/488-4640, 800/729-4640. Fax 504/488-4639. www.historiclodging.com. 547 Esplanade Ave., 70116. 1 room, 2 suites, 1 cottage. AE, DC, DISC, MC, V. $$$–$$$$$*

See Map 3 on p. 33.

Le Pavillon (p. 24) CBD Close to the Superdome and New Orleans Center shops, this fancy property offers a lot for your money, including an open-air rooftop pool with cabanas and the Crystal Room, a restaurant with one of the city's best bargain-lunch buffets. Outside are awnings and a porte-cochère with massive Corinthian columns; inside, the European-style lobby is lovely, with oil paintings, lots of marble, and imported crystal chandeliers. True, the rooms are identical, with traditional mahogany furnishings, though some have big bay windows, but they all offer high-speed Internet access. The suites are sumptuously decked out in satins and velvet.... *Tel 504/581-3111, 800/535-9095. Fax 504/522-5543. www.lepavillon.com. 833 Poydras St., 70140. 119 rooms, 7 suites. AE, DC, DISC, MC, V. $$$–$$$$$*

See Map 4 on p. 34.

Le Richelieu (p. 32) FRENCH QUARTER Without a doubt, this is the best buy in town. It's a small hotel in the lower Quarter, with rooms and suites all done up differently, and extra features such as walk-in closets, ceiling fans, and mirrored walls. The restaurant and bar are just off the courtyard and pool, and free parking is on-site in a patrolled parking lot.... *Tel 504/529-2492, 800/535-9653. Fax 504/524-8179. www.lerichelieuhotel.com. 1234 Chartres St., 70116. 69 rooms, 17 suites. AE, DC, DISC, MC, V. $$–$$$$$*

See Map 3 on p. 33.

Loews Hotel (p. 25) CBD Another luxury hotel testing its luck in the Big Easy, the extremely new Loews has a few things going for it: location, location, location. Just a couple blocks from the convention center, across the street from Harrah's, and easy walking distance to the Quarter, it will undoubtedly attract a lot of the doctors and lawyers in town for their annual meetings. It, of course, has the expected amenities—large rooms, king beds, turndown, free morning coffee and newspaper—along with some unexpected ones like free shoeshines, four spa treatment rooms, and babysitting.... *Tel 504/595-3300, 800/235-6397. Fax 504/595-3310. www.loewshotels.com. 300 Poydras St., 70130. 273 rooms, 12 suites. AE, DC, DISC, MC, V. $$$$–$$$$$*

See Map 2 on p. 18.

Loft 523 (p. 23) CBD Probably the highest concept lodging in the city, this hotel subscribes to a very minimalist/haute design philosophy. Rooms are large and full of open space, as the name would indicate. Furniture is sparse and architectural with Fortuny lamps, whirlybird ceiling fans, Agape Spoon tubs, Vola bath accessories, and Mondo beds. If these names mean nothing to you, then it's not your kind of hotel. Each guest gets the card of his or her "personal assistant" who is supposed to tend to your every need during your stay. There's also a dark and trendy bar downstairs.... *Tel 504/200-6523. Fax 504/200-6522. www.loft523.com. 523 Gravier St., 70130. 16 rooms, 2 suites. AE, DC, DISC, MC, V. $$$–$$$$$*

See Map 4 on p. 34.

Maison Orleans (p. 23) FRENCH QUARTER This posh sister of the Ritz-Carlton raises the bar on the company's service standards.

A boutique hotel upgraded to Club Level, it offers intensely personalized service—including your own Club Concierge—with access to the luxuries of the bigger Ritz next door: the bars, restaurant, shopping, and spa. If you're rich, famous, and discreet (a small group, we know), this is your spot.... *Tel 504/254-9431, 800/241-3333. Fax 504/670-2910. www.maisonorleans.com. 904 Iberville St. 70112. 75 rooms. AE, DC, DISC, MC, V. $$$$-$$$$$*

See Map 3 on p. 33.

The McKendrick-Breaux House (p. 29) LOWER GARDEN DISTRICT Two beautifully restored 1865 Greek Revivals offering nine lushly furnished rooms—you just can't miss here. The rooms bear extravagant touches like floor-to-ceiling silk dupioni drapes and fresh flowers. Bathtime is a pleasure here; each bathroom is notable for its size, pedestal sinks, and claw-foot tubs. And the covered patio, equipped with fans and tons of comfy seating, is an excellent spot for kicking back at the end of a long day of touring.... *Tel 504/586-1700, 888/570-1700. Fax 504/522-7138. www.mckendrick-breaux.com. 1474 Magazine St., 70130. 9 rooms. AE, DC, DISC, MC, V. $$$$-$$$$$*

See Map 2 on p. 18.

Moreau Townhouse (p. 27) LOWER GARDEN DISTRICT If you opt for optimum privacy, consider staying in one of these super-swank apartments. Not a hotel, the Townhouse offers stunning suites with full kitchens (including dishwasher, coffeemaker, microwave, iron, and ironing board) or kitchenettes, king beds with down pillows and down comforters, cable TV, CD player, and private balcony. Owner Heather Moreau caters to long-term guests, and has hosted a number of celebs who've desired absolute anonymity. Don't expect amenities such as room service; there isn't even a switchboard—guests are given a private phone number and have their own answering machine. The property is half a block from the St. Charles streetcar. Posh, pricey, and very private. No kids or pets; no smoking indoors.... *Tel 504/527-5037, 888/815-5037. Fax 504/593-9079. www.moreautownhouse.com. 1404 Prytania St., 70130. 7 suites. No credit cards. $$$-$$$$$*

See Map 2 on p. 18.

New Orleans Hilton Riverside (p. 24) CBD Near the convention center in the CBD, the Hilton is one of the biggest and splashiest of the convention-cum-tour-group hotels. Sightseeing paddle-wheelers dock smack at its side door, and the hotel itself is awash with restaurants, bars, and lounges, including the rooftop Executive Lounge. You can wear yourself completely out in the rooftop Rivercenter Racquet and Health Club, or you can just flop down and fatten up in the various restaurants, lounges, and bars.... *Tel 504/561-0500, 800/445-8667. Fax 504/568-1721.*

www.hilton.com. 2 Poydras St., 70140. 1,600 rooms, 89 suites. AE, DC, DISC, MC, V. $$$–$$$$$

See Map 2 on p. 18.

New Orleans Marriott (p. 24) CBD This is a major CBD convention hotel, but it's not to be confused with one of the Marriott's luxurious resorts. And you'll be shelling out a lot for a place that could as easily be in Kansas City. But it comes with the works: pool, health club, lounges, cafe, and a lobby the size of a football field.... *Tel 504/581-1000, 800/228-9290. Fax 504/523-6755. www.marriott.com. 555 Canal St., 70130. 1,329 rooms, 54 suites. AE, DC, DISC, MC, V. $$–$$$$$*

See Map 4 on p. 34.

Olivier House Hotel (p. 26) FRENCH QUARTER This is a somewhat quirky family-run guesthouse that's well located in the Quarter, and whose loyal repeat guests eschew the big luxury hotels in favor of the very laid-back style. The general ambience might be termed Caribbean-cum-southern Italy. The assortment of rooms and suites includes a secluded cottage just off the courtyard and pool, and a rear courtyard that's been enclosed and transformed into a large two-story suite, with a skylight, a fountain, and banana trees. Others range from split-level suites and lofts to small darkish inside rooms with old brick walls. Almost all have microwaves and some sort of kitchen facilities; there's no restaurant, but Antoine's is only a block and a half away.... *Tel 504/525-8456, 866/525-9748. Fax 504/529-2006. www.olivierhouse.com. 828 Toulouse St., 70112. 42 rooms. AE, DC, MC, V. $$–$$$$$*

See Map 3 on p. 33.

Omni Royal Crescent (p. 31) CBD A chic kid sister to the Quarter's Royal O., this boutique hotel boasts marble bathrooms and Egyptian cotton sheets. Robes and slippers are provided for snuggling up and listening to the bedside tape cassette player, which is replete with classical music selections. Suites have VCRs and Jacuzzi baths. There is a well-equipped fitness center (with sauna), and the sixth-floor wading pool is done up like a Roman bath. The in-hotel restaurant, Benjarong, serves Thai food.... *Tel 504/527-0006 or 800/THE-OMNI. Fax 504/571-7575. www.omnihotels.com. 535 Gravier St., 70130. 91 rooms, 7 suites. AE, DC, DISC, MC, V. $$–$$$$$*

See Map 4 on p. 34.

Omni Royal Orleans (p. 22) FRENCH QUARTER Smack in the center of the Quarter, the Royal O. is an upscale hotel in which gilded statues guard marbled halls laid with Oriental rugs and hung with immense crystal chandeliers. Suites here are knee-weakening, with canopied beds only slightly smaller than your average Boy Scout tent, but regular rooms are on the smallish side, though still grandly decorated. The lobby's Esplanade lounge is fine for winding down after a hard night of jazz and zydeco, and the Rib Room (see Dining) is a favored place for power breakfasting and dining. There's a pool at the rooftop La Riviera Club.... *Tel 504/529-5333, 800/THE-OMNI. Fax 504/529-7089. www.omniroyalorleans.com. 621 St. Louis St., 70140. 330 rooms, 16 suites. AE, DC, DISC, MC, V. $$$–$$$$$*

See Map 3 on p. 33.

Pontchartrain Hotel (p. 25) GARDEN DISTRICT This venerable hotel is too sedate for newfangled frills like a pool and health club. The friendly staff is accustomed to catering to the whims of celebrity guests, and elegant suites are named for stellar personages who have occupied them (Anne Rice, Richard Burton, and Tennessee Williams among them). But no one fails to turn down your bed if you opt for the less luxurious and far-less-expensive pension rooms, which have shower baths and nary a grand piano or solarium.... *Tel 504/524-0581, 800/777-6193. Fax 504/529-1165. www.pontchartrainhotel.com. 2031 St. Charles Ave., 70140. 118 rooms,19 suites. AE, DC, DISC, MC, V. $$–$$$$$*

See Map 2 on p. 18.

Queen & Crescent Hotel (p. 31) WAREHOUSE DISTRICT Styled along the lines of a small European hotel, the Q&C is a conversion of a 12-story turn-of-the-century office building. Beyond the marbled lobby, rooms provide plush robes and minibars, safes and coffeemakers, two phone lines with dataports, and irons and ironing boards. Makeup mirrors add a convenient touch, and nightly turndown service is provided. There is not a restaurant here, or a pool; however, there's a fitness center and a guest laundry.... *Tel 504/587-9700, 800/975-6652. Fax 504/587-9701. www.queenandcrescent.com. 344 Camp St., 70130. 196 rooms. AE, DC, DISC, MC, V. $$–$$$$$*

See Map 4 on p. 34.

Renaissance Arts Hotel (p. 22) WAREHOUSE DISTRICT This very new spot has appropriately decked itself out in original works of art, a homage to its creative 'hood. There's a gallery off the lobby and a sculpture garden on the second floor. Even the cheerful rooms are kitted out with local art and bold fabrics.... *Tel 504/613-2330, 800/468-3571. Fax 504/613-2331. www.renaissancehotels.com. 700 Tchoupitoulas St., 70130. 217 rooms, 11 suites. AE, DC, DISC, MC, V. $$$–$$$$$*

See Map 2 on p. 18.

Renaissance Pere Marquette Hotel (p. 26) CBD Renaissance hotels are part of the Marriott family, but you'd never guess their super-chain roots once you get inside. The Pere Marquette is smack in the middle of the bustling corporate CBD, so it's near the Quarter, but without the constant din of nighttime revelers. The guest rooms are ultra modern with Henry Miller Aeron desk chairs, dataports, cordless phones, and in-room safes sized to fit your laptop. There's also the requisite pool and an excellent French restaurant, Rene Bistro (see Dining).... *Tel 504/525-1111, 800/HOTELS1. Fax 504/252-0688. www.renaissancehotels.com. 817 Common St., 70112. 280 rooms, 6 suites. AE, DC, DISC, MC, V. $$$$-$$$$$*

See Map 4 on p. 34.

Ritz-Carlton New Orleans (p. 23) CBD Renowned for its employee empowerment and focus on high service, the R-C had its work cut out for it trying to train the sometimes unruly Big Easy workforce. Sure, our people are friendly, but just try getting them to come to work on time. For the most part the R-C is a success story, with its beautiful rooms, usually impeccable service, and very warm staff. Its French Quarter Bar (see nightlife) is a hot spot for locals and tourists alike. Of course, the spa is one of the main things to recommend the Ritz: Myriad services in the most beautiful treatment rooms the city has to offer.... *Tel 504/524-1331, 800/241-3333. Fax 504/524-7675. www.ritzcarlton.com. 921 Canal St., 70112. 490 rooms, 37 suites. AE, DC, DISC, MC, V. $$$$-$$$$$*

See Map 3 on p. 33.

Royal Sonesta Hotel (p. 25) FRENCH QUARTER The front doors open onto Bourbon Street, but the Sonesta staff works hard to preserve a sense of peace and serenity. Rooms are average-sized; avoid those with balconies on the front and sides unless it's Mardi Gras. Those with balconies on the courtyard overlook the pool and orange trees. There are ground-floor shops purveying luxury items; a well-equipped business center; and sundry bars, lounges, a casual eatery, and an overpriced restaurant.... *Tel 504/586-0300, 800/SONESTA. Fax 504/586-0335. www.royalsonestano.com. 300 Bourbon St., 70140. 480 rooms, 20 suites. AE, DC, DISC, MC, V. $$$-$$$$$*

See Map 3 on p. 33.

St. Charles Guest House (p. 29) LOWER GARDEN DISTRICT A lovely entranceway with a small crystal chandelier and attractive wallpaper ushers you into Joanne and Dennis Hilton's unpretentious guesthouse. It ambles all over the place, with simple, functional rooms for backpackers—a few without air-conditioning (a major negative in summer). A low-key bakery breakfast is served.... *Tel 504/523-6556. Fax 504/522-6340. www.stcharlesguesthouse.com. 1748 Prytania St., 70130. 35 rooms. AE, DC, DISC, MC, V. $-$$$$*

See Map 2 on p. 18.

Saint Louis Hotel (p. 26) FRENCH QUARTER The location is excellent—in the Quarter, and two blocks from the CBD—but the 1960s hotel hasn't much in the way of character. Its main attractions are the stunning courtyard and the fine French restaurant, Louis XVI (see Dining).... *Tel 504/581-7300, 888/508-3980. Fax 504/524-8925. www.stlouishotel.com. 730 Bienville St., 70130. 83 rooms, 4 suites. AE, DISC, MC, V. $$$–$$$$*

See Map 3 on p. 33.

Sheraton New Orleans (p. 25) CBD True, the lobby is usually crowded with conventioneers and tour groups, but the high-rise Sheraton somehow seems to rise above it all. A huge plate-glass window facing Canal Street allows plenty of light into the splashy lobby, which houses a Starbucks and a bar. The rooms are above-average rooms, plus there's an excellent health club, a pool, a restaurant, and lounges. It's directly across the street from the Marriott.... *Tel 504/525-2500, 800/325-3535. Fax 504/595-5222. www.sheraton.com. 500 Canal St., 70130. 1,110 rooms, 56 suites. AE, DC, DISC, MC, V. $$$–$$$$$*

See Map 4 on p. 34.

Soniat House (p. 28) FRENCH QUARTER In the quiet lower Quarter, this fine small hotel occupies two adjoining early 19th-century town houses with a flower-filled courtyard. Across the street are six Jacuzzi suites, and three premier rooms. All are expensively dressed in antiques, Oriental rugs, and framed contemporary prints. There's no pool or restaurant, but there is a 24-hour concierge; continental breakfast (not included in the rate) is café au lait and plump biscuits with homemade strawberry preserves and freshly squeezed orange juice.... *Tel 504/522-0570, 800/544-8808. Fax 504/522-7208. www.soniathouse.com. 1133 Chartres St., 70116. 23 rooms, 11 suites. AE, DC, DISC, MC, V. $$$$–$$$$$*

See Map 3 on p. 33.

Sully Mansion (p. 29) UPTOWN/GARDEN DISTRICT In the Garden District, a block from the St. Charles streetcar, this bed-and-breakfast is in a handsome Queen Anne mansion. The house dates from the 1890s, and has the original stained-glass windows. The whimsical assortment of rooms ranges from large suites with four-posters, new draperies, and antiques, to a tiny room you can hardly turn around in. The staff is friendly and helpful.... *Tel 504/891-0457, 800/364-2414. Fax 504/269-0793. www.sullymansion.com. 2631 Prytania St., 70130. 5 rooms, 2 suites. AE, DISC, MC, V. $$–$$$$$*

See Map 2 on p. 18.

W New Orleans (p. 22) CBD The designs are bold—such as the black bedroom wall and cherry-red shower curtains—and the target is the business traveler: All rooms have 27-inch TVs with Internet access via infrared keyboard; CD players; and two phones. Cabanas in the pool area are equipped for laptops and

TV. Some of the rooms have a fax, printer, copier, and scanner. Ah, me. You don't actually have to work when you stay here. Creature comforts, too, are aplenty, such as luxurious beds dressed with pillowtop mattresses, 250 thread-count sheets, and goose-down comforters and pillows; Aveda bath toiletries; stocked minibars (which sell voodoo dolls); and terry-lined robes to wrap yourself in after that chocolate-milk bath. The lobby lounge features the W Hotel's living room design signature board games; Whiskey Blue is the bar; and Zöe Bistro is a Parisian-style brasserie.... *Tel 504/525-9444, 800/522-6963. Fax 504/581-7179. www.whotels.com. 333 Poydras St., 70130. 400 rooms, 23 suites. AE, DC, DISC, MC, V. $$$$–$$$$$*

See Map 4 on p. 34.

W New Orleans–French Quarter (p. 23) FRENCH QUARTER Ideally located in the Quarter, three blocks from Canal Street, this luxe hotel features top-quality fabrics in bold colors, plush bedding and bathrobes, stocked minibars, CD players, and 27-inch cable TVs. The property boasts a glamorous courtyard and pool, behind which are carriage houses containing even more comfy accommodations. The restaurant is the estimable Tuscan establishment Bacco, owned by Ralph and Cindy Brennan.... *Tel 504/581-1200, 800/WHOTELS. Fax 504/523-2910. www.whotels.com. 316 Chartres St., 70130. 100 rooms, 2 suites, 4 carriage houses. AE, DC, DISC, MC, V. $$$–$$$$$*

See Map 3 on p. 33.

Windsor Court Hotel (p. 23) CBD This luxury hotel has something in the neighborhood of $7 million worth of art from the British Empire and antiques displayed in public rooms throughout. The theme, as the name suggests, is the "House of Windsor." Most rooms are suites done up with four-poster beds. Dipping is done in an oversized pool, and a health club has plenty of machines for working off all the weight you'll put on in the New Orleans Grill (see Dining). The swells do deals over champagne and scones in Le Salon, which by night doubles as the only smoke-free lounge with live jazz in the city.... *Tel 504/523-6000, 800/262-2662. Fax 504/596-4513. www.windsorcourthotel.com. 300 Gravier St., 70130. 58 rooms, 266 suites. AE, DC, DISC, MC, V. $$$$$*

See Map 4 on p. 34.

Woods Hole Inn (p. 24) NORTH SHORE An hour from New Orleans, cozy private accommodations are in two suites and a 100-year-old cabin. Among the charming features are an antique queen-size bed, a four-poster bed, wood-burning fireplaces, hardwood floors, patchwork quilts, and old-fashioned claw-foot tubs. The cabin has a beamed ceiling and tin roof, as well as a full kitchen. Modern conveniences include cable TV, coffeemakers, and fridges that are filled with everything you need for a continental breakfast, which you prepare at your leisure. The home of proprietors Marsha and Sam Smalley is a discreet distance from the cottages.... *Tel 985/796-9077. www.woodsholeinn.com. 78253 Woods Hole Lane, Folsom, 70437. 2 suites, 1 cabin. No pets or small children. AE, DISC, MC, V (for online reservations only). Personal checks accepted. Cash discount. $$–$$$$*

See Map 2 on p. 18.

Wyndham New Orleans (p. 22) FRENCH QUARTER The large and luxurious hotel soars to 29 floors above the tiny Canal Place mall, with an 11th-floor lobby, where arched 26-foot-high windows frame the river and the French Quarter. Each room and suite has a marble foyer, pristine white millwork, and soothing-on-the-eyes shades of peach, rose, or green. There's a rooftop pool; a good restaurant, River 127 (see Dining); and some 40 or so shops beneath your feet.... *Tel 504/566-7006, 800/WYNDHAM. Fax 504/553-5120. www.wyndham.com. 100 Iberville St., 70130. 438 rooms, 41 suites. AE, DISC, MC, V. $$$$–$$$$$*

See Map 3 on p. 33.

D I N

ING

2

Map 5: New Orleans Dining Orientation

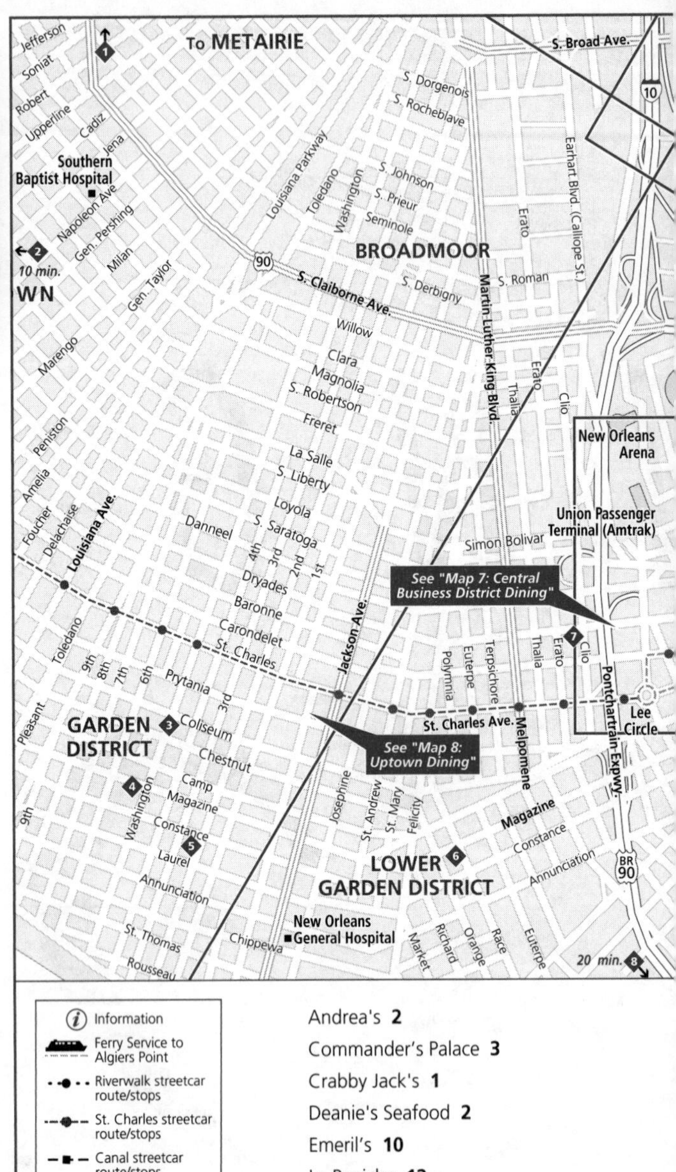

Information

Ferry Service to Algiers Point

Riverwalk streetcar route/stops

St. Charles streetcar route/stops

Canal streetcar route/stops

Vieux Carre loop route/stops

Andrea's **2**

Commander's Palace **3**

Crabby Jack's **1**

Deanie's Seafood **2**

Emeril's **10**

La Peniche **12**

Mosca's **8**

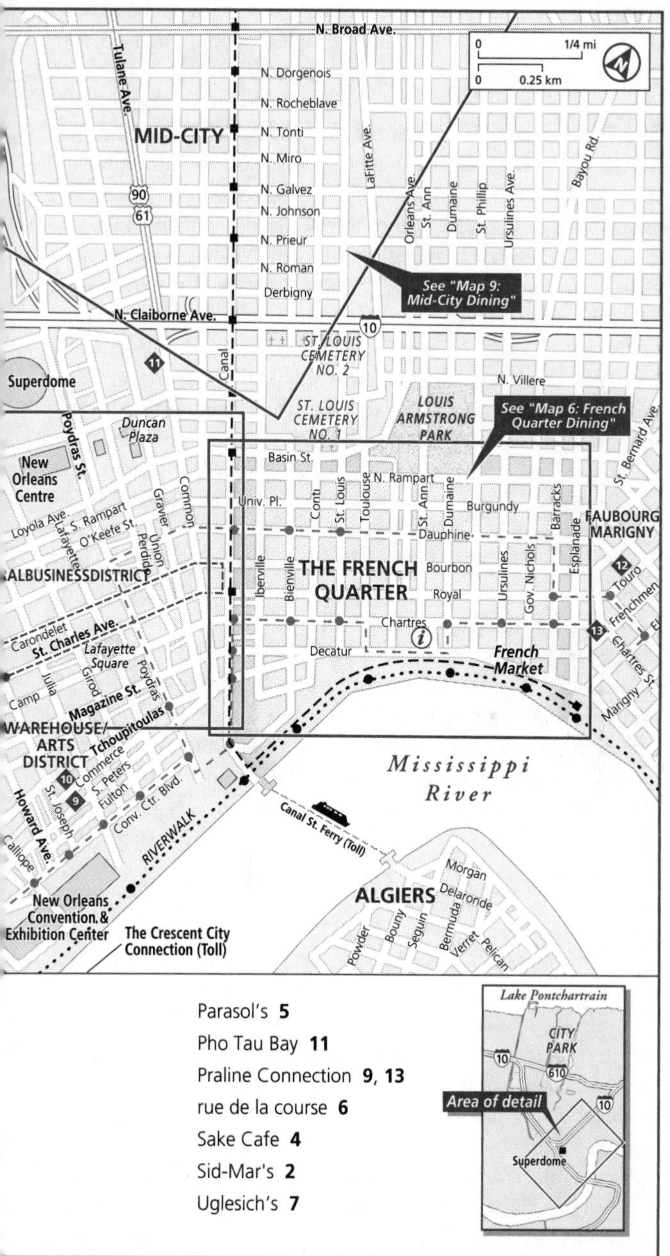

Parasol's **5**

Pho Tau Bay **11**

Praline Connection **9, 13**

rue de la course **6**

Sake Cafe **4**

Sid-Mar's **2**

Uglesich's **7**

Basic Stuff

New Orleans usually ranks near the top of the list of the nation's fattest cities, and it's no wonder. People here are obsessed with food. The city is replete with edibles: red beans and rice with sausage on Mondays, seafood gumbo or fried catfish on Fridays, King Cakes during Carnival, crawfish and Ponchatoula strawberries in the spring. Come March, people are already obsessing about the crawfish beignets, mango freezes, crawfish Monica, and other delicacies served at the New Orleans Jazz and Heritage Festival. We're not talking about food snobs; even average New Orleanians have strong opinions about the best way to make a roux (the oil-and-flour base for gumbo), or how to peel a crawfish, or which bakery makes the best King Cake. People here talk about food the way people elsewhere talk about sports, art, theater, or politics. Contributing to the girth of many New Orleanians is a single culinary rule of thumb: If it tastes good, eat it.

If you come for just a weekend, even a long one, prepare to be full the whole time. You'll want to eat as much as possible. And we're not just talking about big meals at Galatoire's or Commander's Palace. You'll probably want to try a muffaletta from Central Grocery, or beignets and café au lait at Café du Monde, or both. And what about a po'boy? Fried shrimp or roast beef? For a quick snack in the Quarter, you'll want to gobble a Lucky Dog, if only so you can tell your friends you ate something from a street cart shaped like a giant hot dog. And, depending on the season, you'll want to try some raw oysters, right? And boiled crawfish. And what about those celebrity chefs? Are Emeril Lagasse and Paul Prudhomme really the best in the city? What about Susan Spicer? Anne Kearney? John Besh? Don't you want to try at least one of these? By now you get the point. If you come here, you should expect something akin to a food orgy.

Since there's no way to cover every restaurant during one visit, you need to be strategic. If you want to sample Creole cooking, go to Galatoire's or Antoine's or Arnaud's or Commander's Palace, but not all of them. For contrast, pick one of the several restaurants that specialize in New South Louisiana cuisine. You get the picture. A truism about New Orleans is that change comes slowly here, so most of the places you'll want to visit will still be here when you return.

No one has ever done a study on why Orleanians are so fixated on food, but they are. They analyze food, argue about food, and, especially, pontificate about food. And complain about food. Everybody's a critic here, and whining about the food seems to be a part of the Orleanian psyche, like grousing about politics. (Makes you wonder how they'd react if they were ever served truly bad food.) In truth, these people are very well satisfied; they love New Orleans's food and New Orleans's restaurants. So it wouldn't be wise to chime in and agree with them about the "inedible" food they're bashing.

The opening of a new restaurant gets Orleanians all a-quiver, similar to the way some folks get in anticipation of a new play on Broadway. While openings are rather frequent, closings are rare. New Orleanians eat out a lot and are far more supportive of restaurants than they are, say, of the ballet or the opera. The dining-out mood is usually festive. Again, it's similar to theatergoing in New York, and some spots are as splashy and bright as a Broadway musical (well, almost).

The greatest concentration of restaurants lies in the French Quarter, where there is at least some kind of food available on virtually every block, even if it's just one of the Lucky Dog carts. The Central Business District (CBD) is likewise bursting with everything from smart hotel dining rooms to skid row dives. Seafood, of course, is ubiquitous in this port city in the swamps; practically every place serves some manifestation thereof, but the really hard-core fish eaters' havens are out in the West End and Bucktown, where there are scads of family restaurants and seafood shacks.

Local tastes are wide-ranging. Sure, locals go to Commander's and Galatoire's. But they also go to places like Parasol's, an

Cajun Country

Contrary to what many people seem to think, New Orleans is not a Cajun city. It was French Creoles who colonized New Orleans—the Cajuns were another group of French-speaking folk who migrated down here about 40 years later. They came from Canada and settled in 22 parishes (the Louisiana term for counties) to the west of the New Orleans colony, in an area now known as Cajun Country, or Acadiana, or French Louisiana. These French Catholics were descendants of a group of settlers from northwest France who, in 1603, had colonized a section of present-day Nova Scotia, which they called l'Acadie—or Acadia. These Acadians were kicked out in the mid–18th century when the English conquered that territory and demanded that the French settlers relinquish their religion and pledge allegiance to the British crown. The Longfellow poem "Evangeline" (a classic that nobody reads anymore) is about this exodus, known as Le Grand Derangement. In 1763, 3,000 Acadians were welcomed in Louisiana, then under the rule of Spaniards sympathetic to the Catholics' dilemma. "Acadian" became corrupted into "Cajun."

uptown Irish restaurant and bar known for its heavenly po'boys and raucous St. Patty's day partying. People here are food lovers, not food snobs.

Only in New Orleans

Don't get a headache trying to figure out the difference between Creole and Cajun food. Leave it to locals to sweat the nuances (something they love to do). Both cuisines have French roots, but Creole food evolved in the city kitchens of New Orleans and Cajun cooking developed in the parishes (counties) of Acadian country to the west. There are no pure Cajun restaurants in New Orleans, even though there are several Cajun chefs. Most Cajun foods, if properly prepared, would be too time-consuming for restaurant kitchens—and besides, all that bacon fat, lard, and butter (that authentic dishes call for) have, shall we say, fallen out of favor. Paul Prudhomme almost single-handedly kicked off the nationwide Cajun craze of the 1980s, but though he himself is a card-carrying Cajun, the food he serves is an elaborate embellishment of the real thing. "Blackening"—as in blackened redfish—is a Prudhomme invention, not a traditional Cajun preparation. Cajun chefs owe a lot to Chef Paul, however, since he popularized all things Cajun and thus attracted customers to Cajun restaurants. Nowadays, people expect—and usually get—at least a few blackened dishes in any Cajun restaurant. Several local chefs also prepare what they call "South Louisiana cooking," which combines elements of Cajun with Creole and other traditions.

Pralines are far more prevalent in New Orleans than black-eyed peas—proof, if it's needed, that New Orleans is not really a southern city. Pralines are sweet candies made of butter, pecans, and sugar, and they, too, come in many different manifestations. (To buy a box, visit Aunt Sally's Praline Shop at 810 Decatur St.—see Shopping.)

Indigenous Ingredients & Such

Everybody's doing arugula, Shiitake, and cilantro—New Orleans's chefs see those ingredients and up the ante. Here are some local terms that may not be so familiar:

Andouille: Cajun pork sausage, kin to kielbasa. Emeril Lagasse, of Emeril's and Nola, makes a pretty mean andouille.

Bananas Foster: A rich dessert made of sliced bananas sautéed in butter with brown sugar, cinnamon, and banana liqueur, then flamed with white rum and served over vanilla ice cream. Invented at Brennan's, but possibly even better at Arnaud's.

Barbecue shrimp: Do not be fooled. This is barbecue in name only. It's really peel 'n' eat boiled shrimp in a garlicky sauce. Pascal's Manale claims to be the originator of this dish, but now many restaurants serve it.

Beignets: Best known as the deep-fried dough squares smothered in powdered sugar served at Café du Monde, but appetizers of fried seafood are sometimes also called beignets.

Boudin: Cajun smoked pork sausage.

Bouillabaisse: A stew made of spicy broth and seafood.

Café au lait: Half strong, hot chicory coffee and half hot milk. Get the best at Café du Monde.

Crawfish: Affectionately called mudbugs (they live in the mud of freshwater streams), these tiny crustaceans are known to Yankees as crawdads. Or, worse, crayfish.

Debris: Sounds awful, but it's biscuits soaked in gravy and bits of roast beef, or whatever was cooked. Mother's is known for its delectable Debris po'boy.

Etouffée: A spicy, long-simmered stew of shrimp or crawfish, served over rice. French for "smothered." Galatoire's serves a crawfish étouffée that's a classic.

Filé: Ground sassafras leaves used for seasoning and thickening.

Gumbo: A thick soup, always served with rice, plus seafood, chicken, sausage, and filé. Many variations. The Gumbo Shop and Gabrielle are prime places to sample this.

Jambalaya: Not quite paella, but in that family. This typical Cajun dish uses simple ingredients (yellow rice, tomatoes, bits of shrimp, ham, andouille, and onions) to create (sometimes) a masterpiece.

Mirliton: A squashlike vegetable pear. Yankees call it a chayote; in the Caribbean it's a christophene.

Muffaletta: A giant sandwich piled with Italian meats and cheeses. Don't miss Central Grocery's.

Pain perdu: Literally "lost bread," what Anglos know as French toast. Here, it's usually made with French bread.

Plantain: Kissing cousin of the banana, but less sweet, often served as a side dish.

Soul Creole: In any other Southern city this would be called Southern cooking but, of course, New Orleans is not any other Southern city; fried chicken, stewed okra, turnip greens, and cornbread are called...soul Creole. Go to the Praline Connection if you want to learn what this is all about.

Tasso: Smoked, spicy Cajun ham, used for seasoning.

How to Dress

New Orleans is a casual town, and the French Quarter is especially so—in many cafes and restaurants, jeans and even shorts are perfectly okay. But New Orleanians also like to get all gussied up on occasion; if you're going to eat in the high-end restaurants, somewhat more formal wear is advised, and sometimes required. Ties are rarely required, but jackets frequently are. (Acts of God notwithstanding: During one deluge, a group of men dining at Arnaud's saw that the restaurant was in danger of being flooded, so they stripped down to their skivvies, put their suits in plastic trash bags, and finished eating.) The listings below tell you which of our recommended restaurants require a jacket and/or tie for men. If you're dining someplace we don't list, ask about the dress code when you call to reserve a table, or ask your hotel concierge.

Tips About Tipping

Tipping here is not much different from tipping in any other American city, and it should always, of course, depend upon the service. Locals tend to tip 15% in low-end eateries and 20% in the most upscale places. If there are six or more in your party, a service charge of 15% to 20% may be added to your bill. It's relatively rare, but some restaurants will tack on a 15% service charge without bothering to mention it. Always check.

Getting the Right Table

Cozy up to your concierge. They are very buddy-buddy with restaurateurs, and always have their fingers placed on the proverbial pulses. To be on the safe side, call before you arrive in New Orleans for a reservation at any restaurant you really want to eat at; however, unless Mardi Gras, Jazz Fest, or a huge convention is in town, you should be able to get a table.

At a few top restaurants, there may be certain rooms to which tourists and unfamiliar-looking locals are relegated. A prime example is the front room at Antoine's, which is locally known as Siberia and which Orleanians bypass using a side door. A concierge's knowledge and pull could really help you. Unfortunately, once you've been shown to a table it's pretty gauche to request another one, unless it's to move to a smoking or nonsmoking section.

The Lowdown

The Royal Brennanbaums... New Orleans's restaurant royalty is the Brennan family, whose members own and operate a slew of eateries. Like many royal dynasties, the Brennan family has demonstrated its share of dysfunction. This hasn't affected their food, but the background is worth noting, not only for the trivia, but also so you know whose restaurant you're eating at. Some family members have literally made this issue into a federal case. Owen Brennan, Sr., founded the original **Brennan's** restaurant, which is located on Royal Street in the French Quarter. This is the famous Brennan's known for its brunches and as the birthplace of Bananas Foster and some fancy egg dishes. Despite its waned popularity among locals, Brennan's is a fine place for a pricey, special-occasion meal. The wine list is extraordinary; the building is beautiful; and its location, in the heart of the French Quarter, is outstanding.

When Owen, Sr., died, he left the property to his wife, Maude, and their sons, Jimmy, Ted, and Pip. Owen, Sr.'s brothers and sisters worked in the restaurant but didn't own it. However, in order to raise money at one point, Maude sold shares in the restaurant to her father-in-law, Owen Patrick Brennan, who then left these shares to his kids: Owen, Sr.'s siblings Ella, John, and Adelaide. This set the stage for the feud that would later ensue.

By the early 1970s the family had opened Brennan's restaurants in Atlanta, Dallas, and Houston, as well as **Commander's Palace,** which is widely considered one of the city's finest restaurants—perhaps the finest depending on which critic you read. Located in a rambling aqua blue-and-white Garden District mansion across from the historic Lafayette cemetery, Commander's is popular with locals and tourists alike. Some of the city's most famous chefs, including Paul Prudhomme, Emeril Lagasse, Frank Brigtsen of Brigtsen's, and Richard Benz of Dick & Jenny's, apprenticed at Commander's before going on to become local and national stars. The restaurant is a shrine of Creole, French, and American cuisine.

In 1974, the Brennan family split up. Ted, Pip, and Jimmy took control of the original Brennan's, while Ella and her siblings got the rest of the empire, including Commander's Palace. The branches are now known colloquially as the Royal Street Brennans and the Commander's Brennans.

Considering the family traditions, it's not surprising that the latest generation of Brennans has carried on the family business and expanded further. Ralph Brennan, a nephew of Ella, owns, co-owns, or operates **Bacco,** a fine French Quarter Italian eatery; **Ralph Brennan's Red Fish Grill,** on Bourbon Street; **Mr. B's Bistro,** up Royal Street from the original Brennan's; and the newly opened **Ralph's on the Park** near City Park. Dickie Brennan—a much younger cousin of Ted, Jimmy, and Pip—runs **Dickie Brennan's Steakhouse** in the Quarter; **Bourbon House Seafood,** a fine seafood place with an elegant oyster bar; and **Dickie Brennan's Palace Café** on Canal Street (this one with his sister, Lauren Brennan Brower). Demonstrating the immensity of the Brennan family's restaurant empire, the *Times-Picayune* recently estimated the family's various white-tablecloth restaurants could serve 2,000 diners in a single seating.

Although the younger Brennans seem willing to let bygones be bygone and are friendly with their cousins, the rift between the Royal Street and some Commander's Brennans appears to be as wide as ever. As recently as 2002, the Royal Street Brennans were in federal court suing Dickie Brennan for trademark violations surrounding the use of his name in the names of his restaurants. The plaintiffs alleged Dickie had created confusion in the marketplace by leading diners to think his restaurants were the original Brennan's. A jury awarded the plaintiff Brennan's $250,000, far from the $2.3 million they had sought, and ruled that Dickie had not committed fraud by using his own name.

Despite the bad blood, you won't find a bad meal at any of the Brennan family's restaurants.

Mollusk mavens... When Louisiana oystermen went to court claiming their beds had been ruined by the state government's decision to divert fresh water from the Mississippi River system into the places where they fished for oysters, the jury responded with a $1.3 billion verdict that threatens to bankrupt the state treasury. While the state has appealed to the Louisiana Supreme Court, which could overturn the verdict, the case shows just how much people around here value the salty bivalves. So where can you sample these tasty treats? All over the place. French Quarter spots like **Acme Oyster House** and **Felix's** serve them up cold and salty with few frills. **Dickie Brennan's Bourbon House Seafood** on Bourbon is a swankier space that serves oysters plump and juicy with the respect of the purest purists. **Uglesich's** in Central City serves oysters on the half shell. **Deanie's Seafood Restaurant** in the Metairie is a casual, family-style spot, teeming with locals feasting on the catch of the day. Uptown there's **Casamento's,** worth the trip for the tiled-wall decor alone, but call ahead to make sure they're open. Also Uptown at the river's bend is **Cooter Brown's,** a college dive where you can get oysters with just about any beer there is. Want them cooked? Go to **Antoine's.** Founded in 1840, Antoine's is the oldest restaurant in the U.S. operated by the same family, and it's also home of the classic oysters Rockefeller. For a less formal affair, try **Jacques-Imo's** fried oyster appetizer served with garlic sauce, a simple dish that's a perennial favorite. Jacques-Imo himself, aka Jack Leonardi, also owns **Crabby Jack's,** a roadside diner on an industrial stretch of Jefferson Highway. The average tourist won't have much reason to be in the neighborhood, but those on a New Orleans food safari will delight in amazingly good food of a quality inversely proportional to the atmosphere and prices. On the other end of the price spectrum, everything on the menu at **GW Fins** will set you back, but it's worth it. Their smoked and sizzling oysters on the appetizer menu are especially good. Finally, for a truly decadent oyster dish, drive out to the middle of nowhere to **Mosca's** and get the Mosca's Italian oysters, baked in a huge metal pan with bread crumbs, garlic, olive oil and various herbs. If you die of a heart attack immediately after consuming this dish, your dying thought might well be: "It was worth it."

Stars and star-gawkers... Given the city's obsession with food, it's no surprise that New Orleans has a coterie of chefs viewed with the respect that some communities reserve for local star athletes, titans of business or, in the case of small towns, their clergy. Near the top of the list, at least those known best outside the city, are Paul Prudhomme and Emeril Lagasse. Chef Paul's **K-Paul's Louisiana Kitchen** in the French Quarter draws throngs wanting Cajun fare, and his own creations, such as blackened fish. The avuncular Emeril, known nationally because of his television show, runs **Emeril's** in the Warehouse District, **Emeril's Delmonico** on St. Charles, and **Nola** in the Quarter. Susan Spicer's **Bayona** entices tourists and locals alike, and the coconut pie served at Spicer's **Herbsaint** is a cloud of paradise rich and fluffy as a goose-down pillow. Spicer's influence also extends to **Cobalt** in the Hotel Monaco, where she trained the head chef. Anne Kearney's **Peristyle** ranks with Commander's Palace among the city's top eateries, although its intimate size and popularity makes reservations tough to get. (***Note:*** At press time, Peristyle switched owners, which may or may not affect the restaurant's popularity and availability.) John Besh's **Restaurant August** has also emerged as one of the city's finest restaurants, and former Grill Room chef Rene Bajeux has built a name for himself and his French fare at **Rene Bistrot**.

Chefs aren't the only stars you'll find at New Orleans restaurants. Louisiana recently passed a package of tax incentives designed to attract film productions, and since the passage, Hollywood had come en masse to the Big Easy to make movies. John Cusack showed up at the Ritz-Carlton's **French Quarter Bar** while he was shooting *The Runaway Jury* here. And Francis Ford Coppola, who owns a house in the French Quarter, was said to have swooned over the Italian food served at **Andrea's** during a recent visit. Julia Roberts, Lyle Lovett, and Kevin Costner have all been spotted at one time or another at the **Napoleon House,** which is also a favorite of Dick Cavett's. Alec Baldwin and Kim Basinger (when they were together) have made the scene at Emeril's, and Denzel Washington has been seen at Nola. Tom Cruise and Nicole Kidman were spotted at Emeril's Delmonico in happier days, and Tom Hanks, Heather Graham, Mariah Carey, and Christopher Walken have all feasted on the French Creole fare at **Arnaud's.** Both Matt Damon and John Cusack have turned up at various times at **Peristyle,** and **K-Paul's** has hosted Helen Hunt, Hank Azaria, Denzel Washington, Samuel L. Jackson, Tom Brokaw, and Steven Spielberg. Paul Newman, Joanne Woodward, Ellen Barkin, and Dennis Quaid are on a very long list of movie stars, prime ministers, presidents, and kings who've dined at **Antoine's**—a list that literally fills a booklet. The same restaurant whose waiters so blatantly ignore tourists actually publishes a brochure, filled with factoids and famous names, which is handed out to those very same tourists as they depart! The **House of Blues,** part of a chain that started in Cambridge,

Massachusetts, is a $7-million maze with a 260-seat restaurant and cavernous high-decibel concert hall, both of which are done with an overkill of Louisiana folk art and sculptures. Part-owner Dan Aykroyd stops in from time to time, and Dennis Quaid, Sting, and Britney Spears have also checked out the action. **HOB** is so popular with locals that it forced Tipitina's (see Nightlife), a veritable shrine to New Orleans funk and R&B, to open another location, which happens to be right around the corner.

Classic New Orleans... A classic, turn-of-the century Creole bistro, **Galatoire's** sits amid the daiquiri shops, sex-toy emporiums, and grime of Bourbon Street like some bourgeois Frenchman in a bowler hat surrounded by prostitutes in hot pants and pasties. On Friday, Galatoire's is the power-lunch spot for old-line New Orleanians. The menu, with dishes like trout Amandine and oysters and bacon en brochette, is a living artifact of the city's Creole heritage. For visitors seeking a glimpse of the lifestyle and aesthetic of the New Orleans bourgeoisie, Galatoire's is a must-see. Of course, Galatoire's is hardly the only old-line restaurant serving Creole fare. **Antoine's** is actually older than Galatoire's and does notable Creole. Second only to Antoine's in age, is **Tujague's** (say "two jacks"). Tourists and a certain class of locals flock here and order the table

THEY LOVE GILBERTO

When a popular waiter at ***Galatoire's*** *restaurant was fired a few years ago after allegations that he had sexually harassed two women on the staff, the incident became one of those anecdotes that showed much about the soul of New Orleans: its love of food and tradition, its resistance to change, and a laissez-faire attitude toward such modern notions as a hostile work environment. Rather than expressing outrage at Gilberto Eyzaguirre's alleged boorish behavior, many loyal patrons rallied around him, writing letters of support and expressing nostalgia that bordered on obsession. Gilberto fans even launched a website,* ***www.welovegilberto.com****. Supporters included prominent doctors and lawyers, as well as academics and writers such as Richard Ford, the Pulitzer Prize–winning novelist who lives here. Among the musings were discussions about the superiority of Galatoire's old-style hand-crushed ice over its newer woefully inferior machine-crushed variety. The incident even inspired a local play, a comedy of manners in which performers simply read the letters verbatim, as well as perhaps the greatest of New Orleans tributes: a Mardi Gras float with a giant fiberglass likeness of Gilberto's head.*

d'hote. **Arnaud's,** founded in 1918, offers a time-machine trip back to days gone by. Although not as old as some of these, **Commander's Palace** also offers outstanding Creole food, such as turtle soup and an exquisite bread pudding souffle, along with superlative service.

No first trip to New Orleans would be complete without a visit to one of these restaurants.

Beyond Creole... Given New Orleans's many cultural peculiarities, it's understandable that visitors might confuse Cajun and Creole as being the same thing. They're not. To get a sense of the difference, check out the menu at **K-Paul's,** the restaurant credited with popularizing the spicy regional cuisine in the 1980s. While he has branched out a lot, you'll still find honest representations of classic Cajun fare like chicken and andouille gumbo and jambalaya. Clearly we ain't talking about oysters Rockefeller here.

Beyond K-Paul's, you can find excellent examples of Cajun eats at **Alex Patout's Louisiana Restaurant** on St. Louis Street. Fans rave over Patout's gumbo, as well as his roast duck and eggplant with shrimp and crabmeat. The **Bon Ton** has been serving traditional Cajun food since 1953. Red beans and rice, crawfish étouffé, and bread pudding are served in this upmarket but casual place, with old brick walls, and red-and-white checked tablecloths.

At many other places, the distinctions become blurry, and influences merge and meld. For instance, although **Brigtsen's** restaurant Uptown is identified in this book's listings as a Creole restaurant, it could also be described as an elegant restaurant inspired by Cajun country. Indeed, Chef Frank Brigtsen was a protege of Chef Paul, and his menu includes dishes like blackened yellowfin tuna with roasted corn sauce and roast duck with cornbread dressing, as well as butternut shrimp bisque. Other restaurants are described as New South Louisiana, a moniker that acknowledges the influences of the region's cuisines and traditional ingredients without getting boxed into one category.

Dick and Jenny's, an unpretentious-but-polished Uptown restaurant, is such an example. Here, Commander's Palace and Upperline alumnus Richard Benz serves wonderful fish and duck dishes, mouthwatering crab cakes, and tangy cold shrimp remoulade over crispy hot fried green tomatoes. This last dish, it should be noted, originated at **Upperline,** also Uptown, where the colorful proprietress

JoAnne Clevenger holds court with tourists and loyalist locals over yummy gumbo, andouille, and crawfish étouffée, all served in a homey space decorated with works by local artists. For an equally intimate experience with South Louisiana food, try **Gabrielle** in Mid-City. Although Greg and Mary Sonnier don't have the celebrity status of Emeril, they stand at the top of the list as restaurateurs—and people. Their roasted duck dish can't be beat. Another restaurant rooted firmly in Southeastern Louisiana is **Jacques-Imo's** on Oak Street. There you can find amazing fresh seafood dishes and extraordinary Southern fried chicken served with sides like corn *maque choux.* It wasn't so long ago that Jacques-Imo's was so off the beaten path that chef Jack Leonardi would give extra food to patrons rather than let it go to waste. But times have changed dramatically, and Jacques-Imo's is now almost always packed with patrons looking for great food at great prices. Fortunately, the bar is well stocked and the friendly atmosphere tends to infect the hordes of customers waiting for tables.

Where the locals go... When you live in the midst of ubiquitous culinary excellence, where do you go and how do you choose? Often, locals choose the same restaurants that savvy tourists do: showplaces of celebrity chefs like Restaurant August, Bayona, Nola, and Peristyle, as well as old-style eateries like Commander's and Galatoire's. Given this cross-pollination, it's hard to point to a place that's a locals-only spot. Still, a few places spring to mind when facing the question, "Where do you go out for dinner?" Near the top of the list is **Crepe Nanou.** This French bistro located Uptown offers true French cooking in a cozy atmosphere straight out of Paris. After a glass of pastis and the pâté plate, followed by lamb chops with cognac sauce and pommes frites and a crepe for dessert, you'll feel like you've crossed the Atlantic for a spell. Plus the prices will make your wallet reasonably happy. **Gautreau's** also finds its way onto the short list of places for a quiet dinner. This is considerably pricier than Crepe Nanou, but the clubby atmosphere of the oak-paneled dining room, service that's attentive but not overbearing, and high-quality ingredients make the experience at Gautreau's superlative. This fish is always fresh and cooked to perfection; the gnocchi like puffy balls of heaven. Don't expect a scene here; if you're looking for that, go to Nola or Emeril's. The food, not the people or atmosphere, takes center stage. The opposite could be said of **Clancy's**, where the Continental food is fine, but the scene is the real draw. Locals table hop and gossip like guests at a Hamptons wedding. (Recently, actress/singer/bimbo Jessica Simpson dined here and had predictable trouble with the menu. According to local gossip columnist Chris Rose, she asked if the grilled drum was like drumsticks and whether sweetbreads were like French toast. Needless to say, she took a pass on both. No wonder she's so skinny.) More "Gautreau" than "Clancy" in its respect for ingredients, **Lilette** is another local favorite. Chef John Harris prepares dishes that seem seasoned by the sea breezes and bright clean light of the Mediterranean. For Asian food, **Sake Café** is a cavernous sushi joint with ultra-mod decor and space-age music playing on the stereo system. Their fish is so fresh, you'll routinely see fish deliveries on Saturday nights. If it's particularly late on said Saturday night and you've been shaking your thang in the Faubourg, then try **La Peniche** for a midnight snack. It's one of the city's surprisingly few 24-hour spots.

Where the locals don't go... Locals usually leave the weekend brunches to the tourists, and in this particular case, it's a good idea not to do as the locals do. Practically every restaurant in town does some sort of Sunday jazz brunch, but the idea originated with **Commander's,** which is about the only place in town that also does one on Saturday. Balloons festoon the tables, and a peripatetic jazz trio wanders from room to room. Locals, mind you, have no quarrel with the food here—but they think the brunches are way touristy. Likewise, no self-respecting New Orleanian would be caught dead at the **Court of Two Sisters** jazz buffet, which runs from 9am to 3pm. The food is fine, and heaven knows there's plenty of it—a huge spread that includes étouffées, shrimp Creole, jambalaya, and other regional specialties—but it's considered merely a tourist attraction by locals. **Pascal's Manale** is an Uptown tourist spot that's built a reputation on the back of its famous creation: barbecue shrimp. **Muriel's** gorgeously Gothic decor and killer location on the corner of Jackson Square make it popular with the out-of-towners. It's not the best eatery in town, but it's handy and pretty, and rarely disappoints visitors.

Keeping it real... What makes New Orleans such an impressive food city is not so much its universe of exceptional, high-end restaurants, but the lower-key places as ubiquitous as the musicians that seem to magically grow out of the sidewalks. To get a sense of just how good the average food in New Orleans really is, go to a modest neighborhood restaurant off the beaten tourist path. It's these spots that will give you a real sense of the city's pervasive joie de vivre when it comes to food. A classic example is **Uglesich's.** The decor is nothing to brag about; it has all the charm of the junk pile in your grandmother's basement. But the seafood dishes are exceptional. For artery-clogging fried everything and red-and-white checked plastic tablecloths, try **Frankie and Johnny's** Uptown. **Parasol's** in the Irish Channel has one of the city's best roast beef po'boys. (If your timing is right, they also have a humdinger of a St. Patty's party.) If your budget is aching and you're longing for some fresh and healthy Vietnamese, try **Pho Tau Bay** on Tulane Avenue in the medical district. **Dunbar's** is an Uptown luncheonette with tables unembellished except for juicy po'boys and big bowls steaming with red beans and rice. Another fairly cheap takeout spot is the **Whole Foods Market.** Although some locals jokingly refer to it as Whole Paycheck because of the way your money can go quickly if you yield to temptation and do all your grocery shopping there, and despite others who resent the fact that it's a chain store, Whole Foods's new Arabella Station store on Magazine Street has an amazing variety of prepared foods, fancy olives and cheeses, wines, imported beer, and bakery items perfect to take out for a picnic at Audubon Park. Where can you get something filling and reasonably priced in the French Quarter? Perhaps the best deal is **Central Grocery,** an Italian deli on Decatur Street specializing in the muffaletta: a sandwich of salami, ham, and other meats, and provolone cheese, with fragrant olive relish served on a giant round loaf of bread. Take one to the river with a bottle of Barq's and a bag of Zapp's chips and watch the ships go by while you dine alfresco. **Port of Call** on Esplanade Avenue is considered one of the city's better burger joints. **Johnny's Po'Boys,** also in the Quarter, is an institution for its classic sandwiches. Beefeaters will be happy to know about **Poppy's Grill** on St. Peter Street, which is open all day and night. Another option open 24/7 is **Angeli on Decatur** Street which has salads, sandwiches, and pizza. The **Gumbo Shop** has solid gumbo, jambalaya, and other New Orleans food at a good price.

People looking for something simple but with more atmosphere than, say, Angeli, might opt for **Napoleon House.** Though it is good, the food hardly matters in this atmospheric restaurant and bar that, the story goes, was built to be a home for Napoleon Bonaparte after he was rescued from exile in a scheme hatched by the pirate Lafitte brothers. Like so many other well-laid plans, it never came to fruition. **House of Blues** is also lots of fun—kids love it —and the food is much better than the food at an average theme restaurant. In a pinch, you can always get a **Lucky Dog** from a street vendor.

Where's the beef?... By this time, you might be wondering, "Is there anywhere in this bloody town where you can just get a steak?" The answer is, "You betchya, cowboy!" Ruth Fertel, the late, great patron saint of New Orleans beef-lovers, founded **Ruth's Chris Steakhouse** here and turned it into an international chain. The formula is pretty simple: Ruth's Chris serves aged prime beef and sides in big portions. And it's one of the city's power-lunch spots. Another power spot for carnivores is **Crescent City Steaks.** An old-style joint with a tile floor, Crescent City Steaks is popular with the city's politicos. Indeed, you might well see City Councilman Eddie Sapir there along with his right-hand man, Billy Broadhurst, a high-powered Louisiana fixer who earned a footnote in U.S. political history for being aboard the *Monkey Business* charter boat on the ill-fated trip when one-time Democratic presidential hopeful Gary Hart was caught with model Donna Rice. The booths at Crescent City Steaks have little curtains so scheming politicos and trysting lovers can eat with relative privacy (if only the *Monkey Business* had had the same...). Speaking of hiding the beef, **Victor's Grill** in the Ritz-Carlton Hotel on Canal Street offers curtained booths big enough to contain couches, so patrons can really stretch out over basic steakhouse fare. When you consider the prices and the expectations that come from dining at a Ritz-Carlton, the food here is only okay. Still, thrill-seekers and exhibitionists might enjoy testing just how much privacy these booths really offer by engaging in some extra-culinary canoodling between courses. You'll probably never see any of these waiters again if you're caught, so why not? And if you're looking for a different beef experience for nearly every night of the week, then check out **Dickie Brennan's** eponymous steakhouse on Iberville Street, which also offers good steakhouse food in an old-timey environment, and **Smith & Wollensky,** a national chain, with an outlet near the Superdome.

Diners and grills... After a long night of drinking, few things battle a hangover like a big greasy breakfast followed by a nap. This section doesn't address the nap, but for breakfast, there are plenty of places where the Big Easy becomes the Big Greasy. And that's a good thing. **The Clover Grill** in the French Quarter serves a $5 breakfast special from 5am to 11am. The Clover also makes good burgers, which are cooked under a hubcap. Open 24 hours, it's worth a visit at the end of a late-nighter, or on the morning after one. Another great breakfast spot is the **Bluebird Cafe,** located Uptown on Prytania Street. The line out the door will give you the sense that this is a popular spot, especially with the college set. And the food, served by a staff that's clearly done its own share of partying the night before, will confirm what the line implies. The Bluebird serves a strong huevos rancheros and a tasty, homemade hash with poached eggs. Get there early to avoid the lines. Another place you're likely to find a line is the **Camellia Grill.** This old-style '50s diner serves eggs, omelets, and burgers at the counter, as well as pecan pie with ice cream warmed on the grill where the burgers are fried. Chili cheese fries and milkshakes are other specialties.

Java joints... When Starbucks first eye-balled New Orleans in the mid-'90s, the developers looked at a building that once housed a florist's shop on St. Charles Avenue. This was during a time when preservationists were alarmed at a flurry of developments, including Harrah's New Orleans Casino, that they believed threatened to kill the soul of the city. After a brief but bloody fight with preservationists and the neighborhood groups, the Starbucks folks crept away with their tail between their legs, and it was years before the Seattle chain opened its first store in New Orleans. One reason Starbucks was so roundly rejected was because of the local culture. New Orleans has been a coffee town long before Starbucks came along. Some of the city's coffee brokers are family-owned businesses going back five generations; indeed, some of the city's most socially prominent families built their fortunes on the coffee trade. The port of New Orleans remains the nation's largest coffee port, and the city is also home of the nation's largest roasting facility, owned by Folger's. New Orleans even has its own special blend; coffee and chicory might be an acquired taste, but brewed right and served with steamed milk, the bitter cup has a flavor as unique as the city itself. The high temple of New Orleans's retail coffee culture is **Café du Monde.** Across from Jackson Square, Café du Monde's green-and-white striped awnings are practically a symbol of New Orleans, and its beignets, fried dough with powdered sugar, are a tribute to the city's decadent culinary traditions: They're simple, fattening, and delicious. When the weather's nice, it's hard to beat sitting outside under the canopy with a cafe au lait and a beignet, watching the world go by to a live jazz soundtrack. And it's one of the best bargains in town. Unless you've been before, no trip to New Orleans would be complete without a visit. And a tip for neophytes: Never wear black when Café du Monde is on your itinerary. Those beignets have so much powdered sugar piled on them that a small, poorly timed exhale will leave you dusted in the white stuff. A sneeze spells certain disaster. CDM is hardly the city's only indigenous coffeehouse. **Croissant d'Or** and its sister **La Marquise,** both in the Quarter, have excellent coffee and pastries. And **Community Coffee**'s retail outlets, called CC's, have fine coffee and fun coffee gewgaws much like the merchandise sold at Starbucks. Phyllis Jordan's **PJ's Coffee & Tea Co.** stores also make Starbucks something of an afterthought here. And there's the local **rue de la course** chain. After starting on Magazine Street, rue, as the kids call it, has locations throughout the city, where the boho baristas can sell java without selling out.

Soul Creole... In any other city, what New Orleanians call "soul Creole" is simply down-home Southern cooking, but this isn't any other city. **Dooky Chase** exemplifies the genre. Come here for such Southern standbys as filé gumbo, stewed okra, and sweet potatoes. **The Praline Connection,** in the Faubourg Marigny, is another down-home room serving terrific fried chicken and barbecued ribs, this one with waiters wearing black derbies. The restaurant is named for the candy store in a separate room at the rear. The Praline Connection also has a connection in the Warehouse/Arts District, with the same eats and a soulful Sunday gospel brunch to boot. Another option is **Dunbar's** on Freret Street. The red beans and rice with fried chicken on Mondays is a great deal.

Decor to die for... Long as you're paying top dollar, besides getting superb, sophisticated food, you might as well get a beautiful setting as well. Famous for its classic French cuisine, **Louis XVI** is a sedate, understated room with Art Deco flourishes, such as the polished brass wall sconces. Chairs are upholstered in velvet, carpeting is almost thick enough to sink into, and tall French windows dressed with richly textured drapes overlook a lavish courtyard with a big stone fountain surrounded by tropical greenery. In addition to its fine French Creole fare, **Arnaud's** is a stunning restaurant, with lovely mosaic tile floors, beveled windows, and potted palms. **Commander's Palace**, an old aqua-colored mansion in the Garden District, is broken into scads of small, parlorlike rooms, each with its own colors and accessories. Talk to the staff when making your reservations and see what room might best suit your sensibilities. **Emeril's Delmonico** is housed in a fully rehabbed Edwardian building on the edge of the Garden District, and decor is opulent but understated. Think ivory suede drapes and extensive faux bois detailing. For more old Orleans feel, try **Restaurant August** with towering ceilings and blinding chandeliers. **Cuvee** in the CBD offers dinner and top-tier wine in a dark wood and redbrick setting that recalls a wine cellar (in a good way). **Lilette** and **Zoë Bistrot** both offer the modern chicness of sleek Parisian bistros, with banquettes and big-brasserie-style touches.

A taste of Italy... Andrea Apuzzo, a native of Capri, is the chef/owner of **Andrea's,** in suburban Metairie, in which he uses local ingredients and imports from his homeland to create regional Italian dishes. You can feast on fine osso buco Milanese as well as dishes with a Continental flair, such as angel hair pasta tossed with salmon. The draws at **Bacco** are pizzas baked in a wood-fired oven, homemade pastas, and great garlic mashed potatoes accompanying a thick and juicy rosemary-flavored pork tenderloin. The fine porcelain at **Cafe Giovanni** is as dressed up as the crowd, with regional Italian offerings such as spaghetti alla

Bolognese. At **Mosca's,** a roadhouse on the West Bank, there is plenty of garlic and olive oil in the restaurant's renditions of spaghetti and meatballs, chicken cacciatore, and Cornish hen. On a quiet street in the lower Quarter, **Irene's Cuisine** keeps the locals coming back for more country Italian fare. Save room for dessert at the Sicilian landmark **Angelo Brocato's Ice Cream,** which has been satisfying New Orleanians' sweet tooths for over 100 years with such flavors as tiramisu, Italian chocolate chip, and cannoli.

Best jazz dining... At the **Palm Court Jazz Café,** you can listen to traditional jazz while sampling traditional Creole cooking in an upscale, L-shaped room. Musicians take to the tiny stage and raise the rafters, while the waitstaff tries hard to hear what customers are ordering. Proprietor Nina Buck is always up to speed on local acts and where they're playing, and local musicians often hang out at the bar. But don't come here for inventive cuisine, swift service, or quiet conversation. **Arnaud's** serves fine French Creole fare to the tune of live jazz in its Jazz Bistro, where dress is more casual than in the main dining rooms—though this is not the place for jeans and cutoffs. On the fringe of the Quarter, **Funky Butt,** named for a turn-of-the-century New Orleans jazz hall, offers a roster of top local musicians, as well as a fine eclectic menu of regional, Middle Eastern, and Mediterranean dishes.

Best jazz brunching... No one does a jazz brunch better than **Commander's Palace,** which originated the concept. This Garden District outpost of the Brennans' empire is in a marvelous Victorian mansion whose seven dining rooms are done up with pretty wallpaper, curtained windows, and cloth-covered tables; at 11:30am on Saturday and 10:30am on Sunday, balloons festoon the tables, a jazz trio ambles from room to room, and the kitchen turns out superb egg dishes. The venerable Creole **Arnaud's** is a close runner-up for best jazz brunch, and it is, after all, right here in the Quarter.

Music and meals on paddle wheels... The **Steamboat *Natchez*** and the ***Creole Queen,*** both replicas of the old floating palaces, do 2-hour nighttime cruises, with traditional jazz, banjos, straw boaters, and tables almost sagging under jambalaya, red beans and rice, shrimp Creole, crawfish and shrimp étouffée, and bread pudding. This kind of food translates well into buffets, and they don't scale back the spices for unaccustomed palates. It's a very touristy experience, but you get a lot for your money—food, music, and a river cruise.

Best people-watching... Sometimes the food isn't the thing. Opposite Jackson Square, right in the thick of things, **Café du Monde** is an open-air pavilion with a jumble of bare tables both indoor and out adorned only with paper-napkin holders. Sidewalk mimes and musicians vie for loose change while a polyglot crowd chatters over café au lait and beignets. An interesting array of Quarterite characters weave in and out of **Poppy's Grill,** across the street from Pat O'Briens and Preservation Hall. If the weather's nice, grab a po'boy or muffaletta and head to Jackson Square for a picnic. There on the flagstones in front of St. Louis Cathedral you'll see musicians, mimes, jugglers, fortune-tellers, and sidewalk artists vying for the attention of tourists. It's one of the great public spaces in the United States. For a glimpse of the city's movers and shakers, try **Le Salon,** the Windsor Court's luxe lobby lounge, where teatime has evolved into primetime business entertaining. Groupings of richly upholstered settees and armchairs are carefully arranged around marble-topped coffee tables—perfect for scooping out who else is there negotiating with whom. Classical music and trays of pastries help to soothe late-in-the-workday frazzled nerves. In the CBD, office workers crowd into the no-nonsense **Mother's** for po'boys and other cheap eats.

For a different scene, take out something from **Whole Foods Market**'s Arabella Station store (which is built in an old streetcar barn on Magazine St.) and go to Audubon Park. On the levee behind the zoo (known as the Fly or the Butterfly to locals) on weekends, you'll see families having picnics, college students sunbathing over their books, kids and grown-ups playing pickup soccer, and giant freighters gliding past on the huge expanse of the Mississippi River. It's a scene of the everyday life of the city that visitors rarely see.

Map 6: French Quarter Dining

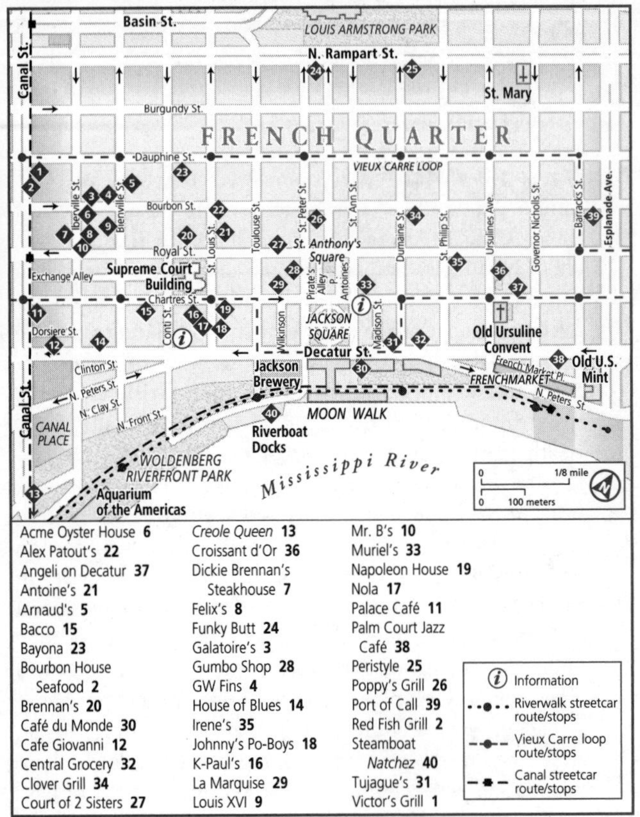

Map 7: Central Business District Dining

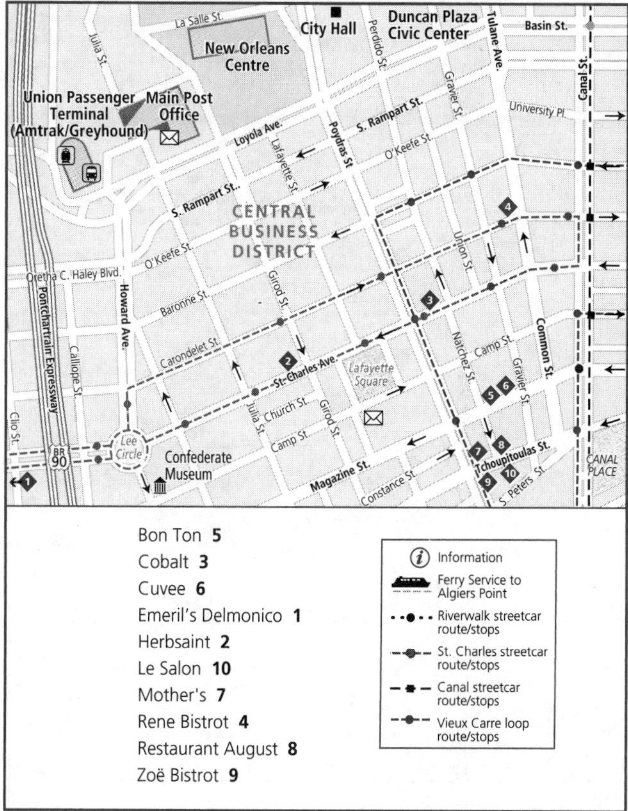

Bon Ton **5**
Cobalt **3**
Cuvee **6**
Emeril's Delmonico **1**
Herbsaint **2**
Le Salon **10**
Mother's **7**
Rene Bistrot **4**
Restaurant August **8**
Zoë Bistrot **9**

Information
Ferry Service to Algiers Point
Riverwalk streetcar route/stops
St. Charles streetcar route/stops
Canal streetcar route/stops
Vieux Carre loop route/stops

Map 8: Uptown Dining

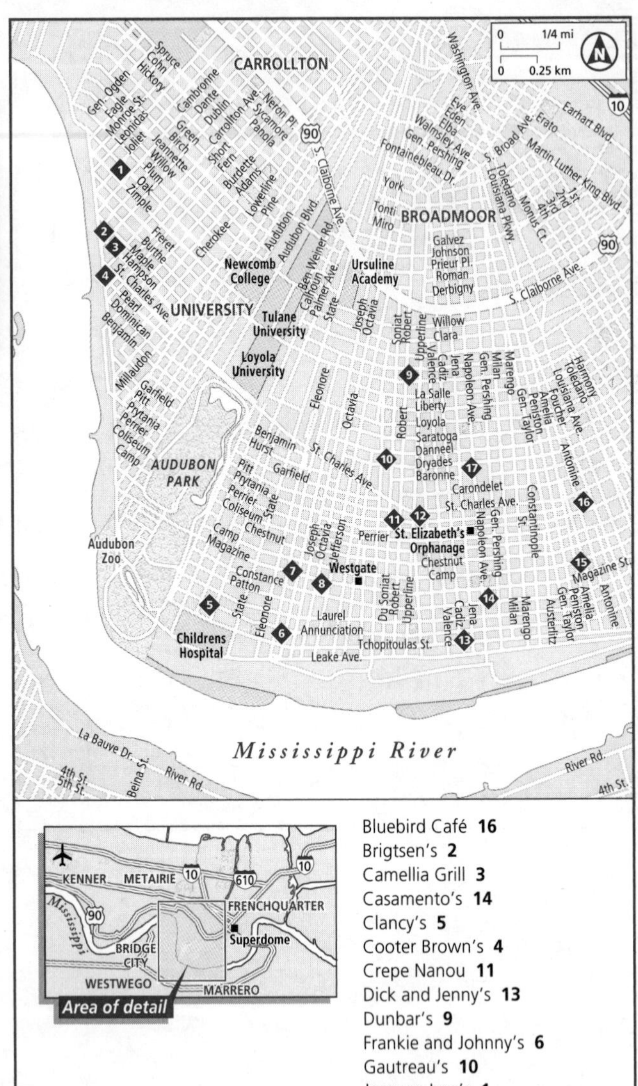

Bluebird Café **16**
Brigtsen's **2**
Camellia Grill **3**
Casamento's **14**
Clancy's **5**
Cooter Brown's **4**
Crepe Nanou **11**
Dick and Jenny's **13**
Dunbar's **9**
Frankie and Johnny's **6**
Gautreau's **10**
Jacques-Imo's **1**
Lilette **15**
Pascal's Manale **17**
PJ's Coffee & Tea Co. **8**
Upperline **12**
Whole Foods Market–
Arabella Station **7**

Map 9: Mid-City Dining

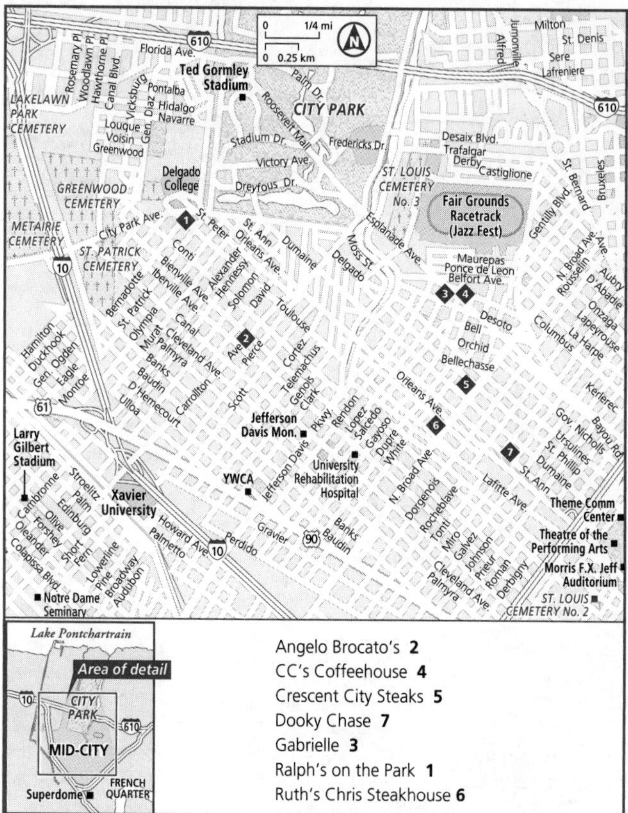

DINING

The Index

$$$$$	over $40
$$$$	$30–$40
$$$	$20–$30
$$	$12–$20
$	under $12

Prices given are per person for entrees only.

The following abbreviations are used for credit cards:

AE	American Express
DC	Diners Club
DISC	Discover
MC	MasterCard
V	Visa

Acme Oyster House (p. 62) FRENCH QUARTER *SEAFOOD* At this down-home old-timer with black-and-white tablecloths and a long marble bar, the big draw is salty oysters on the half shell, knocked back with ice-cold beer. Acme lures legions of loyal Orleanians, which means you'll probably have to line up. By all means, join 'em.... *Tel 504/522-5973. www.acmeoyster.com. 724 Iberville St. AE, DC, DISC, MC, V. $$*

See Map 6 on p. 76.

Alex Patout's Louisiana Restaurant (p. 66) FRENCH QUARTER *CAJUN* Chef Patout's roots are deep in Cajun country and his cuisine here is South Louisiana. His version of gumbo, that ubiquitous dish, is thick and hearty. Roast duck is served with oyster dressing, and eggplant with shrimp and crabmeat comes with eggplant dressing. The mashed sweet potatoes are divine. The restaurant's handsome design is second only to the food.... *Tel 504/525-7788. www.patout.com. 720 St. Louis St. Reservations advised. AE, DC, DISC, MC, V. $$$*

See Map 6 on p. 76.

Andrea's (p. 64) METAIRIE *ITALIAN* Inside this ranch-style suburban house, it's a surprise to find crystal chandeliers and fine china and crystal. You'll know it's Italian when you see the huge platters of antipasti and a crowd feasting on osso buco Milanese and angel-hair pasta dressed up with salmon and flamed with brandy; another recommended dish is roast Long Island duckling, with raspberry sauce and rice dressing. Take I-10 West to the Causeway Boulevard North exit, turn right, drive to 19th Street, and turn right again. Andrea's is on the right side of the street.... *Tel 504/834-8583. 3100 19th St. Reservations advised. AE, DC, DISC, MC, V. $$$$*

See Map 5 on p. 54.

Angeli on Decatur (p. 70) FRENCH QUARTER *SANDWICHES* Where the hipster, freaky Quarter people meet to eat and get served by other hipster freaky Quarter people, 24 hours a day. Excellent salads, big ole sandwiches, and tasty pizzas. Surprisingly good fare in fairly run-down surroundings.... *Tel 504/566-0077. 1141 Decatur St. AE, MC, V. $$*

See Map 6 on p. 76.

Angelo Brocato's Ice Cream (p. 74) MID-CITY *SWEETS* One hundred years ago, Sicilian immigrant Brocato opened up an Italian-style ice cream emporium that has been satisfying the sweet tooths of New Orleanians ever since. Old-time locals each have a favorite flavor they will fiercely defend: Italian chocolate chip, tiramisu. And they do mean cannoli and spumoni. This place is really an institution.... *Tel 504/486-0078. www.angelobrocatoicecream.com. 214 N. Carrollton Ave. DC, DISC, MC, V. $*

See Map 9 on p. 79.

Antoine's (p. 63) FRENCH QUARTER *CREOLE* This traditional Creole restaurant first opened in 1840. It only recently loosened up enough to add English subtitles to the French. The 15 rooms range from a huge main dining room with dimly lit chandeliers and walls lined with celebrity caricatures to the smaller Rex Room, all aglitter with crowns, scepters, and Carnival memorabilia. Yes, the tuxedoed waiters can be stuffy here, and they do cater to the old-line regulars. But to eat here is to have a truly Nouvelle Orleans experience. The salty puffed potatoes are better than even those at Arnaud's. Oysters Rockefeller originated here; so did *pompano en papillote* (fish baked in a paper bag). Save room for the fantastic baked Alaska.... *Tel 504/581-4422. www.antoines.com. 713 St. Louis St. Reservations advised. AE, DC, MC, V. $$$$$*

See Map 6 on p. 76.

Arnaud's (p. 64) FRENCH QUARTER *CREOLE* Famous Arnaud's is a large, lovely, rambling restaurant that's been serving Creole specialties since 1918. The light, airy puffed potatoes are addictive, and you can easily wolf down too many before forking into the shrimp Arnaud, served in a very spicy rémoulade sauce. The house veal specialty is tournedos, served with crab cake and crawfish O'Connor. You're safe ordering any of the flaming desserts.... *Tel 504/523-0611. www.arnauds.com. 813 Bienville St. Reservations requested. AE, DC, DISC, MC, V. $$$$$*

See Map 6 on p. 76.

Bacco (p. 62) FRENCH QUARTER *ITALIAN/CREOLE* The Brennan family's Italian entry has four swanky rooms in which locals chatter noisily beneath hand-painted Venetian silk chandeliers and high ceilings studded with ersatz stars. Homemade pastas and designer pizzas from a wood-fired oven are among the standouts.... *Tel 504/522-2426. www.bacco.com. 310 Chartres St. Reservations recommended. AE, DISC, MC, V. $$$$$*

See Map 6 on p. 76.

Bayona (p. 64) FRENCH QUARTER *INTERNATIONAL* Chef/owner Susan Spicer's followers are almost religious in their devotion. She calls her cuisine "New World," but it's mostly French-Mediterranean and all designer-nouvelle. Consistent winners are her cream of garlic soup, grilled duck breast glazed with pepper jelly, and grilled shrimp in coriander sauce. The setting is a restored Creole cottage, decorated with elaborate floral arrangements, photographs of New Orleans, and a *trompe l'oeil* painting of the Mediterranean. But note: They really pack them in when the city is full, and you may feel rushed by the waitstaff.... *Tel 504/525-4455. www.bayona.com. 430 Dauphine St. Reservations required. AE, DC, DISC, MC, V. $$$*

See Map 6 on p. 76.

Bluebird Café (p. 71) UPTOWN *BREAKFAST* Sleepy students and lazy locals line up to get into this greasy but lovely breakfast-only diner/cafe they affectionately call "the Bird." The skanky/funky cooks make a mean *huevos rancheros,* their hash is chunky and out of this world, and sugarphiles love the waffles. They close at 3pm.... *Tel 504/895-7166. 3625 Prytania St. No credit cards. $*

See Map 8 on p. 78.

Bon Ton (p. 66) CBD *CAJUN* Since 1953, this cozy, down-home place with its red-and-white checked tablecloths has been serving Pierce family Cajun recipes for jambalaya, crawfish *étouffée,* hearty gumbo, butter-drenched broiled seafood, shrimp and crab okra, and warm bread pudding with whiskey sauce. Jammed at lunch with CBD office types, and closed weekends.... *Tel 504/524-3386. 401 Magazine St. Reservations recommended. AE, DC, MC, V. $$$*

See Map 7 on p. 77.

Bourbon House Seafood (p. 62) FRENCH QUARTER *SEAFOOD* Dickie Brennan's newest offering—and maybe the best one yet. A backdrop of high ceilings and white tablecloths sets the scene for a plethora of fishy dishes: Start with raw or flash-fried oysters, or the gumbo du jour. Then choose from Gulf fish prepared five different ways, or down-home catfish, or even veal smothered in lump crabmeat.... *Tel 504/522-0111. 144 Bourbon St. Reservations recommended. AE, DC, DISC, MC, V. $$$$*

See Map 6 on p. 76.

Brennan's (p. 61) FRENCH QUARTER *FRENCH/CREOLE* Not overly popular with locals—prices are sky-high and there are almost always throngs of tourists—Brennan's is nevertheless worth a trip for its classic French Creole breakfasts (brunch, really): sherry-spiked turtle soup, apples in double cream, and poached eggs drenched in superb hollandaise sauce. The signature dessert is bananas Foster, which originated here. At night things are somewhat more subdued, and they've even foregone their "no jeans" policy. Brennan's is set in an 18th-century mansion, with a gorgeous courtyard and fountain; flocked wallpaper and crystal chandeliers abound.... *Tel 504/525-9711. www.brennansneworleans.com. 417 Royal St. Reservations advised. AE, DC, DISC, MC, V. $$$$$*

See Map 6 on p. 76.

Brigtsen's (p. 66) UPTOWN *CREOLE* Frank Brigtsen, protégé of Paul Prudhomme and all-around good guy, serves creative South Louisiana dishes in a little shotgun house near the Mississippi River. The menu changes daily, but you can usually bank on blackened yellowfin tuna with smoked corn sauce, roast duck with a corn bread dressing, Brigtsen's delectable butternut shrimp bisque, and homemade ice cream.... *Tel 504/861-7610. www.brigtsens.com. 723 Dante St. Reservations highly advised. AE, DC, MC, V. $$$$*

See Map 8 on p. 78.

Café du Monde (p. 72) FRENCH QUARTER *BEIGNETS/COFFEE* It would be hard to figure out how many paper napkins have wiped how many fingers and faces in this open-air pavilion over the last century or so. Every T-shirt and dashiki, every miniskirt and Mardi Gras getup rises from the bare tables wearing a liberal dusting of powdered sugar, thanks to the irresistible beignets (so don't wear black). Café au lait (frozen and iced in summertime), orange juice, and chocolate milk make up the rest of the menu. Much of the world comes here at least once. Open 24 hours a day. On the edge of Jackson Square.... *Tel 504/525-4544, 800/772-2927. www.cafedumonde.com. 800 Decatur St. No credit cards. $*

See Map 6 on p. 76.

Cafe Giovanni (p. 73) FRENCH QUARTER *ITALIAN* Well-located in the Quarter, this convivial New World Italian features opera singers on Wednesday, Friday, and Saturday nights. The hot prosciutto pinwheel, an elaborate concoction featuring puff pastry stuffed with goat cheese and fresh basil, is a favorite. The veal LoCicero (named for chef Duke), sautéed with shrimp in a lemon sauce, is also a crowd pleaser, and there's a lengthy list of classic Italian specialties like Hunter's Cannelloni.... *Tel 504/529-2154. www.cafegiovanni.com. 117 Decatur St. Reservations advised. AE, DC, DISC, MC, V. $$$$*

See Map 6 on p. 76.

Camellia Grill (p. 71) UPTOWN *DINER* Sooner or later everybody in town eats at this counter-only diner, with its tuxedoed waiters, maitre d', and occasional long lines. The main attractions are some of the city's best burgers and fries, substantial breakfasts (with great waffles), and heavenly banana cream pie.... *Tel 504/866-9573. 626 S. Carrollton Ave. No credit cards. $*

See Map 8 on p. 78.

Casamento's (p. 63) UPTOWN *PO'BOYS* Beauty of a po'boy shop, covered floor to ceiling in immaculately kept tile work. This joint serves up excellent fried seafood and, of course, po'boys to tourists and locals alike. They are especially famous for their oyster loaf—fried ersters placed between two thick slices of white bread, but don't miss a cup of the gumbo.... *Tel 504/895-9761. www.casamentosrestaurant.com. 4300 Magazine St. No credit cards. Closed June, July, and Aug, and every Mon. $$*

See Map 8 on p. 78.

C.C.'s Coffeehouse MID-CITY *COFFEE* New Orleanians do love their community coffee, and consume gallons of it at sundry branches of C.C.'s Coffeehouse. In addition to great coffee and pastries, the Esplanade Avenue branch has a large "yard"—not quite a courtyard—with wrought-iron tables for alfresco imbibing. Indoors, in the air-conditioning, there is ample seating, including a couple of cushy leather chairs near the entrance.... *Tel 504/465-0527. 2800 Esplanade Ave. AE, DC, MC, V. $*

See Map 9 on p. 79.

Central Grocery Store (p. 69) FRENCH QUARTER *SANDWICHES* Belly up to the rear counter and have the Sicilian grocer wrap you a plate-sized muffaletta—a half or quarter order can fill you up. Fresh whole rounds of Italian bread are stuffed to bursting with imported Italian meats and cheeses and spicy olive salad. Get a Barq's root beer and then go munch your lunch on a park bench on the Moonwalk, watching the Mississippi's parade of tugs and riverboats.... *Tel 504/523-1620. 923 Decatur St. AE, DISC, MC, V. $*

See Map 6 on p. 76.

Clancy's (p. 68) UPTOWN *CONTINENTAL* Set in a very residential spot, Clancy's is the place where chattering Uptowners meet to dine. Nary a tourist can find it, and few would dare to try to break into what feels like a private club. The food is fine; call it New New Orleans cuisine. Don't miss the oyster and brie starter.... *Tel 504/895-1111. 6100 Annunciation St. Reservations accepted. AE, DC, DISC, MC, V. $$$$*

See Map 8 on p. 78.

Clover Grill (p. 71) FRENCH QUARTER *BURGERS* This place is so campy and fun, even the website merits a visit! It's 24-hour diner bliss at the Clover, where the burgers are what's for dinner. They purport to cook them under a hubcap. Whatever!

They're juicy and delicious. The $5 breakfast special is a swell choice for revelers who've been out all night, served from 5am to 11am.... *Tel 504/5981010. www.clovergrill.com. 900 Bourbon St. AE, DC, MC, V. $*

See Map 6 on p. 76.

Cobalt (p. 64) CBD *NEW SOUTH LOUISIANA* Set in the ground floor of a former Masonic temple–cum–Hotel Monaco, Cobalt offers three meals a day, but is much more enticing for dinner. That's when the live music is going and the cocktails are flowing from the bustling bar. The room is chic with tile and steel and the food is contemporary Southern with offerings like crispy bacon, sweet hot pickled green tomatoes, and the "Big Ass" BBQ rib-eye with country mashed potatoes, skillet-seared mushrooms, and crispy asparagus.... *Tel 504/565-5595. www.cobaltrestaurant.com. 333 St. Charles Ave. Reservations recommended. AE, DC, DISC, MC, V. $$$$$*

See Map 7 on p. 77.

Commander's Palace (p. 61) GARDEN DISTRICT *CREOLE* This distinguished restaurant, whose menu blends Creole, French, and American traditions, is perennially one of the country's best. It's housed in a marvelous Victorian mansion in the Garden District. Try for a window table in the second-floor Garden Room, overlooking the attractive courtyard, but you'll be vying with a host of locals, and they get priority. Top menu choices are turtle soup laced with sherry, trout wrapped in a crispy pecan crust, and a sinful Creole bread pudding soufflé served with whiskey sauce. Commander's originated the now-ubiquitous jazz brunch, and they do a fun one, with festive balloons and a trio.... *Tel 504/899-8221. www.commanderspalace.com. 1403 Washington Ave. Reservations required. Jackets preferred for dinner. AE, DC, DISC, MC, V. $$$$$*

See Map 5 on p. 54.

Cooter Brown's Tavern and Oyster Bar (p. 63) UPTOWN *BAR FOOD* Cooter's is a college drinking spot that happens also to do excellent, affordable raw oysters. It also has a formidable beer selection—400 different brews in all. If pool tables and sports-spewing wide-screen tellies are your scene, this is your place.... *Tel 504/866-9104. www.cooterbrowns.com. 509 S. Carrollton Ave. AE, DC, DISC, MC, V. $$*

See Map 8 on p. 78.

Court of Two Sisters (p. 68) FRENCH QUARTER *CREOLE* Before you start filling your plate at the jazz brunch buffet (tourists galore 9am–3am), stroll around the 80-odd dishes and consider your options: In addition to the usual suspects—jambalaya, boiled crawfish, shrimp Creole, étouffées, and every other imaginable regional specialty—there are carving boards of roast beef, turkey, duck à l'órange, oysters Bienville, barbecued ribs, and several different kinds of desserts. The mind boggles. Dinner is more sedate, with candlelight, escargots in mushroom caps, roasted duck, and trout Picasso, which comes with bananas, kiwi, strawberries, and honeydew.... *Tel 504/522-7261. www.courtoftwosisters.com. 613 Royal St. AE, DC, DISC, MC, V. $$$*

See Map 6 on p. 76.

Crabby Jack's (p. 63) JEFFERSON *SEAFOOD* Set way off the beaten path on nasty old Jeff Highway, Crabby Jack's happens to do the fattest, tastiest po'boys around. Besides fried shrimp and oyster, they also cook up a roast duck po'boy and a lamb version that are out of this world. Since they also sell fresh seafood, you can't miss if you try the blackened Gulf fish or the fish tacos. It's owned by Jack Leonardo, colorful chef at Jacque's Imo, so when the wait's too long there, skip it and hit Crabby Jack's the next day for lunch. Tip: Take it to go and picnic somewhere; it's not made for dining in.... *Tel 504/833-2722. 428 Jefferson Hwy. Walk-ins welcome. AE, DC, DISC, MC, V. $$*

See Map 5 on p. 54.

***Creole Queen* (p. 74)** CANAL ST. WHARF *CREOLE* A sleek replica of a 19th-century riverboat, replete with a big red paddle churning up the Big Muddy, the *Queen* does nightly 2-hour cruises with traditional jazz (and gangs of tourists) aboard. She begins boarding at 7pm and departs about an hour later. Dinner is a buffet of jambalaya, shrimp Creole, red beans and rice, étouffées, gumbo, and bread pudding.... *Tel 504/529-4567, 800/445-4109. www.neworleanspaddlewheels.com. Canal St. Wharf. Reservations required. AE, DC, DISC, MC, V. $$$$$*

See Map 6 on p. 76.

Crepe Nanou (p. 67) UPTOWN *FRENCH* Très Deco on the outside and très French on the inside, this tiny, beloved eatery churns out consistently excellent crepes and other Gallic specialties for an avid local following. The crepes are the thing here, but lamb and beef also glide to the cramped tables cooked to perfection. Save room for the dessert crepes—especially the namesake Crepe Nanou, crammed with three kinds of ice cream, chocolate sauce, and almonds.... *Tel 504/899-2670. 1410 Robert St. AE, DC, MC, V. $$*

See Map 8 on p. 78.

Crescent City Steaks (p. 70) MID-CITY *STEAK* Serving carnivores for 67 years straight, this fabulous relic puts other steakhouses to shame. They have not deigned to fluff the menu with anything but U.S. prime aged corn-fed beef, which you can get in any of five cuts. Potatoes come six different ways, and veggies are often served au gratin. The best thing about the place is the totally spare, old-school interior which includes curtained booths where local politicos love to make their deals.... *Tel 504/821-3271. www.crescentcitysteaks.com. 1001 N. Broad St. Reservations accepted. AE, DC, DISC, MC, V. $$$$*

See Map 9 on p. 79.

Croissant d'Or (p. 72) FRENCH QUARTER *PASTRIES* In this wildly popular little patisserie with tiny marble-topped tables, choose fresh-from-the-oven raspberry, almond, apple, and blueberry croissants from the display case, along with plump brioches, chocolaty eclairs, and various other cream-filled and fattening French pastries. Good cappuccino, too. For lunch you can get croissant sandwiches, soup, and sundry salads.... *Tel 504/524-4663. 617 Ursulines St. AE, MC, V. $*

See Map 6 on p. 76.

Cuvee (p. 73) CBD *CREOLE CONTINENTAL* From a $1,500 '85 Mondavi-Rothschild "Opus One" to a $20 '99 Sierra Cantabria "Tinto" Rioja, Cuvee's wine shelves run wide and deep. Hence the oenophilic name. The decor is also evocative—dark wood, red brick, and massive magnums of champagne bottles–cum–chandeliers almost make you feel you're dining in an actual cellar. The food here is good, and though some kitchen upheavals have made locals nervous, this restaurant's vintage is on the rise again.... *Tel 504/587-9001. 322 Magazine St. Reservations recommended. AE, DC, MC, V. $$$$–$$$$$*

See Map 7 on p. 77.

Deanie's Seafood Restaurant (p. 63) METAIRIE/FRENCH QUARTER *SEAFOOD* Bowls of seasoned boiled new potatoes start things off, and your fingers will already be sticky before your barbecue shrimp arrives, served in a hot cauldron with butter and garlic sauce—a typical New Orleans peel 'n' eat dish. There's a prodigious listing of other fried, boiled, and broiled seafood (including on pizza) in a cavernous, unpretentious space.... *Metairie: Tel 504/831-4141, 800/66–CAJUN; 1713 Lake Ave. Take I-10W to West End Blvd., then drive north on West End Blvd. for about 1.5 miles to Robert E. Lee Blvd.; drive west on R. E. Lee Blvd. across the 17th St. Canal Bridge. R. E. Lee Blvd. becomes Old Hammond Hwy. across the bridge; go 1 block and turn left. Deanie's is at Lake Ave. and Plaquemine St. French Quarter: Tel 504/581-1316; 841 Iberville St. AE, DC, DISC, MC, V. $$*

See Map 5 on p. 54.

Dick and Jenny's (p. 66) UPTOWN *NEW SOUTH LOUISIANA* Once the wunderkind of Upperline, Richard Benz left that Uptown Victorian several years ago for a charming cottage farther downtown. Foodies clamor for a taste of his shrimp or duck dishes, but he has a way with fish as well. The no-reservation policy means there is almost always a wait for din-din, unless you get there at opening. So have a snack first, then have a drink on the patio and wait your turn.... *Tel 504/894-9880. 4501 Tchoupitoulas St. AE, DISC, MC, V. $$$$*

See Map 8 on p. 78.

Dickie Brennan's Steakhouse (p. 62) FRENCH QUARTER *STEAK* "Straightforward steaks with a New Orleans touch" is the, um, prime attraction, accompanied by potatoes—fried, au gratin, baked, or Lyonnaise. There's a grand five-onion soup among the starters, and generous servings of sides like fried onion rings. Sea creatures include whole lobster, flown in daily, and a vegetable platter is available, with mashed sweet potatoes. Locals have flocked here since its 1998 opening.... *Tel 504/522-2467. www.dickiebrennanssteakhouse.com. 716 Iberville St. Reservations suggested. AE, DC, DISC, MC, V. $$$$$*

See Map 6 on p. 76.

Dooky Chase (p. 72) TREME *CREOLE/SOUL FOOD* A down-home place where the main attractions are chicken breast stuffed with oyster dressing and baked in *marchand de vin* sauce (called Chicken à la Dooky), filé gumbo, stewed okra, sweet potatoes, and grilled pork chops. The dining room is decorated with paintings by local African American artists.... *Tel 504/821-2294. 2301 Orleans Ave. Reservations advised. AE, DC, DISC, MC, V. $$*

See Map 9 on p. 79.

Dunbar's (p. 69) UPTOWN *CREOLE/SOUL FOOD* This is an unadorned luncheonette on a run-down strip of Freret Street, but the crunchy fried chicken comes three pieces per plate, the corn bread is sweet and fluffy, and there are terrific po'boys, smoked sausage, and red beans and rice.... *Tel 504/899-0734. 4927 Freret St. AE, DISC, MC, V. $*

See Map 8 on p. 78.

Emeril's (p. 63) WAREHOUSE DISTRICT *NEW SOUTH LOUISIANA* Housed in a restored warehouse, Emeril's showcases splashy expressionist art on plain adobe walls. Chef/owner Emeril Lagasse is renowned for his homemade everything: andouille, pasta, Worcestershire sauce, ice cream, you name it. One of his signature salads is warm wilted spinach dressed with homemade goat cheese and andouille sausage vinaigrette. Creole meunière butter sauce tops the andouille-crusted Texas redfish, and green chile mole covers the grilled double-cut pork chops.... *Tel 504/528-9393. www.emerils.com. 800 Tchoupitoulas St. Jackets optional. AE, DC, DISC, MC, V. $$$$*

See Map 5 on p. 54.

Emeril's Delmonico (p. 63) LOWER GARDEN DISTRICT *CREOLE* Delmonico has been on this site since the late 19th century, but in 1997 the ubiquitous Emeril Lagasse purchased it and poured millions into a glamorous renovation. (Take a gander at the restrooms before you leave.) Ceilings are sky-high, and so is the noise level, so don't expect a quiet tête-à-tête here. Also plan to rent a U-Haul to use as a doggie bag. Emeril's portions are always gargantuan. Dinner entrees include veal Marcelle with sautéed jumbo lump crabmeat and grilled shrimp Bordelaise with dill roasted new potatoes. The waitstaff, dressed to the nines, does deft tableside preparation of Caesar salad and bananas Foster for dessert.... *Tel 504/525-4937. www.emerils.com. 1300 St.*

Charles Ave. Reservations recommended. AE, DC, DISC, MC, V. $$$$$

See Map 7 on p. 77.

Felix's Restaurant and Oyster Bar (p. 62) FRENCH QUARTER *SEAFOOD* A casual seafood place across the street from the Acme Oyster House, and with a somewhat lengthier menu, Felix's has a good oyster bar and cooked-to-order fresh seafood.... *Tel 504/522-4440. www.felixs.com. 739 Iberville St. AE, DC, DISC, MC, V. $$*

See Map 6 on p. 76.

Frankie and Johnny's (p. 69) UPTOWN *SEAFOOD* An Uptown bastion of fried seafood for locals and tourists alike. On weekends and during special events, this down-home, dark, divey grease palace gets packed, and with its no-reservation policy that means waits can be epic. Luckily they have a pretty big bar area where would-be eaters drink 'til they're called up. Menus are up on the wall, and plastic tablecloths cover eating surfaces. It ain't pretty, but it's good.... *Tel 504/899-9146. 321 Arabella St. AE, DISC, MC, V. $*

See Map 8 on p. 78.

Funky Butt (p. 74) FRENCH QUARTER *CREOLE/CAJUN* Locals remember this venue as the very elegant and Art Deco restaurant Jonathan. Some of the Deco remains, in etched glass mirrors and other touches, but these days the place is home to a wildly popular music club. It's named for a similarly popular turn-of-the-century music hall where Buddy Bolden played—the man most folks credit with playing the first jazz licks. Nowadays you can listen to jazz while feasting on blackened chicken and crawfish linguine.... *Tel 504/558-0872. www.funkybutt.com. 714 N. Rampart St. No credit cards. $*

See Map 6 on p. 76.

Gabrielle (p. 67) MID-CITY *NEW SOUTH LOUISIANA* Shaped like a triangle, this tiny 70-seat restaurant is the bastion of Greg Sonnier, one of the most consistently fabulous chefs in the city. His wife Mary makes those fiendishly delicious carrot cakes and cobblers. Both worked for Paul Prudhomme back in those days. The rack o' lamb comes crusted in Creole cream cheese with black grape sauce, and the slow-roasted duck comes in an orange-sherry sauce over vermicelli.... *Tel 504/948-6233. www.gabriellerestaurant.com. 3201 Esplanade Ave. Reservations recommended. AE, DC, DISC, MC, V. $$$$*

See Map 9 on p. 79.

Galatoire's (p. 65) FRENCH QUARTER *FRENCH CREOLE* Open since 1905, this is a classic French Creole bistro with polished brass rails, mirrored walls, white tablecloths, tuxedoed waiters, and hordes of old-line Orleanians patiently lined up on the littered Bourbon Street sidewalk outside. Fried oysters and bacon en brochette, broiled pompano, trout amandine, and excellent chicken dishes are all winners on the five-page menu. Crawfish *étouffée* is a popular off-the-menu special.... *Tel 504/525-2021. www.galatoires.com. 209 Bourbon St. Reservations for upstairs. Jackets required for dinner and all day Sun; no jeans. AE, DC, DISC, MC, V. $$$$*

See Map 6 on p. 76.

Gautreau's (p. 67) UPTOWN *CREOLE* This local favorite is housed in an erstwhile pharmacy, with polished wood, a pressed-tin ceiling, and wonderful photographs of Old New Orleans. Shrimp and fennel bisque, grilled sea scallops with marinated peppers, and a marvelous duck confit are top appetizers; then try roasted chicken with wild mushrooms, green beans, and garlic mashed potatoes. There's also a wonderful lineup of filets mignon. Leave room for any of the desserts that involve chocolate, like the warm flourless cake.... *Tel 504/899-7397. 1728 Soniat St. Reservations recommended. DC, DISC, MC, V. $$$$$*

See Map 8 on p. 78.

Gumbo Shop (p. 70) FRENCH QUARTER *CREOLE/CAJUN* Stroll down the narrow alley at the side to reach this easygoing neighborhood eatery. Best known, of course, for gumbo, and for the sampler of New Orleans specialties: shrimp Creole, jambalaya, and red beans and rice.... *Tel 504/525-1486. www.gumboshop.com. 630 St. Peter St. AE, DC, DISC, MC, V. $$*

See Map 6 on p. 76.

GW Fins (p. 63) FRENCH QUARTER *SEAFOOD* It's not surprising to find excellent seafood in this Gulf state. What is surprising though, is the type and quality of the fish dished out at this newish Quarter eatery: Scottish salmon, Alaskan halibut, Hawaiian mahimahi, all flown in cold and fresh and ready to be turned into bouillabaisse; wood-grilled sea scallops; lobster dumplings; or some other mouthwatering preparation. If you love high-end seafood, don't miss Fins.... *Tel 504/581-3467. www.gwfins.com. 808 Bienville St. AE, DC, DISC, MC, V. $$$$$*

See Map 6 on p. 76.

Herbsaint (p. 64) WAREHOUSE DISTRICT *FRENCH/AMERICAN* In this little French-American bistro, on a corner of St. Charles Avenue, chefs Susan Spicer and Donald Link turn out wonderful renditions of tomato and shrimp bisque, double-cut pork chops, and shrimp and chile grits cake topped with their own unique "gravy".... *Tel 504/524-4114. www.herbsaint.com 701 St. Charles Ave. Reservations suggested. AE, DC, DISC, MC, V. $$*

See Map 7 on p. 77.

House of Blues (p. 64) FRENCH QUARTER *SOUTHERN/AMERICAN* The kitchen is surprisingly good, considering that this is first and foremost a live music venue. Southern-style cooking dominates, with the star attraction being baby back ribs, slow-smoked over mesquite and hickory, served with turnip greens and sweet mashed potatoes spiked with Jack Daniel's. Sautéed North Atlantic salmon is done with shrimp and eggplant stuffing, and crab claws are done in a balsamic butter sauce. Gospel music makes the Sunday brunch a soulful affair.... *Tel 504/529-2583. 225 Decatur St. Reservations recommended. AE, DC, DISC, MC, V. $$$*

See Map 6 on p. 76.

Irene's Cuisine (p. 74) FRENCH QUARTER *ITALIAN* Tiny, cluttered, and noisy though it is, Irene DiPietro packs 'em in to feast on her robust and garlicky country Italian fare. Steamed mussels are done in a marinara sauce, and roast duck is flavored with spinach and mustard. There's a good selection of oyster dishes, as well as fried soft-shell crab and rack of lamb. If the front room appears to be too noisy, ask for seating in the back room.... *Tel 504/529-8811. 539 St. Philip St. No reservations. AE, DC, DISC, MC, V. $$$*

See Map 6 on p. 76.

Jacques-Imo's (p. 63) UPTOWN *CREOLE/SOUL FOOD* It's hard to believe that less than a decade ago, chef Jack Leonardi would routinely send his staff home early for lack of customers. Nowadays, people will wait 3 hours for a table at this raucous Uptown joint, and Jack has even taken over the building next door. It's the kind of place you never forget: oysters fried till they're perfectly crisp outside and juicy inside without seeming the least bit greasy; giant hunks of Escobar; and a chef who wears hot pepper shorts to work and dances on the busy bar.... *Tel 504/861-0886. www.jacquesimoscafe.com. 716 Iberville St. Reservations for 5 or more. AE, DC, DISC, MC, V. $$$*

See Map 8 on p. 78.

Johnny's Po-Boys (p. 69) FRENCH QUARTER *PO'BOYS* Not much in the way of decor, but this place has been around more than half a century. The roast beef and gravy, oyster, shrimp, and other po'boys are popular with Quarterites, and breakfast is until midnight, closing time.... *Tel 504/524-8129. 511 St. Louis St. No credit cards. $*

See Map 6 on p. 76.

K-Paul's Louisiana Kitchen (p. 63) FRENCH QUARTER *CAJUN/CREOLE* Cajun celebrity chef Paul Prudhomme no longer presides over the kitchen at this famous down-home cafe, but it's still his, and his interpretation of Acadian cooking is the star attraction. The menu includes good gumbo, crawfish étouffée, blackened yellowfin tuna, corn bisque, and sweet potato–pecan pie. Skip lunch, when the downstairs room has only community seating, and reserve a table for dinner.... *Tel 504/524-7394. www.chefpaul.com. 416 Chartres St. AE, DC, DISC, MC, V. Open for dinner only. $$$$$*

See Map 6 on p. 76.

La Marquise (p. 72) FRENCH QUARTER *COFFEE/PASTRIES* This little patisserie, just off Jackson Square, is a sister to Croissant d'Or on Ursulines St.... *Tel 504/524-0420. 625 Chartes St. Weekdays 7am–7pm, weekends until 8pm, Sun until 5pm. $*

See Map 6 on p. 76.

La Peniche (p. 68) FAUBOURG MARIGNY *AMERICAN* In a city that never sleeps, all-nighter eats are surprisingly hard to find. Look no further: Late-night comfort food is what's on the menu at this wacky little spot nestled on a quiet street in the Marigny. Pork chops, burgers, omelets, pancakes, Oreo pie—whatever you need to console yourself with here, they probably have it.... *Tel 504/943-1460. 1940 Dauphine St. AE, DC, DISC, MC, V. $*

See Map 5 on p. 54.

Le Salon (p. 75) CBD *TEA* The ritzy lobby lounge of the very British Windsor Court Hotel has cushy settees, armchairs, and a smoke-free environment for live jazz in the evening. Classical music plays when you take tea (served twice daily) accompanied by plump scones, dainty little finger sandwiches, cookies, and chocolate truffles.... *Tel 504/523-6000. 300 Gravier St. Reservations advised. AE, DC, DISC, MC, V. Reservations advised. $$$*

See Map 7 on p. 77.

Lilette (p. 68) UPTOWN *FRENCH/ITALIAN/NEW SOUTH LOUISIANA* Visually elegant, gastronomically divine. Ivory booths, high ceilings, a lengthy wine list, and John Harris, a nationally recognized chef, make this once cursed spot one of the city's hottest reservations. Spinach gnocchi, boudin noir, sautéed Gulf fish, or the deliciously heavy braciola (a roulade of veal, prosciutto, and pine nuts, with tomato sauce and polenta)—come, eat, and just *try* not to weep with pleasure.... *Tel 504/895-1636. 3637 Magazine St. Reservations recommended. AE, DC, DISC, MC, V. $$$*

See Map 8 on p. 78.

Louis XVI (p. 73) FRENCH QUARTER *FRENCH* The design is Art Deco, the mood subdued, and the cuisine classic French, with expert tableside service. Onion soup gratinée, roasted breast of duckling in Escoffier sauce, beef Wellington with vegetables and perigourdine sauce, exceptional veggies, and flaming desserts are all presented with great panache.... *Tel 504/581-7000, 800/535-9707. www.louisxvi.com. St. Louis Hotel, 730 Bienville St. Reservations advised. AE, DC, MC, V. $$$$*

See Map 6 on p. 76.

Mr. B's Bistro (p. 62) FRENCH QUARTER *CREOLE* Noted for its hickory grill, Ralph and Cindy Brennan's sleek bistro is all done up with etched glass, white cloths, fresh flower arrangements, and an open kitchen. Panned chicken fettuccine and barbecue shrimp are excellent; jambalaya here is made with pasta, andouille, and shrimp. Warm bread pudding soaked in Irish whiskey sauce is a standout, but there are also some chocolate desserts that will knock your socks off.... *Tel 504/523-2078.*

www.mrbsbistro.com. 201 Royal St. Reservations advised for dinner. AE, DC, DISC, MC, V. $$$$

See Map 6 on p. 76.

Mosca's (p. 63) WEST BANK *ITALIAN* Garlic is king here, and the kitchen turns out splendid renditions of chicken, spaghetti and meatballs, quail, and Cornish hen. There's a great crab salad, with lumps of white crabmeat, iceberg lettuce, and green olives, served in a bracing vinaigrette. Rather than oysters on the half shell, oysters Mosca are baked en casserole, with bread crumbs, garlic, olive oil, and herbs; a succulent reason why locals make the 30-minute drive across the death-defying Huey P. Long Bridge. From downtown, take U.S. 90 across Huey P. Long. Continue on U.S. 90 west for 4.5 miles, and keep an eye peeled on the left side of the road.... *Tel 504/436-9942. 4137 U.S. 90 W. Reservations advised. No credit cards. $$$$*

See Map 5 on p. 54.

Mother's (p. 75) CBD *PO'BOYS* The ladies behind the steam tables stay busy cooking the roast beef, baked ham, and turkey po'boys for which this blue-collar spot is famous. Stake out a table before lining up at the cafeteria for plates of spicy jambalaya, red beans and rice, po'boys, and bread pudding. Great for cheap, hearty breakfasts, too.... *Tel 504/523-9656. 401 Poydras St. D, AE, DC, DISC, MC, V. $*

See Map 7 on p. 77.

Muriel's (p. 68) FRENCH QUARTER *NEW SOUTH LOUISIANA* Perched as it is on a to-die-for corner of Jackson Square, Muriel's is a slam dunk for hungry tourists. Its decor is best described as New Orleans Gothic (without being too campy), and its menu is an ambitious affair bursting with poached oysters, crawfish pie, rabbit, duck, and other local delectables. It's a fun spot to pop into for a lunch after a psychic reading in the Square.... *Tel 504/568-1885. www.muriels.com. 801 Chartres St. AE, DC, DISC, MC, V. $$$*

See Map 6 on p. 76.

Napoleon House (p. 64) FRENCH QUARTER *CREOLE* This beloved institution defines old New Orleans atmosphere—worn wooden tables, peeling sepia walls hung with pictures of Napoleon, and canned classical music. Some amount of time will be frittered away waiting for a waiter, but no one—patrons or staff—is in a hurry here. Pimm's Cup, served with a garnish of cucumber, is the featured beverage; po'boys and warm muffalettas are the main fare.... *Tel 504/524-9752. www.napoleonhouse.com. 500 Chartres St. AE, DC, DISC, MC, V. $*

See Map 6 on p. 76.

Nola (p. 63) FRENCH QUARTER *CREOLE/AMERICAN* Some people think Emeril Lagasse's split-level French Quarter entry is even better than his eponymous Warehouse District restaurant—witness the crowds and clatter. Among the popular entrees is a mixed grill of herb-marinated filet mignon, brochette, homemade chorizo, and Gulf shrimp with a roasted garlic potato cake. The wood-fueled oven turns out cedar plank–roasted redfish accompanied by a Vietnamese seafood salad. Emeril's tuber specials include pecan-glazed sweet potatoes and roasted-garlic creamed potatoes.... *Tel 504/522-6652. www.emerils.com. 534 St. Louis St. Reservations advised for dinner. AE, DC, DISC, MC, V. $$$$$*

See Map 6 on p. 76.

Palace Café (p. 62) FRENCH QUARTER *CREOLE* The Palace Café, designed along the lines of a big Parisian bistro, is in a historic Italianate/baroque building that once housed the Werlein Music Co. One of the Brennan family's restaurants, it's a big, boisterous place with a grand spiral stairway, tile floors, and splashy murals of homegrown musicians. Tops are the crabmeat cheesecake appetizer and shrimp *Tchefuncte.* Seafood is king here, but the kitchen turns out a mean filet mignon, too. The white chocolate bread pudding became a legend about 10 minutes after it was first served.... *Tel 504/523-1661. www.palacecafe.com. 605 Canal St. Reservations recommended. AE, DC, DISC, MC, V. $$$$*

See Map 6 on p. 76.

Palm Court Jazz Cafe (p. 74) FRENCH QUARTER *CREOLE/AMERICAN* Tile floors, pretty cafe curtains, ceiling fans, and white-clothed tables are the setting at one of the surprisingly few places in town where you can have dinner while listening to traditional jazz. Dig into oysters Bordelaise, steak and mushroom pie, jambalaya, red beans and rice, and bread pudding, of course.... *Tel 504/525-0200. www.palmcourtjazzcafe.com. 1204 Decatur St. Reservations suggested. AE, DC, DISC, MC, V. $$*

See Map 6 on p. 76.

Parasol's (p. 69) UPTOWN *PO'BOYS* An ages-old stomping ground during annual St. Patrick's Day festivities, Parasol's is a local favorite for po'boys. There's nothing fancy here, and you should not plan to stroll around the neighborhood, but the roast beef and the meatball po'boys are made by celestial beings.... *Tel 504/899-2054. www.parasols.com. 2533 Constance St. AE, DC, MC, V. $*

See Map 5 on p. 54.

Pascal's Manale (p. 68) UPTOWN *CREOLE/ITALIAN* Famous as the self-proclaimed inventor of barbecue shrimp—which, by the way is not barbecued at all—Manale's has been resting on its laurels and its advertising campaign with not-culinarily-inquisitive tourists for years. Nonetheless, if you simply must have the original version of this now ubiquitous shrimp dish, this is where you come.... *Tel 504/895-4877. 1838 Napoleon Ave. Reservations suggested. AE, DC, DISC, MC, V. $$$*

See Map 8 on p. 78.

Peristyle (p. 64) FRENCH QUARTER *CONTINENTAL* Small (62 seats) and smart, Peristyle is the home court of proprietor/chef Anne Kearney, who used to work at the food bar at Emeril's. She says she loves the close proximity to the customers, and her love of food preparation is clearly evident. Her changing menu might include, for starters, pan-seared foie gras with strawberry reduction; main events may be grilled duck breast with picholine olives and peaches. Seafood is always featured: mussels bourride in saffron shellfish broth, or grilled sea scallops in lemon and white-wine sauce. For the carnivorous, there's pan-seared lamb loin chops with herb Dijon reduction. Very popular with table-hopping Orleanians. Better at dinner, but they do have a Friday lunch service.... *Tel 504/593-9535. 1041 Dumaine St. Reservations required. AE, DC, DISC, MC, V. Closed Sun and Mon. $$$$$*

See Map 6 on p. 76.

Pho Tau Bay (p. 69) CBD *VIETNAMESE* If you don't have time to drive out to the West Bank or New Orleans East, but you want to try some of New Orleans's surprisingly excellent Vietnamese food, this is the place for you. It's just a takeout shack, but, oh, the chargrilled meats! Oh, the feathery rice noodles! Basil, lemon grass, mint! What's not to love about a light, healthy snack in this city of heavy-duty meals?.... *Tel 504/524-4669. 1565 Tulane Ave. AE, DC, DISC, MC, V. $*

See Map 5 on p. 54.

PJ's Coffee & Tea Co. (p. 72) UPTOWN *COFFEE/TEA* Once local, now national, PJ's has many locations around town. The one we list is on the way to the zoo and smack in the midst of a great shopping area. Granitas are especially good on a hot Nola day, and their chai is pretty refreshing, too. They also have the requisite selection of baked goods.... *Tel 504/895-0273. 5432 Magazine St. AE, MC, V. $*

See Map 8 on p. 78.

Poppy's Grill (p. 69) FRENCH QUARTER *24-HOUR GRILL* If you stagger out of Pat O'Brien's at 3am in search of a burger and fries, cross the street to this 24-hour grill. No decor except for some neon and a jukebox. Cheap breakfast specials begin at 5am.... *Tel 504/524-3287. 717 St. Peter St. AE, DC, DISC, MC, V. $*

See Map 6 on p. 76.

Port of Call (p. 69) FRENCH QUARTER *STEAK/HAMBURGERS* At this funky dive with a nautical motif, the juicy two-fisted burger—a half-pound of freshly ground chuck served with a huge, baked potato—is among the best of the genre. No-nonsense pizzas, New York strip, filet mignon, rib-eye, and mushrooms sautéed in red-wine sauce are other attractions.... *Tel 504/523-0120. www.portofcallneworleans.com. 838 Esplanade Ave. AE, DC, DISC, MC, V. $*

See Map 6 on p. 76.

Praline Connection (p. 72) FAUBOURG MARIGNY/WAREHOUSE DISTRICT *SOUL FOOD* All of the waiters wear black derbies at this small, crowded neighborhood soul food joint. Smothered pork chops, stewed or fried chicken, mustard greens, barbecued ribs, corn bread, sweet potato pie, and bread pudding are among the down-home offerings.... Faubourg Marigny: *Tel 504/943-3934, 800/392-0362; www.pralineconnection.com; 542 Frenchmen St. Warehouse District: Tel 504/523–3973; 901 S. Peters St. AE, DC, DISC, MC, V. $*

See Map 5 on p. 54.

Ralph's on the Park (p. 62) MID-CITY *NEW SOUTH LOUISIANA* The Ralph in question is Ralph Brennan, one of the storied clan that dominates the restaurant scene out here. The second-generation restaurateur has learned a thing or two about the biz. His spanking-new venture employs the talents of chef Gerard Maras, an excellent local talent who has cooked at many of the city's best eateries. The place is located in a historical building with many great stories to tell, two of which are depicted in grand murals by artist Tony Green. The food makes use of local ingredients and shows them off well: fried green tomatoes with lump crabmeat, oysters with bacon and jalapeño cream sauce, baked black drum with béarnaise sauce. *Tel 504/488-1000. www.ralphsonthepark.com. 900 City Park Ave. Reservations suggested. AE, DC, DISC, MC, V. $$$*

See Map 9 on p. 79.

Red Fish Grill (p. 62) FRENCH QUARTER *SEAFOOD* A huge room with soaring ceilings and a roaring noise level, Ralph Brennan's entry into the seafood scene has a lengthy listing of sea critters done up in imaginative costumes. The signature dish is sweet potato catfish, served with an andouille cream drizzle. If you'd like to shop around, order the Bourbon Street sampler (coconut-crusted Gulf shrimp, grilled alligator sausage, barbecued oysters, and crawfish au gratin), which serves two hearty souls. Those who eschew seafood have several options, including honey-glazed chicken, pork chops, and hickory-grilled filet mignon. The restaurant says it welcomes walk-ins, but take our advice: Make a reservation.... *Tel 504/598-1200. www.redfishgrill.com. 115 Bourbon St. Reservations suggested. AE, DC, DISC, MC, V. $$$*

See Map 6 on p. 76.

Rene Bistrot (p. 64) CBD *FRENCH* Rene Bajeux left a sweet gig at the renowned Grill Room to open up his eponymous bistrot several years ago, and he's never regretted it. Some of his food—mainly the Alsatian stuff—can get a bit heavy in the thick of summer, but he gets points for making his own pâtés, sausages, and smoked salmon in-house. For our climate, veer towards his Provençal selections like the bouillabaisse, the salade Niçoise, or the grilled sardines with baby octopus salad.... *Tel 504/412-2580. www.renebistrot.com. 817 Common St. Reservations suggested. AE, DC, DISC, MC, V. $$$*

See Map 7 on p. 77.

Restaurant August (p. 64) WAREHOUSE DISTRICT *CONTINENTAL/NEW SOUTH LOUISIANA* Run by nationally recognized local chef John Besh, August attracts the flush and fabulous to its Old World dining rooms. Under glimmering chandeliers suspended from towering ceilings, guests munch on buster crabs with lettuce and heirloom tomatoes on a *pain perdu* (lost bread) crouton; braised veal short-rib ravioli with hen-of-the-woods mushrooms and sherry vinaigrette; and game bird pâté with cornichon, fig, and watermelon.... *Tel 504/299-9777. www.rest-august.com. 301 Tchoupitoulas St. Reservations highly recommended. AE, DC, MC, V. $$$$$*

See Map 7 on p. 77.

rue de la course (p. 72) LOWER GARDEN DISTRICT *COFFEE/TEA* On a quiet corner of the LGD, the original rue, as locals affectionately call it, serves up coffees of all sorts: iced, flavored, cappuccino, latte, espresso, plus a host of teas, herbal and not. Baked goods abound too. This is a classic local coffeehouse with savants and weirdoes, students, and soccer moms crammed together for a bracing cup.... *Tel 504/899-0242. 1500 Magazine St. No credit cards. $*

See Map 5 on p. 54.

Ruth's Chris Steakhouse (p. 70) MID-CITY *STEAK* In a big unadorned room, aged prime beef, thick-cut fries, and green salad all arrive in prodigious portions. Excellent food, pricey but popular with politicos and Saints players.... *Tel 504/486-0810, 800/544-0808. www.ruthschris.com. 711 N. Broad St. Reservations suggested. AE, DC, DISC, MC, V. $$$$$*

See Map 9 on p. 79.

Sake Café (p. 68) GARDEN DISTRICT *JAPANESE/SUSHI* Those who know have proclaimed Sake the best sushi joint in town. First off, the setting is modern and cool, with space age music playing on the sound system. More importantly though, the seafood is wonderfully fresh—no fishy smell greets you at the door—and the sushi is made in perfect little servings, both aesthetically and gastronomically pleasing. They also dish out an array of soups, tempura and teriyaki dinners, and specialty dishes like the Japanese pizza. Their lunch special is also one of the best deals in town.... *Tel 504/894-0033. www.sakecafeuptown.com. 2830 Magazine St. Reservations accepted. AE, DC, DISC, MC, V. $$$*

See Map 5 on p. 54.

Sid-Mar's BUCKTOWN *SEAFOOD* The screened porch of this ramshackle roadhouse is a favorite place for boiled crawfish and the fresh seafood caught almost at the front door.... *Tel 504/831-9541. www.sidmarsofbucktown.com. 1824 Orpheum Ave. Take I-10 West to West End Blvd., go north on West End Blvd. about 1.5 miles to Robert E. Lee Blvd., and turn left onto R. E. Lee. Go straight on R. E. Lee Blvd. until you get to the red light* *at the 17th St. Canal, then turn right—don't cross the bridge—onto Orpheum Avenue. You'll see fishing boats on the right along the canal, and Sid-Mar's on the left. AE, DC, DISC, MC, V. Closed Mon. $$*

See Map 5 on p. 54.

Steamboat *Natchez* (p. 74) FRENCH QUARTER *CREOLE/CAJUN* A floating palace in the 19th-century riverboat tradition, the 1,600-passenger *Natchez* is a steam-powered beauty decked out—so to speak—in gingerbread trim, wood paneling, brass wall sconces, and antique chandeliers. At 6pm she begins boarding to the tune of a shrill calliope, and departs at 7 for a 2-hour harbor cruise with Dixieland bands and a huge buffet of Creole and Cajun specialties—jambalaya, red beans and rice, étouffées..... *Tel 504/586-8777, 800/233-BOAT. Fax 504/587-0708. www.steamboatnatchez.com. Toulouse St. Wharf behind the Jax Brewery. Reservations recommended. AE, DC, DISC, MC, V. $$$$$*

See Map 6 on p. 76.

Tujague's (p. 65) FRENCH QUARTER *FRENCH CREOLE* "Two jacks," as it's pronounced, opened in 1856, and is the city's second-oldest restaurant (after Antoine's). It has black-and-white tile floors, crisp white napery, and photos of Old New Orleans lining the walls. The menu is French Creole; a five-course table d'hôte meal features soup, shrimp rémoulade, boiled brisket of beef in Creole sauce, a choice of four entrees, and dessert—with bread pudding the top seller. A classic New Orleans experience.... *Tel 504/525-8676. www.tujagues.com. 823 Decatur St. Dinner reservations advised. AE, DC, DISC, MC, V. $$$*

See Map 6 on p. 76.

Uglesich's (p. 63) CENTRAL CITY *SEAFOOD* No more than a shack built in such a sketchy neighborhood, it only stays open for lunch, but this is still probably one of the best restaurants for down-home seafood in the country. So renowned is their grub—like trout with jalapeños, soft-shell crab po'boys, and barbecue oysters—that people come from far and wide, and wait for hours just for a plate of it. Domestic goddess–turned–convict Martha Stewart even made the trek. The proprietors, Mr. and Mrs. Uggie, as they are lovingly called, are getting ready to call it quits, but nobody knows exactly when, so put this at the top of your "must-eat" list.... *Tel 504/523-8571 or 504/525-4925. www.uglesichs.com. 1238 Baronne St. Reservations not accepted. Open for lunch only. No credit cards. $$*

See Map 5 on p. 54.

Upperline (p. 66) UPTOWN *CREOLE* Dining in this white-frame cottage is almost like eating at someone's home; paintings from owner JoAnne Clevenger's private collection of works by regional artists line the walls. "A Taste of New Orleans" is the restaurant's best-seller, with samples of seafood gumbo, Creole white bean soup, fried green tomatoes with shrimp remoulade, andouille, and crawfish étouffée. A favorite dessert is warm bread pudding with toffee sauce.... *Tel 504/891-9822. www.upperline.com. 1413 Upperline St. Reservations advised. AE, DC, MC, V. Open for dinner only, Wed–Sun. $$$*

See Map 8 on p. 78.

Victor's Grill (p. 70) FRENCH QUARTER *STEAK/CHOPHOUSE* Set amidst lustrous salmon and gold fabrics, crystal chandeliers, and bushels of fresh flowers, Victor's sure shows a pretty face. And the menu is heavy duty: lump crab remoulade with fried capers, 14-ounce rib-eyes with a selection of sauces, and profiteroles for dessert. For the prices, the service isn't what you might expect, though you might be okay with the lack of attention if you happen to get seated in one of their curtained-off booths.... *Tel 504/524-1331, 800/241-3333. www.ritzcarlton.com. 921 Canal St. Reservations advised. AE, DC, DISC, M, V. $$$$$*

See Map 6 on p. 76.

Whole Foods Market–Arabella Station (p. 69) UPTOWN *GROCERY/DELI* Makin' groceries has been elevated to art for Uptowners who shop at Whole Foods. Sure lotsa locals laughingly call it "Whole Paycheck" because its organic produce and free-range meats cost way more than the local Winn-Dixie. But the fruits and veggies are pristine, the cheeses are otherworldly, the meat is hormone free, and that kinda quality just doesn't come cheap. The deli overflows with sandwiches, sushi, brick-oven pizza, an organic salad bar, and tons of premade noshes, which is great for visitors looking to grab a picnic on the fly.... *Tel 504/899-9119. 5600 Magazine St. AE, DISC, MC, V. $–$$$$$*

See Map 8 on p. 78.

Zoë Bistrot (p. 73) CBD *BRASSERIE* The dining room of the W New Orleans Hotel looks for all the world like a sleek Parisian brasserie, from the deep burgundy banquettes to the tall tapers, right down to the big-brasserie-style white plates. You can get a bacon cheeseburger, if you're willing to pay a steep price. But you can also get good, moderately priced renditions of steak frites, filet and brie crêpes, Bourbon glazed pork, shrimp with wild mushrooms and pasta, and redfish served with lump crabmeat in brown-butter sauce. You'll probably have to mull a moment or two over the desserts, as the choices include a strawberry meringue cookie with dark chocolate mousse, and vanilla bean ice cream profiteroles. The bistro has a very impressive wine list.... *Tel 504/525-9444. www.zoebistrot.com. 333 Poydras St. AE, DC, DISC, MC, V. $$$*

See Map 7 on p. 77.

DIVER

SIONS

3

Map 10: New Orleans Diversions Orientation

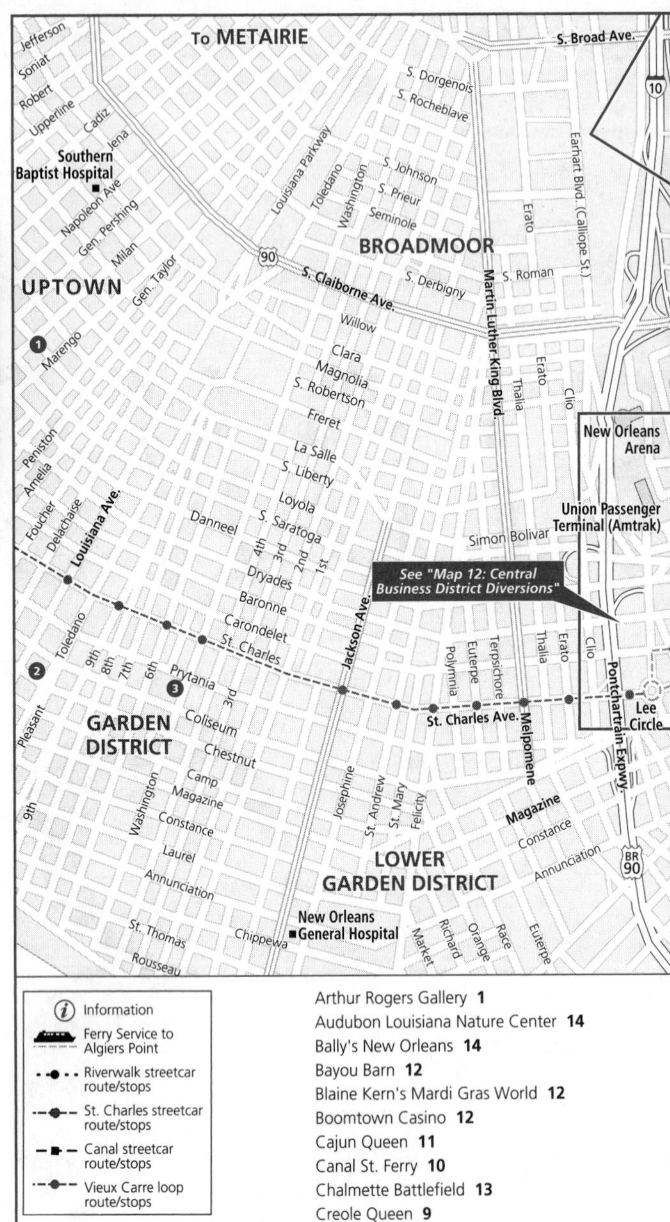

Information
Ferry Service to Algiers Point
Riverwalk streetcar route/stops
St. Charles streetcar route/stops
Canal streetcar route/stops
Vieux Carre loop route/stops

Arthur Rogers Gallery **1**
Audubon Louisiana Nature Center **14**
Bally's New Orleans **14**
Bayou Barn **12**
Blaine Kern's Mardi Gras World **12**
Boomtown Casino **12**
Cajun Queen **11**
Canal St. Ferry **10**
Chalmette Battlefield **13**
Creole Queen **9**
Honey Island Swamp Tours **16**

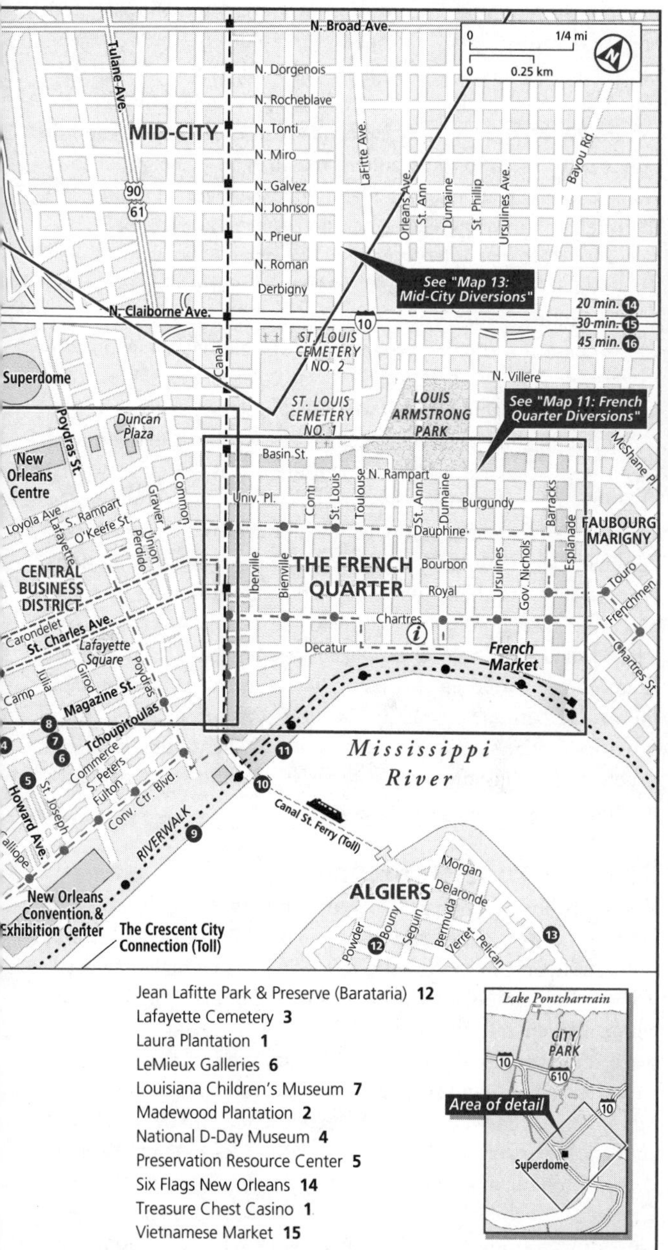
N. Broad Ave.
0 1/4 mi
0 0.25 km
Tulane Ave.
MID-CITY
N. Dorgenois
N. Rocheblave
N. Tonti
N. Miro
N. Galvez
N. Johnson
N. Prieur
N. Roman
Derbigny
LaFitte Ave.
Orleans Ave.
St. Ann
Dumaine
St. Phillip
Ursulines Ave.
Bayou Rd.
90
61
See "Map 13: Mid-City Diversions"
N. Claiborne Ave.
10
20 min. 14
30 min. 15
45 min. 16
ST. LOUIS CEMETERY NO. 2
Canal
Superdome
N. Villere
ST. LOUIS CEMETERY NO. 1
LOUIS ARMSTRONG PARK
See "Map 11: French Quarter Diversions"
Poydras St.
Duncan Plaza
New Orleans Centre
Basin St.
N. Rampart
McShane Pl.
Common
Gravier
Union
Perdido
Loyola Ave
Lafayette
S. Rampart
O'Keefe St.
Univ. Pl.
Conti
St. Louis
Toulouse
St. Ann
Dumaine
Burgundy
Barracks
Esplanade
FAUBOURG MARIGNY
Dauphine
CENTRAL BUSINESS DISTRICT
Iberville
Bienville
THE FRENCH QUARTER
Bourbon
Royal
Ursulines
Gov. Nichols
Touro
Frenchmen
Carondelet
St. Charles Ave.
Lafayette Square
Chartres
Decatur
French Market
Chartres St.
Camp
Julia
Girod
Poydras
Magazine St.
Tchoupitoulas
Mississippi River
Commerce
S. Peters
Fulton
Conv. Ctr. Blvd.
Howard Ave.
St. Joseph
Calliope
RIVERWALK
Canal St. Ferry (Toll)
Morgan
Delaronde
ALGIERS
Bermuda
Verret
Pelican
Powder
Bouny
Seguin
New Orleans Convention & Exhibition Center
The Crescent City Connection (Toll)
Jean Lafitte Park & Preserve (Barataria) 12
Lafayette Cemetery 3
Laura Plantation 1
LeMieux Galleries 6
Louisiana Children's Museum 7
Madewood Plantation 2
National D-Day Museum 4
Preservation Resource Center 5
Six Flags New Orleans 14
Treasure Chest Casino 1
Vietnamese Market 15
Lake Pontchartrain
CITY PARK
10
610
Area of detail
Superdome

Basic Stuff

Conventioneers, jazz freaks, European package tourists, frat boys and sorority girls, tattooed gutter punks, exotic dancers, Dutch oil workers, and just plain folks. All types hear the Big Easy's siren call, and often for variations of three basic themes: to carouse the strange and beautiful Vieux Carré with a cup full of booze, to listen to transcendent music in seedy neighborhood clubs, or to eat all manner of gorgeously high-fat food until their belts pop. New Orleans has always been a place for people to cut loose, to be someone else, to live like a bon vivant for just a few days before going back to Kansas and selling vacuums door to door.

Luckily, for the people who live here and visitors who care to get past "the good time girl" surface of the city, there's a lot more than just the Trinity of food, drink, and jazz.

Here in the City That Care Forgot where so many norms are turned on their heads, *our* subculture consists of velvety public golf courses, primeval wetlands, super funky shopping, an abundance of art and antiques, lush parks, and a long list of family activities. Unless you need a vacation from the kids, don't hesitate to bring them. There are, after all, little ones who live here, and they don't all grow up inside a Bourbon Street bar. The Monday edition of the *Times-Picayune* carries a full page of "Parents and Children" happenings in the Living section, and the Friday edition's Lagniappe section runs a calendar of kids' activities. There's a top-notch zoo, an excellent aquarium, fun streetcars to clang around on, a Six Flags, and great parks for relaxing or exploring.

Getting Your Bearings

You probably will not get your bearings in New Orleans—at least, not if you depend upon mundane directions like north, south, east, and west. Nobody in town knows which way is up, if you ask directions by compass points. The Mississippi River, which carved out this crescent-shaped landmass in the first place, cuts an S-shaped swath through the city and creates chaos with such conventional directions. The sun rises in the east here, just like it does anywhere else, but in New Orleans it appears first over the West Bank. Which is east of the East Bank. You'll make yourself crazy if you try to outsmart the river. Creative Orleanians go with the river's flow: Uptown is upriver, Downtown is downriver, "lakeside" is toward Lake Pontchartrain, and "riverside" is toward the Ol' Man.

The French Quarter nestles up against a great bend in the Mississippi. The Quarter's downriver border is Esplanade Avenue, Rampart Street runs lakeside, and Iberville Street is the Uptown border. (By some accounts, Canal St. is the Uptown border, but not according to the Vieux Carré Commission, a body set up in 1936 by the state legislature to oversee the preservation of the Quarter. The blocks between Iberville and Canal streets are not under the jurisdiction of the VCC, and tend to be on the raunchy side.) The French Quarter's streets—laid out by French engineers in 1721, back when the French Quarter was called "La Nouvelle Orleans"—are designed in a regimental grid, covering about 1 square mile. The Vieux Carré, as the Quarter is also called, means Old Square, but this term is misleading—it's more a parallelogram than a square. The centerpiece is Jackson Square, neatly hemmed in by Decatur, St. Ann, St. Peter, and Chartres streets.

The Central Business District (CBD) is adjacent to the French Quarter, and Canal Street is the great divide between the two. The somewhat loosely defined boundaries of the CBD are Canal Street, Loyola Avenue, Howard Avenue, and the river. Within the CBD lies the Warehouse District, a pocket of abandoned 19th-century warehouses now renovated as restaurants, nightclubs, art galleries, and apartments.

Just uptown of the CBD—starting unofficially on the other side of the freeway underpass—is the Lower Garden District. Filled with super-funky shops, a Wal-Mart (soon), and decrepit houses right next door to meticulously restored mansions, it's sort of the trying-to-get-her-act-together stepsister to the Belle of New Orleans, the Garden District. Continuing uptown beyond the Garden District, you come to "Uptown," which is everything above Louisiana Avenue. At the high end of Uptown, you hit the University area, home to Loyola and Tulane, as well as the stunning Audubon Park and its terrific zoo. With its proliferation of kinetic college kids, the university section has some of the best and grungiest bars and music clubs. New Orleans proper, which is all of Orleans Parish, extends across the river to include Algiers, an old neighborhood on the West Bank, as well as up to Lake Pontchartrain. The big soup bowl called Mid-City stretches between Downtown and Lake Pontchartrain. Much of New Orleans lies 5 to 8 feet below sea level, and much of New Orleans is Mid-City. This is where the first French settlers camped, along Bayou St. John, before moving along a Native American portage (now called Bayou Rd.)

toward the river to stake out the colony that is now the French Quarter. Mid-City is predominantly residential, but within its borders are the 1,500 green acres of **City Park,** a slew of cemeteries, and the Fair Grounds, headquarters not only of thoroughbred racehorses but of the Jazz Fest.

Normal directions get a little easier once you get away from the serpentine river. Lake Pontchartrain forms the northern border of the city proper; on its north shore lies St. Tammany Parish, with its homes, pretty parks, and pine trees. On the south shore, Lakeshore Drive laces alongside the lake, running about 5 miles from Lakefront Airport to the West End. (The lake is big with locals for fishing, boating, and picnicking; swimming, however, is officially banned in its polluted waters.) The West End is awash with seafood restaurants, some of the city's best. Orleanians will drive out to the West End and just cruise the parking lots, checking to see which seafood shack they can get into with the least amount of waiting time.

The greater New Orleans metropolitan area includes, to the west, Jefferson Parish (home to much of the metro's malls and chain restaurants) and, to the east, St. Bernard Parish, which is of vital interest to people who live there but has almost nothing of interest to visitors. If you fly into town, as most people do, you'll land at Louis Armstrong International Airport, which occupies a good chunk of Kenner, a Jefferson Parish town about 15 miles west of downtown New Orleans. After landing, the smart tourist will grab a cab, get on the I-10, and close his eyes 'til he's within sight of the Superdome. The drive through Kenner and Metairie sure ain't pretty.

A Madness Called Mardi Gras

While the rest of the country is recovering from the bustle of their abbreviated holiday season—those measly days between Thanksgiving and New Year's—New Orleanians are only halfway through their 6-month-long party. Only a day or so after the fresh year has been welcomed, city workers are erecting barricades that will separate the madding crowds from the marching bands, flambeaux bearers, and three-story floats making their way toward Canal Street for what is surely America's biggest street party: Mardi Gras.

The official start of the season is January 6—aka Twelfth Night—when a gang of masked nuts calling themselves the "Phunny Phorty Phellows" hijacks a St. Charles Streetcar and makes a circuit while sipping champagne, eating King cake, and chucking beads.

Soon after that, the Living section of the *Times-Picayune* started running black-and-white photos of graceful young debs and middle-aged gentlemen dressed in bedazzled finery—sometimes the men wore creepy masks to hide their identities—indicating that the first Mardi Gras balls had begun.

But don't get out your white gloves yet. Most of the parties and balls are private, invitation-only affairs, so you'll have to content yourself with the fun and snippy task of paging through the morning paper over a café au lait and mocking the society crowd on its pages.

No, you really do not need to start flying, walking, or driving here until approximately 2 weeks before Mardi Gras Day, which changes from year to year, but is always sometime in February or March. Consult a Catholic Church near you and inquire as to the date of Ash Wednesday. Mardi Gras—which literally means Fat Tuesday—is the day before that, and the plebeian part of the fiesta really cranks up in New Orleans the fortnight before.

That's when most of the krewes (see "Learn the Lingo" box below) start parading. Members have spent the previous year developing overall themes such as A Tribute to Movie Musicals or Childhood Memories, and then building and painting floats that carry out the theme—well, actually, having them built and painted. The krewes have anywhere between 15 and 39 floats in their parades, along with scads of uniformed high school marching

Mardi Gras Roots

Mardi Gras came to Louisiana from France. On March 3, 1699, when French-Canadian Pierre LeMoyne, Sieur d'Iberville, the founder of Louisiana, made camp south of the present city, he noted in his diary that the day was Mardi Gras, and christened the site Pointe du Mardi Gras. By most accounts, the early celebrations of the occasion were little more than rowdy street brawls. The modern tradition of Mardi Gras began in 1857, when six Englishmen joined with 13 French Creoles to form a secret men's society—the Mystick Krewe of Comus (note the Olde English spelling)—and staged the first Mardi Gras parade. The first daytime procession was hastily thrown together in 1872 to entertain a royal visitor, the Russian Grand Duke Alexei Alexandrovich Romanov, and became known as the Rex parade. Rex began some of the enduring customs—the Mardi Gras colors of purple, gold, and green; and the "theme" song, "If Ever I Cease to Love," with ridiculous lyrics like "If ever I cease to love, may sheep's heads grow on apple trees." A fittingly absurd song for this madcap season.

bands, enthusiastic baton twirlers, crack flag corps, and sequined dance squads. During the week, the parades go on at night only, lit by streetlamps and men bearing cumbersome gas torches called flambeaux. While these men dance down the route, parade watchers toss coins their way, rewarding them for carrying out their arduous, enthusiastically executed task.

Everyone loves a parade—but why are these parades different from, say, the Macy's Thanksgiving Day parade in New York? Well, in the Big Easy, masked and costumed float riders throw trinkets to the roadside revelers. Plastic bead necklaces, stuffed animals, panties, Frisbees, plastic go-cups, spears, golden coconuts, aluminum coins called doubloons, and moon pies are just some of the truck that comes off those floats. This is where the Mardi Gras magic comes in, because in real life, who on earth would care about all that "Made in China" schlock?

But just you try to stand through a whole parade without getting caught up in the acquisitive insanity. Sweet old grandmothers clutching shopping bags and screaming "Throw me somethin', Mistah!" will knock out your front teeth to catch a strand. Grown men will body-block toddlers to get their share. It's a melee, though usually all in good fun. Generally the knocking about is accidental, and the knockers will profusely apologize and compensate the knockees with a strand of pearls or a doubloon.

Learn the Lingo

If you're in town more than 10 or 15 minutes you'll probably hear the word ***krewe*** *bandied about. Krewes (pronounced "crews") are the social and civic clubs that mastermind, pay for, and "put on" the 60 or so Mardi Gras parades. They also host elaborate—and usually private—Carnival balls, with royal courts, masked men, and highly choreographed* ***tableaux*** *you need to see to believe. Members must know someone in the krewe to join, and often they're invited. Once in, they pay annual dues—in some cases, they're pretty stiff—which go toward the cost of the floats, the costumes, and the souvenirs, called* ***throws,*** *that they toss to the crowds. Notables: Krewe D'tat is an all-male group that spoofs politics and is famous for its light-up skull beads. Krewe of Muses, the all-female satirical krewe, throws various lipstick and stiletto necklaces. The funniest group is usually Krewe de Vieux, which is comprised of various sub-krewes that pick raunchy, silly themes. There's no shortage of silliness elsewhere: Krewe de Poo tosses beads laced with plastic dog turds, and Krewe de Jew once threw bagels.*

Early in the fortnight, the parades are smaller and the floats less grandiose. But in the second week, the parades get longer, the floats bigger, and the grand marshals more famous. In the last weekend, the groups dubbed the super krewes make their appearances—Endymion, Bacchus, and Orpheus—with dozens of floats, thousands of riders, and what seems like millions of beads.

Once you've acquired a stash of beads, your Mardi Gras options can expand, depending on what kind of person you are. If you are the family, G-rated sort, you are probably watching the parades from Uptown—or at least you should be. That's where the kiddies and mommies and daddies belong, among locals who live near the route and are just out for an evening's enjoyment. In fact, one year an overly enthusiastic college coed was seen baring her breasts at an Uptown parade and the scowls she got from her fellow parade-goers were enough to melt rocks. She stowed her girls forthwith and headed for the Quarter...

...which, if you're after the Mardi Gras portrayed on the Fox Network and the Girls Gone Wild videos, is where *you* belong. And that's where you can make good use of your hard-won beads. Because it is in the French Quarter where women—and increasingly men—are willing to show the goods for a 5-cent strand of beads.

Now, pay attention, because this is the part where we help keep you out of jail: In recent years during the lead-up to Mardi Gras, the New Orleans Police Department has issued stern official warnings against public nudity and lewd behavior. (These warnings started in earnest the year after one uniformed NOPD officer was pictured on the front page of the local paper snapping a shot of a boob-flashing woman. Coincidence? You make the call.) In reality, the cops have mostly limited their arrests to people who are actually engaged in sex acts on the street. Nonetheless, smart money is on taking in the spectacle without making one of yourself.

And in the Quarter, there really is a *lot* to take in. On Mardi Gras day alone, you can catch the climactic home stretches of the funky Zulu and old school Rex parades on Canal Street. Or you can wander to the opposite side of the Quarter around Burgundy and St. Ann to watch the gay and fabulous Bourbon Street awards. Or you can cross Esplanade Avenue into the Faubourg Marigny and ogle part of the Society of St. Ann Walking Parade, a mellower and lesser-known event where the costumes are breathtakingly beautiful and the crowd is hippielike in its peacefulness. Or you can insinuate yourself onto someone's balcony, where you can dangle beads at will, while people on the street bare all in their pursuit.

This hedonistic behavior continues until the stroke of midnight (literally), when brigades of refuse workers, tow trucks, and cops literally begin to dispose of the garbage—both material and human. It's an astonishing sight: In a city that is normally an icon of laid-back inefficiency, these workers sweep in like a horde of fire ants, and by the time you wake up on Ash Wednesday (if you wake up on Ash Wednesday), New Orleans is more or less clean.

With the basics under your belt, it is now time to purchase *Arthur Hardy's Mardi Gras Guide* at the nearest Walgreens, Rite-Aid, or Eckerd's. This Carnival bible delivers all the particulars of every parade in Jefferson and Orleans parishes: routes, dates, times, number of floats, etc. It also gives you fun little historical tidbits and profiles of each krewe.

It's a Festivus Miracle

After Mardi Gras come the small, yet very rowdy, St. Patrick's and St. Joseph's parades, which are really just there to keep the citizenry in shape for the next big throw down: the **New Orleans Jazz and Heritage Festival.**

In case you've been living on the South Pole since 1969 when it was first staged, Jazz Fest is a 10-day, 12-stage music extravaganza held at the New Orleans Fair Grounds on the last weekend of April and the first weekend in May every year.

As it enters it 35th year, Jazz Fest becomes more and more of a misnomer. Oh there's jazz, all right: traditional, Dixieland, straight ahead, BeBop, freestyle, you name it. But in any given year, there's also Cajun and zydeco, African, South American, Caribbean, funk, blues, soul, gospel, rock 'n' roll, and yes, even pop. A profusion of local artists like the Neville Brothers, Irma Thomas, various members of the Marsalis family, Kid Jordan, Los Hombres Calientes, Kermit Ruffins, and Terrence Blanchard keep the Fest true to its local roots. But international musicians from countries like Mali, Haiti, and Brazil, along with famous names like Sting, Paul Simon, Van Morrison, Bob Dylan, Dave Matthews, Bonnie Raitt, and Emmylou Harris give it an appeal that boosted total attendance to more than half a million in 2003.

Of course, there will never be this many folks here on a single day—but it might feel like it. The Fest gets *crowded.* And the city's blast-furnace-on-high-in-a-swamp-shack heat inevitably gets switched on sometime during the 10-day event. Picture this: an un-air-conditioned New York subway car in summer with really good music. If that's not your thing, do not go to the Jazz Fest.

There's another facet to the Fest that often gets eclipsed by the music, and that's the food. There are people—many of them—who go to Jazz Fest for the food first, then the music. In fact, much of the best food can only be had at the Fest, making its fans all the more passionate.

Souvenir hunters will not be disappointed either. Each year the original Fest posters and shirts become hot commodities. And there are several craft areas where artists and craftspeople from all over the country come to sell their wares.

Last but not least, there are lectures and interviews featuring many incredible musicians. Lectures? Well, when you find out that many of them are conducted in the air-conditioned splendor of the grandstand, you may look at them with newfound interest. Attending them is an excellent way to take a break from the heat. And more often than not, you'll get roped into listening to these fascinating artists telling the war stories of their musical pasts.

Best of all, this is just the daytime schedule. During the fest, there are also night concerts at halls, clubs, and auditoriums around the city, and myriad parties and special events open to the public.

For all the nitty-gritty info you could need, call 504/522–4786; write to the New Orleans Jazz and Heritage Festival, 1205 N. Rampart St., 70116; or check out the website at www.nojazzfest.com. Jazz Fest admission is a one-time charge at the gate; once you're inside the Fair Grounds, you don't pay for music. You can avoid the long lines at the gate by purchasing tickets through **Ticketmaster** (tel 504/522-5555). ***But note:*** There are no reserved seats at the Fest, and Ticketmaster charges all kinds of fees. If you don't mind a wait (though *long,* the lines tend to move very fast), pay nothing but the ticket price at the Fair Grounds front entrance.

It goes without saying that Jazz Fest is an unbelievably popular event. Reserving a hotel room a full year in advance is not unheard of. You should reserve as soon as you decide you'd like to be in New Orleans during the Jazz Fest, because rooms are very tight.

The Lowdown

Must-sees for Big Easy virgins... There's only one thing in town that a traveler really can't go home without seeing: the **French Quarter.** One of the nation's favorite partying places, the Quarter is an ongoing show, with a cast of characters right out of a Fellini flick. Pay no mind to the spooky-looking woman with the iron-gray hair, silver-colored crash helmet, and long black clothes—she's but one of the French Quarter fixtures, along with flamboyant transvestites, white-robed priests, gritty skinheads, tattooed bikers in battered jeans, grungy street musicians, and park rangers in their Smoky the Bear hats. Oceans of tourists pour through every day, mixing in with some 5,000 or so Quarterites, who have grown inured to living in this unsanitized, adult equivalent of Disneyland. This movielike setting was, for the most part, designed by the Spanish, not the French—almost all of the original French colony La Nouvelle Orleans burned in the 18th century and was rebuilt by the ruling power at the time, which just happened to be the Spaniards. Narrow, straight-as-an-arrow streets run in front of small, colorful structures that hunker right down flush with the sidewalks, many done up with an overkill of fancy ironwork, galleries, dormers, courtyards, and gingerbread trim. These 19th-century town houses, carriage houses, slave quarters, and stables now house apartments and hotels, restaurants, guest houses, creaky old bookstores, shabby jazz joints, museums, markets, and newsstands.

Perhaps the Quarter's most notorious street is Bourbon Street. It has all the flavor of a carnival midway, including tourists gawking along down the middle of the closed-to-cars-street with a go-cup of booze, craning their necks to peer indoors at a male strip show or a ladies' mud-wrestling competition. Carny-types bark outside many of the joints, extolling the X-rated marvels inside. Doors of music clubs are flung wide to let the sounds out and lure the customers in. Bourbon is actually relatively harmless, as long as you stay aware of where your wallet is, don't volunteer for the mud wrestling, and take care not to trip over all the discarded go-cups. (A tourist once wrote to the *Times-Picayune* suggesting that a ban on go-cups would go far toward cleaning up all that litter on Bourbon. The letter drew shrieks of laughter from Orleanians: Yeah, sure—why not just board up all the bars while you're at it? Close the street altogether. Locals don't walk or drive two blocks without a go-cup of something, even if it's just iced tea.)

And speaking of walking or driving, the former is truly the best way to get around the French Quarter. The narrow streets are pretty hostile to car traffic—unless you enjoy breathing in diesel delivery truck fumes while traveling at 2 mph—the street parking is nonexistent, and the lot parking is strictly for people with the net worth of Bill Gates.

If you're really feeling shameless, mosey up to the river side of Jackson Square, and negotiate a price on one of those corny mule-drawn surrey tours of the Quarter. Thanks to them, Quarter streets smell more like mule-doo than magnolias, but the sharp clip-clop of their hooves echoing off the walls of the quiet, narrow streets does make your heart flip-flop.

Just don't expect textbook history from the drivers. Their raps have been polished to an inaccurate sheen over the years, designed more to entertain than to inform. Oh, and if you do notice mistakes, best not say a word. Several years ago, locals were horrified but not surprised to read about a pedestrian/history buff who called a passing carriage driver on his errors and got beat up on the spot for his academic presumptuousness. (The article was memorably headlined "History Lesson: Don't Bug Buggy Driver.")

Take me to the river... While strolling in the Quarter, you'll suddenly hear a wheezy, off-key calliope belting out the tune to "If You Knew Susie...," and you'll know it's the **Steamboat *Natchez***, warbling away at the Toulouse Street Wharf. The calliope is deliberately tuned wrong, to attract attention and to sound charmingly small-time. The boat itself is a totally slick commercial operation, but somehow that old-timey riverboat song gets you every time.

If, like some, you find the calliope annoying rather than alluring, there are several other river vessels—sans calliopes—from which you might choose. The best way to gander all your options is to walk along the **Woldenberg Riverfront Park** and the **Moonwalk**, where the boats dock between trips.

The riverboat ***Cajun Queen*** and the paddle wheeler ***Creole Queen*** are both owned by local tourism behemoth

Hospitality Enterprises and offer some sweet 19th-century-style riverboat action. If you want the quickie Mighty Miss tour, hop on the *Cajun Queen,* a replica riverboat with cypress bars and faux Victorian frippery. You get a 1-hour tour, enough to give you a good sense of the traffic, the power, and the size of the river.

If you want more of an outing, then make a date with the *Creole Queen,* a more deluxe version of her plainer Jane sister. With her churning red 24-foot-in-diameter paddle wheel on full bore, you'll spend 3 hours chugging around the river and stopping at the Chalmette Battlefield, where in 1814 good ole Andy Jackson "beat the bloody British." The *Creole Queen* also takes an evening voyage replete with dinner and jazz. There are countless restaurants in the city proffering far better fare, and many clubs playing more exciting live music. But if you want both and want them on the river, the *Creole Queen* is your gal.

If you're not in for all that olde decor and history and you've got kids in tow, then your ride would be the ***John James Audubon*** riverboat. It's a modern craft with an easy-to-digest narrated tour up and down the river between the French Quarter and the **Audubon Zoo.** In fact, cruising on the JJA is one facet of one of the most enjoyable full-day adventures a family can have in this city: If you're staying in the Quarters—as locals call it—walk on over to the **Aquarium of the Americas** and give its fish the once-over. Then head out to the river where you board the JJA for an upriver trip to the zoo. Part of the Audubon Institute, the zoo is very well funded and has excellent animals in attractive habitats. Once you've spent yourself at the zoo, walk through Audubon Park to the St. Charles Streetcar and ride it all the way back to the Quarter. It all adds up to a very long day and parents are guaranteed an excellent night's sleep from their tuckered-out tots.

The poor man's answer to those fancy-schmancy riverboat cruises is the **Canal Street Ferry,** which is free and takes you on a 5-minute trip across the river to Old Algiers, a quaint town on the point across from the Vieux Carré. If you want to make the trip a little more interesting, you can grab a free shuttle to **Blaine Kern's Mardi Gras World** and see how all those glitzy parade floats are made.

At the opposite end of the spectrum are the **Delta Queen Steamboat Company**'s overnight river cruises. When you've finished with the Big Easy—or it's finished with you—you and your crew can board one of three elaborate replica steamboats for points north: Natchez, Memphis, Cincinnati, St. Louis, and St. Paul. Cruises last 3 to 8 days and if you really love the river, touring it at 8 miles an hour is hands-down the best way to take it all in.

Don't know much about history?... For obvious reasons, nowhere else can you tour the **Historic New Orleans Collection,** an incredible private archive housed in the beautifully restored 18th-century Merieult House. This Spanish Colonial house survived the fire of 1794 almost intact, and clichéd as it may sound, touring it truly gives you the feeling of stepping back in time. You'll see just enough to marvel at the persistence (some might say obsessiveness) of the late Kemper and Leila Williams, who basically devoted their lives to gathering precious documents and memorabilia pertinent to New Orleans's past, eventually amassing one of the nation's largest such collections. The Williams Gallery on the ground floor mounts changing exhibits of regional interest, and a gift shop sells some uniquely New Orleans items.

So you don't feel like rooting around old papers and living quarters to get your history dose? Then toddle off to Jackson Square, where the important bits will be laid out for you in convenient glass cases with cute little cards explaining what's what. Of the four buildings that comprise the **Louisiana State Museum** complex—the **Cabildo,** the **Presbytère,** the **1850 House,** and the **Old U.S. Mint**—the most interesting is the Cabildo. Built on Jackson Square in 1795 as a home for the cabildo, or Spanish governing council, it replaced an earlier wooden structure that went up in flames in 1788. Eerily, another fire swept through the building almost exactly 200 years later, in 1988, causing enough damage to require 6 years and several million dollars in restoration. Some people think the end result looks far too new and spiffy for so venerable a building—it may be much safer, and it doesn't creak and groan anymore. It's a historic site—transfer papers for the 1803 Louisiana Purchase were signed here in the second-floor sala capitular, and the Marquis de Lafayette stayed here while on a triumphal tour in 1825. The nearby Presbytère, almost an identical twin of the Cabildo (it was originally built as a residence for the priests who served in the adjacent St. Louis

Cathedral, but never was used as such), is given over entirely to an impressive 17,000-square-foot Mardi Gras Museum.

Set in the Lower Pontalba Apartments, the 1850 House is a restored apartment that demonstrates how mid-19th-century Creole city folk lived. If you're on a historical roll with the other two, you might as well stop by here.

The museum's fourth building is a bit farther off on the fringe of the Quarter. The Old U.S. Mint was built in 1835 as a branch of the federal mint and churned out about $300 million in coins during its career. When Louisiana seceded from the Union in 1861, the Yankees shut it down; it reopened in 1879, following Reconstruction, and went out of the coin-minting business for good in 1909. It now houses three exhibits, the best of which is the one on jazz. If you read all the text that goes with the jazz displays and have good reading comprehension, you'll be armed with just enough working knowledge of the genre to be intriguing at a cocktail party. There's also a small area articulating the Mint's history. And finally, there's a pretty but vaguely incongruous section on Newcomb Pottery.

If you're not the sharpest tack in the box, are accompanied by children, or are a "visual learner," better try the "Louisiana Legends" exhibits at the **Musée Conti Wax Museum.** No kidding. New Orleans's answer to Madame Tussaud's displays more than a hundred colorful tableaux of the city's history. All of the legends are here—Lafitte the pirate, Marie Laveau and her voodoo dancers, Louis Armstrong—and wax effigies of more modern figures, such as clarinetist and native son Pete Fountain.

If you're into "old," the **Old Ursuline Convent** on Chartres Street will satisfy your quest for the wonderfully ancient. This is actually the second convent to occupy this site. A magnificent masonry building, with pitched roof and dormer windows, it was begun on orders of Louis XV in 1745 and completed in 1752. The sisters of Ursula arrived from Rouen in 1727, shortly after la Nouvelle Orleans got on its feet, to try to straighten out the sundry convicts, prostitutes, and miscreants who were emptied out of French jails to settle the colony. The sisters operated the first school for Native Americans and the first school for blacks, and taught the young ladies of the colony how to behave in an appropriately aristocratic manner. It's the oldest building in the lower Mississippi valley, the only structure known for certain to have survived the 18th-century conflagrations that destroyed the colony, and thus the only extant example of pure French Creole architecture. Andrew Jackson came to St. Mary's Chapel, a part of the complex, to personally thank the sisters for their prayers for victory in the Battle of New Orleans.

A streetcar named St. Charles... One of the best ways to get an overview of the Garden District, Uptown, and University sections is to take a round-trip ride aboard the streetcar (New Orleanians never say trolley), the city's moving National Historic Landmark. The St. Charles streetcar line is one of the world's oldest street railway systems; it began as a mule-and-carriage line in 1835, linking New Orleans with the little towns of Lafayette and Carrollton, both incorporated into the city in the 1850s. The old-fashioned green cars, with their wooden seats and plank floors, start their clanking and rumbling in the CBD at Canal and Carondelet streets.

Once you cross Jackson Avenue, you'll be rolling through the **Garden District,** the city's ritziest residential district, bounded by Magazine Street and by St. Charles, Louisiana, and Jackson avenues. Settled by the Americans who came barging downriver following the 1803 Louisiana Purchase, the Garden District was developed from an area of former sugar plantations; while the Creoles in the French Quarter hid their courtyards from the streets, notice how the Americans surrounded their palatial homes with magnificent gardens. The most prevalent architectural style here is Greek Revival, but there are also lovely Queen Anne houses, replete with turrets, verandas, and stained-glass windows.

Cross Louisiana, and you are officially Uptown, home to many marvelous manses as well as 400-acre Audubon Park, notable for its live oak trees and the Audubon Zoo. Across the street from the park is Tulane University, founded by a group of doctors in 1834 as the Medical College of Louisiana, and still noted for its medical school as well as its law school. Tulane is Louisiana's largest private university, with a student body of more than 12,000. Loyola University, adjacent to Tulane, is somewhat smaller, with a student body of around 3,500. Louisiana native Edward Douglas White, chief justice of the U.S. Supreme Court from 1910 until 1921, was a Loyola alum. At the great upriver bend in the Mississippi, where St. Charles Avenue dead-ends, the streetcar hangs a right onto Carrollton Avenue, and eventually pulls to a stop at Palmer Park—the end of the line. There, if you're round-tripping, you pay an additional $1.25 (exact change, please!) and reverse the wooden seat so that you face forward for the trip downtown. A round-trip takes about 90 minutes.

Now there's another option for streetcar lovers to return to the Quarter: the Canal Streetcar. When you get off the St. Charles at Palmer Park, hail a cab and ask the driver to take you up Carrollton to Canal Street. From there you can grab the very new Canal Streetcar which will transport you right back to the foot of the river near the aquarium. Mind you, these are both commuter lines for many Orleanians, and you'd be wise to avoid the crowds during morning and afternoon rush hours, as well as around 3pm, when school lets out.

If you loved the movie *Angel Heart*... There are very few things that are normal about this city, which is probably why there is such a profusion of the *paranormal* or just downright freaky here.

The most iconic, of course, are our **Cities of the Dead,** aka our cemeteries. Nearly everyone has heard the rap: The entire city is between 5 to 8 feet below sea level. In the old days before pumps and drainage pipes, folks interred underground had an unnerving way of popping back to the surface after a big rain. So some genius, probably someone who owned a granite pit, came up with the idea of making aboveground tombs to house the dearly departed, thus assuring they would more or less stay put.

The oldest of the city's cemeteries are the St. Louises, established in 1789 beyond the ramparts of Rampart Street. Among the city's early notables interred here, the most famous may be 19th-century voodoo queen Marie Laveau. Look for a whitewashed tomb in **St. Louis No. 1,** engraved "Glapion" (Laveau's married name) and usually decked with flowers, voodoo charms, and crosses scratched with redbrick dust. In the Garden District's **Lafayette Cemetery,** laid out in the early 1800s as the burial ground for Lafayette, at least one wedding has taken place, and scenes from the movie *Interview with the Vampire* were shot. The most famous tomb here is the mass tomb of the Jefferson Fire Company

No. 22, erected in 1852 and featuring a huge bas-relief of a fire engine. **Lakelawn Metairie Cemetery,** the city's largest, was once a racetrack, which accounts for its oval shape. Believe it or not, it's a drive-through and you can pop by the main office for cassette tapes that narrate your tour. Bring your camera along for close-ups of the elaborate statuary. Now it's time to bust a myth about safety in cemeteries: For years guidebooks and tourist mags have been including stark warnings never to set foot into any of the cemeteries unless you are part of a tour group. They say mugging—and imply much worse—is all that awaits you if you do. Yet a call to the First District police station yields no recent reports of mayhem in the cemeteries in their jurisdiction—the St. Louises. Here's the real story: New Orleans is a big city with an unenviable crime rate. In such a place, traveling in a group is always going to mean better security, but it's not always a practical or a preferable option. So, no matter where you go, exercise caution, use your street smarts, and watch your back. And most likely, you won't be joining any of the cemetery's occupants anytime soon.

If you want to go with a group, then by all means do. **Save Our Cemeteries,** a worthy non-profit organization dedicated to preserving the graves and tombs of the city, has guides who can tell you fascinating—and historically accurate—stories. Orleanians themselves visit the cemeteries on All Saints Day, November 1, which is a legal holiday here, and practically a minifestival—folks drive to the graveyards to clean the tombs of their loved ones and lay fresh flowers on them. Families often bring picnics and spend the entire day.

Another spooky facet to New Orleans—as Mickey Rourke will tell you—is voodoo. People who want to get the real lowdown can at least start at the **New Orleans Historic Voodoo Museum.** There you'll get the history of this ever-evolving animistic religion imported with slaves from Africa, via the West Indies, in the 19th century. A real voodoo practitioner resides upstairs and is available for consultations, rituals, "or whatever is necessary," says the woman who answers the phone there.

Hokey-er, **Magic Walking Tours** does two nightly "Ghost Haunt Vampire" tours that are worth a spin. They meet at Lafitte's Blacksmith Shop in the Quarter and stop off at buildings said to be haunted by various ghosts and phantasms. They also do a daytime Garden District tour that takes you to Lafayette cemetery and passes by gothy vampire novelist Anne Rice's home, at 1239 First St. (At the beginning of 2004, Rice put her New Orleans properties on the market and decamped to the "country." No word on where exactly that might be.)

Incidentally, Rice used to have her own tour company that took you to all the spots where her books were set. But her fan base, while disturbingly passionate and loyal, proved too small to keep the tours financially viable.

A River Road ramble... Drive west of New Orleans on Highways 44 or 18, and after anywhere from half an hour to 45 minutes, you'll be in the midst of River Road plantation heaven, where many 19th-century homes have been restored, filled with lovely antiques, and opened for touring. There are about a dozen excellent homes between New Orleans and Baton Rouge, any of which will satisfy your need for Scarlett stuff. Docents with varying degrees of grace and knowledge (depending on the plantation), walk you through nearly all of these houses, cueing you to ooh and aah over the garconnières, pigeonnières, petticoat mirrors, armoires, and testers carved by the top cabinetmaker of the day, Prudent Mallard, and sideboards nearly sagging from the weight of all that silver.

About 60 miles up River Road, **Houmas House** is indeed a gem—a well-preserved Greek Revival mansion famous in these parts for its spiral staircase, and for having been the setting for the gothic movie thriller *Hush...Hush, Sweet Charlotte.* The main problem here is that so many tourists pass through it, the hoop-skirted young docents look glassy-eyed and bored as they recite their canned spiel. (Interrupt them to ask an unscripted question and you'll get a blank stare in reply.) Still, the house is worth the trip, the grounds are gorgeous, and the river looks splendid from atop the levee.

On the opposite side of the grandiose antebellum spectrum is **Laura Plantation**—a complex of 14 Creole structures built in 1805. Owned by French, not English, the house looks Caribbean and blends much better with the Frenchified spirit of la Nouvelle Orleans than any of those big old English-owned plantations do.

Madame Laura is fascinating to visit as a restoration-in-progress, which within the decade may be opened as a bed-and-breakfast. The restoration work is based on 100 pages from the diary of Laura Locoul, great-granddaughter of the commandant who built the house in 1805. Laura was born on the sugar plantation in 1861, inherited the whole shebang when she was 19, and was still alive when JFK was elected president. Life-sized cutouts of family members stand throughout the house and tour guides take on the characters of the people who inhabited the house, telling family secrets and talking about the displays—everything from false teeth to dancing slippers. Historical documents show that Senegalese slaves here first told the folk tales that were later adapted by Joel Chandler Harris as the Br'er Rabbit stories.

If you just can't bear not to overnight in one of these spots, then head up River Road, turn left at Bayou Lafourche, and pull into **Madewood Plantation.** Currently operated as a B&B, it's also open for touring, and it's beautifully restored. The 21-room Greek Revival mansion was designed by Irish architect Henry Howard and "made of wood" (hence the name) in 1846 for Colonel Thomas Pugh. Before you leave, wander out to take a look at the old gravestones in the Pugh family cemetery.

To market, to market... For local color, try the French Quarter's **Old Farmers' Market,** where farmers have been bringing their products for almost 200 years. Less overrun with tourists than the shops and eateries of French Market (also on N. Peters St., but a couple of blocks closer to Jackson Sq.), this produce market is open around the clock. Early in the morning, the chefs compete with one another for the freshest veggies and fruit. From dawn until dusk, more or less, the **Flea Market** also sprawls around the rear of the sheds near Barracks Street. Locals love browsing through the array of old records, paperbacks, jewelry, knickknacks, doodads, and gadgets. (If you hate crowds, this is not the place to be.)

Less than a decade ago, the **Crescent City Farmer's Market** threw up some stalls in a lot on the corner of Magazine and Girod streets, and Voilà! an institution was born. Every Saturday, locals descend on the market to snatch up beautiful artisan cheeses, amazing seasonal produce, kaleidoscope-colored flowers, buckets of fresh seafood, and other locally made, grown, or caught goodies. There's a guest chef cookin' up something yummy every week, and there are occasional special celebrations for holidays like Bastille Day. If you're up early and want to do something culinary and truly native, head over here. (The market has grown so in popularity over the decade that it travels to two other locations during the week. But this is the one that's probably most convenient for visitors.)

When you think of New Orleans, great Vietnamese food is probably not the first thing that crosses your mind. Well, think again. During the mid-'70s, the Catholic church here helped to resettle thousands of Vietnamese refugees—mainly in East New Orleans and on the West Bank. Apart from dining at their excellent restaurants, culinary adventurers can also take a trip to one of the most unexpected sights in Greater New Orleans, **Little Vietnam** and the **Vietnamese Farmer's Market.** Head down Chef Menteur Highway and you'll know you're there when all the shop signs suddenly turn Vietnamese. The market itself starts eye-bulgingly early—5am—and is housed in the ramshackle courtyard of The Versailles Arms. Talk about being transported to another place! Vendors in conical straw hats hawk live ducks, rabbits, chickens, and seafood, along with bushels of basil and chili, piles of okra, and other unidentifiable-to-the-Western-eye foods and plants. If you're in the mood to see something completely out of time and place, this is it.

Kiddie city... As if the French Quarter were not "theme" enough, there is now a full-fledged theme park, replete with hair-raising roller coasters and other death-defying rides—which, of course, make the kiddies shriek and scream. At **Six Flags New Orleans,** which takes up 140 acres of east New Orleans, there's lots of jazz in the air, and plenty of food to consume. Theme-y but far more authentic is **City Park's Carousel Gardens,** where you can set the kids astride one of the wonderful "flying horses." They won't care that the carousel on which they giggle is on the National Register of Historic Places—but it is. The carved-wood carousel was built in 1906, and its giraffes and horses and other critters have all been beautifully restored. Near the carousel, **Storyland** is a children's playground with Mother Goose characters made for scrambling over and into, and a castle for storytelling and puppet shows. There's even more for them to do at the **Louisiana Children's Museum,** in the heart of the Warehouse District. The kid-sized port has a tugboat to be captained and a cargo net to be loaded with sacks of coffee, and there's also a "Body Works," where "Mr. Bones" helps little ones bone up on health and fitness. The **Audubon Louisiana Nature Center,** spread over 86 acres of bottomland hardwood forest in eastern New Orleans, is another place where kids can learn by doing, with nature trails, a children's Discovery Loft with hands-on exhibits, and a planetarium that has weekend laser shows. Riverside of **Audubon Park,** the 58-acre **Audubon Zoo** is home to 1,800 varmints who roam in habitats such as the Louisiana Swamp, the Asian Domain, and the African Savannah. The local story goes that Monkey Hill, in the back of the zoo, was built in the 1930s so schoolchildren in these flatlands could understand what was meant by the word "hill." Downtown, the zoo's sister attraction, the **Aquarium of the Americas,** takes the natural history lesson underwater. It's replete with fish as well as otters, penguins, frogs, a white alligator, and other squishy, scaley swimmers. There's even a shark tank, where a bunch of Aquarium donors took an unscheduled swim after a gangplank collapsed a few years ago at a fundraiser. (Miraculously, no one was hurt and they all got free T-shirts for their trouble.)

When it's too darn hot... When it's so hot and swampy that the air clings to you like a wet wool bodysuit, you really have two choices: put on a tank top (ew!), slather yourself in Right Guard, and just sweat through it; or ditch outdoor stuff for indoor stuff. If you choose option two, you will still find yourself endlessly entertained and much cooler as you drift from one air-conditioned oasis to another. Start at the **National D-Day Museum,** where you can while away an entire day—or two. It opened on June 6, 2000, with much hoopla, including the "largest military parade in America in 40 years" and appearances by former Defense Secretary William Cohen, Steven Spielberg, Tom Hanks (*Saving Private Ryan,* y'know), and Tom Brokaw. The 16,000 square feet of exhibit space is divided into four sections, all loaded with tape-recorded first-person accounts, artifacts, maps, documents, and photographs. The exhibits deal comprehensively with both the European and the Pacific theaters. The cumulative effect is a detailed and devastatingly real picture of what World War II was like for those who lived through it and died in it. It's not uncommon for people to leave the last exhibit area in tears. And while it might stir memories for old-timers, it's also bound to make a lasting impact on younger people who missed the era entirely, which is really one of the best compliments you can give a history museum.

Just round the corner is the newish **Ogden Museum of Southern Art,** a 67,000-square-foot facility designed to house a more than 2,000-piece collection donated to the University of New Orleans by philanthropist Roger Ogden. Recent shows have included artists such as Enrique Alferez, Ida Kohlmeyer, and Jasper Johns, along with exhibits of self-taught artists and blues photographs.

Also nearby is the **Confederate Museum,** hunkered in a forbidding-looking Romanesque Revival building near Lee Circle. During the War Between the States, New Orleans fell to Union troops in 1862 and was occupied longer than any other Southern city. The occupying commander, Gen. Benjamin "Beast" Butler, was so locally hated that ladies lined their chamberpots with pictures of him. There's surprisingly little evidence in the Big Easy of that grim time, but if you are hooked on Civil War history, this is your place. Dedicated in 1891, it's a dank and musty building, full of glass cases containing bloody old battle flags, letters and documents, oil paintings, and weapons. Jefferson Davis's widow donated many of her husband's personal effects to the museum, and parts of Robert E. Lee's silver campaign service are displayed.

Civil War buffs can also pop into the **Old U.S. Customs House** where some 2,000 Confederate prisoners of war were held. It's a huge, Egyptianesque, gray granite building begun before the war, in 1845, but not completed until 1881, well after the war ended. It's still a working customs house today; there's no sign of its wartime role left. But walk inside anyway to see the Great Marble Hall, a splendid Greek Revival room that stretches 95 feet by 125 feet and soars 54 feet high. ***Note:*** As we go to print, the Customs House is closed, and it is not known when it will reopen.

A quick zip over to City Park brings you to the **New Orleans Museum of Art (NOMA),** set in a pretty, white neoclassical building built in 1911. Hot or not, the permanent collection is truly impressive, covering 17th-century to 19th-century European art. Traveling shows here tend to be of high quality too, but the museum's own Fabergé eggs are reason enough for a visit.

Alas, the offbeat **New Orleans Pharmacy Museum** doesn't come with free samples, but it is fascinating. Actually, you'll probably thank that great pharmacist in the sky that you didn't live in the 19th century, when you see the lineup of terrifying medical implements on display. America's first licensed pharmacist, Louis J. Dufilho, had this house built in 1823 as his apothecary shop and home. He lived upstairs, grew things of a medicinal nature in the rear courtyard, and worked in the ground-floor shop.

Swamp thing... Typically, points of embarkation for swamp tours are an hour or two outside of town by car or minivan, and a tool out on the swamp waters lasts about 90 minutes. You're looking at around 4 to 6 hours total, so choose wisely who you bring and when you go. That being said, Louisiana swamplands are eerily beautiful, and tours through them are enormously popular. Independent-minded travelers enjoy going to the Barataria Unit of the **Jean Lafitte National Historical Park** and renting a canoe at **Bayou Barn** to paddle through the wetlands (guided or unguided). You'll need a car, and it entails an hour's drive down to the West Bank. If you'd rather not go it alone, hook up with **Honey Island Swamp Tours** and let wetland ecologist Dr. Paul Wagner point out the blue herons and tell you about the massive alligator he's named El Whoppo. He's a friendly sort and narrates a fascinating—and completely *un*-hokey—trip. For a fee, they'll pick you up at your hotel in a minivan, feed you some red beans and rice, turtle soup, or another local specialty after the tour, and then take you back. Or you can save the dough and drive yourself.

The other big tour companies in town—who shall remain nameless—also do swamp tours. If you like watching the guides feed marshmallows to the alligators (which is ecologically unsound as well as illegal) and having fake snakes thrown at you for a cheap thrill...well, then you deserve these tours.

Home sweet historic home... Of the house museums in the Quarter, the **Gallier House** is the one you should make the effort to see. The private home of architect James Gallier, Jr., who designed and built it in 1857, is a stately place, with wrought-iron galleries outside and Corinthian columns inside. The house is decorated in 19th-century Creole style, meaning very grand: velvet and brocaded antique furnishings, an etched-glass skylight over the stairs, and handsome gas chandeliers hanging from 12-foot ceilings. Docents walk and talk you through it, which is good, because you wouldn't want to miss a single, gorgeous detail.

Just a block away, look for the Greek Revival portico of the **Beauregard-Keyes House,** built in 1826. Though it's pretty and has lovely English gardens, this house is most worthwhile for its relics of two famous former occupants. After the Civil War, Confederate Gen. Pierre Gustav Toutant Beauregard—a native Orleanian (called "the Great Creole" in these parts) and the commander who ordered the first shot fired at Fort Sumter—lived for a short time in the house. It was restored in the 1940s by Frances Parkinson Keyes, the novelist who wrote *Dinner at Antoine's, Steamboat Gothic,* and other tales of the region. (Her books are sold in the gift shop.) She formed a foundation that bought the house and still runs it today. Doll-lovers should not miss Keyes's outstanding doll collection.

And while you're at it, continue on to another house/museum in the neighborhood, the **Hermann-Grima House,** a Federal mansion built in 1831 for a rich Philadelphia merchant named Samuel Hermann. In 1844, it was purchased by Judge Felix Grima. The most memorable thing about this house is the way its curators dress it up for different seasons, changing the upholstery covers and adding various holiday touches—all the historic houses do Creole Christmas decorations, and the Gallier House dresses for summer, but only Hermann-Grima sets up a funeral tableau for Halloween. Pay special note to the formal dining room, laid out with fine crystal, china, and silver. In the rear outbuildings, off the landscaped parterre gardens, Creole cooking demonstrations take place from October through May.

Well worth the cab fare from the Quarter, **Longue Vue House & Gardens** is a bit of an oddity in New

Orleans, designed after a grand English manor rather than a plantation house. This mansion once was home to New Orleans's philanthropist Edgar Stern and his wife, Sears heiress Edith Rosenwald Stern; it's not so much an architectural landmark as a museum of decorative arts. Of all New Orleans's house museums, this one has the best grounds, with 8 acres of manicured theme gardens and a stunning formal Spanish court inspired by the Generalife Gardens of Alhambra, Spain.

If you liked the Louisiana furnishings displayed at the New Orleans Museum of Art, you may want to swing on over to the **Pitot House** nearby, a marvelous old relic that dates from about 1799. Now headquarters of the Louisiana Landmarks Society, which moved the house to its present site in 1962, the creaky place is filled with some knockout Federal antiques. New Orleans mayor James Pitot bought it in 1810, as a quiet retreat for himself and his family.

Gettin' religion... When the Americans came barging down the river in the early 1800s, it seemed to them that in **St. Louis Cathedral,** "God spoke only in French." Sitting placidly between the Cabildo and the Presbytère, St. Louis Cathedral, named for the French saint-king Louis IX, is the third church to occupy this site. The first was a small wooden church, built in 1724 and blown away by a hurricane. The second burned in the fire of Good Friday, 1788, when for fear of disturbing the peace, priests would not allow the church bells to be rung in warning. The present church was dedicated in Christmas Eve services in 1794. Small as it is, it's America's oldest active cathedral, designated a minor basilica by Pope Paul VI in 1964. Pope John Paul II visited in 1987, when the plaza in front was named Place Jean Paul Deux. Inside, it's airy and light, with pastel-colored ceiling frescoes and a large mural over the high altar depicting the saint-king Louis IX announcing the seventh crusade. Notorious 19th-century voodoo queen Marie Laveau was said to have worshipped here, maybe even have married here, and after Napoleon's death, his Orleanian fans staged a huge mock funeral for him here.

Snubbed by the Creoles, the Americans built their own house of worship in their own sector, the area that's now the CBD. On Lafayette Square, which was the Americans' answer to the Place d'Armes, arose **St. Patrick's**

Church, a vastly different house of worship from the French Quarter cathedral. This stark, narrow, gray Gothic church was designed in 1833 by Irishmen James and Charles Dakin, who patterned it after the York Minster cathedral in England. Most of the interior was the work of James Gallier, Sr., another Irishman (christened "Gallagher" in Dublin, he changed his name to Gallier so as to blend in with the Creoles). Much more ornate inside than St. Louis Cathedral, it's also darker and more brooding, whatever that tells you about the difference between the French and American styles of worship. Check out the handsome stained-glass windows and the dramatic murals over the altar, painted in 1841 by Leon Pomerade for a fee of $1,000. While you're here on Lafayette Square, you might as well look over at **Gallier Hall,** a Greek Revival masterpiece (not open to the public for touring) across the square, also designed by James Gallier, Sr. Ionic columns support a pediment with sculptured figures of Justice, Liberty, and Commerce. Built around 1850, this served as City Hall when the three rival municipalities were united in 1852, dealing a bitter blow to the Creoles, who'd expected the city's administration to be run from their former headquarters, the Cabildo on Jackson Square. In the 1950s, City Hall moved to its present location on Loyola Avenue.

Just don't call it gambling... Considering we have four casinos in the New Orleans metro area, it may surprise out-of-towners to hear that gambling is actually illegal in the Big Easy. Luckily for us, *gaming* is not. No, that is not a joke. It's precisely the kind of monkeyshines that give Louisiana politicians such a bad name. Acerbic *Times-Picayune* columnist James Gill explained it best in a 1996 piece: "Unfazed by either constitutional or statutory obstacles, legislators simply decided to make a distinction, unknown to any lexicographer, between 'gambling' and 'gaming.' They declared that 'gaming activities' on a riverboat did not constitute gambling. Thus, they assumed the right to foist any form of gambling they wished on a populace whose judgment was not to be trusted." Yet, despite the brouhaha, gaming has proven to be neither the boon, nor the boondoggle, that was predicted. New Orleans has not become another Atlantic City as the preservationists feared and the casino magnates hoped. It's still the Big

Easy, maybe just a bit bigger (with visiting gamblers) and a bit easier (to fritter away your money, that is). After going bankrupt before they even finished construction on their permanent site, **Harrah's Casino** re-opened in October 1999 in a garishly monstrous building on Canal Street, a die's throw from the Mississippi River. The 100,000-square-foot gambling den is divided into "courts," each of them reflecting a New Orleans theme. Of course, you can see the themes of New Orleans simply by strolling around town. But you don't find 2,900 slot machines and 120 table games in Jackson Square, and that's why the politicians gave us Harrah's, and the three riverboat casinos that preceded it. **Treasure Chest Casino,** on Lake Pontchartrain in Kenner; the **Boomtown Casino,** docked on the Harvey Canal on the West Bank; and **Bally's New Orleans,** also on Lake Pontchartrain in East New Orleans, all have more or less the same complement of slots, gaming tables, entertainment, and eateries.

SoHo in NoLa... In recent years, the city's contemporary art scene has flourished in what is now called the **Warehouse/Arts District.** Some in the local boho crowd like to refer to it as the "SoHo of the South." Manhattanites would undoubtedly scoff at the presumption. In any case, old abandoned warehouses have been, and continue to be, renovated to hold restaurants, nightclubs, museums, and galleries. The most conspicuous of the galleries is the **Contemporary Arts Center.** The big, airy center has 10,000 square feet of space, with several galleries, changing exhibits, and two theaters showcasing the experimental and the avant-garde (see p. 138). Each year, the first Saturday in October is devoted to Art for Art's Sake—a series of gallery openings and parties that draws hundreds, if not thousands, of exuberant artists, art lovers, and dilettantes. The big bash that closes the event is held at the CAC, with revelers pouring out into the streets. Julia Street is the District's main drag, with the largest concentration of galleries, though there are more than a few offshoots on the cross streets. The city's oldest contemporary art gallery, **Galerie Simonne Stern,** one of the first to move from the French Quarter to the Warehouse District, displays the paintings and sculptures of a tri-coastal roster of artists (as in the East Coast, the West Coast, and the Gulf Coast). Abstract paintings and contemporary drawings and sculptures—including the often offensive but locally admired work of George Dureau—are shown at the **Arthur Rogers Gallery.** Small decorative crafts in contemporary designs can be seen at **Ariodante. LeMieux Galleries** shows off its avant-garde credentials with multimedia installations. Paintings, sculpture, prints, and drawings by local and national artists are shown at **Marguerite Oestreicher Fine Arts.** Hand-blown vases and decorative pieces are created and shown at the **New Orleans Glassworks and Printmaking Studio,** a marvelous place with a glassblowing workshop in the rear, and front-room gallery displays of glass sculptures. Call to ask about the daily demonstrations, done in front of the two 800-pound furnaces.

If you'd rather be a follower... Are you curious about vampire chronicler Anne Rice? Want to get the dish on Tennessee Williams? Or hear gruesome tales of below-ground burials in these swamplands? Hook up with a guided tour and you'll learn some of the secrets tucked away in those courtyards and carriage houses. Dr. Kenneth Holditch, a research professor at the University of New Orleans, conducts walking tours of the French Quarter, and if you think "research" and "professor" sound dull, think again—his **Heritage Tours** zero in on the city's rich literary heritage, with quirky and colorful anecdotes about Tennessee Williams, William Faulkner, Sherwood Anderson, Lillian Hellman, and other literati who lived, worked, and hung out in the Quarter. The **Preservation Resource Center,** whose staff is deeply involved in preserving the city's architectural treasures, organizes occasional tours. If you're in town during one of their "Stained Glass in Sacred Places" tours, go along to ooh and aah over the city's church windows. **Hidden Treasures Tours** emphasize influential New Orleans women, during van tours of the Garden District, and **Le'Ob's Tours** focus on African American contributions to the city. If you're carless and hankering to see plantation country to the west of the city with a guide, hook up with **Tours by Isabelle,** which conducts half-day minivan trips to that area, with a lunch stop at Madewood Plantation. For a one-shot overview, nationwide stalwart **Gray Line** or local biggie **Big Easy Tours** offer standard city bus tours, in addition to orientation, plantation, and swamp tours.

Great walks... Royal Street in the Quarter is row after row of galleries and antiques stores and upscale poke-around places. At night the street is lit by antique street lanterns, and buskers, mellowed out after a hard day's hustling, hunker down in doorways and on street corners to softly strum guitars or coax the last few songs from a saxophone. Tawdry Bourbon Street is a blast at any hour of the day or night, even if you don't go inside any of its tourist-trap bars or burlesque shows. When you take the St. Charles Streetcar up to the zoo, you can catch the free shuttle that runs from the streetcar stop to the zoo, but you can also opt to saunter through the park. Get off the streetcar in front of **Tulane University,** cross St. Charles Avenue, and take the paved path that leads alongside the park golf course, beneath great gnarled live oak trees overdressed in Spanish moss. Riverside of the zoo is what locals call the fly, a wonderful stretch of green with a playground, soccer fields, restrooms, and plenty of flat green grass for picnicking along the river as massive ships with exotic names slip soundlessly by on their way to port.

Map 11: French Quarter Diversions

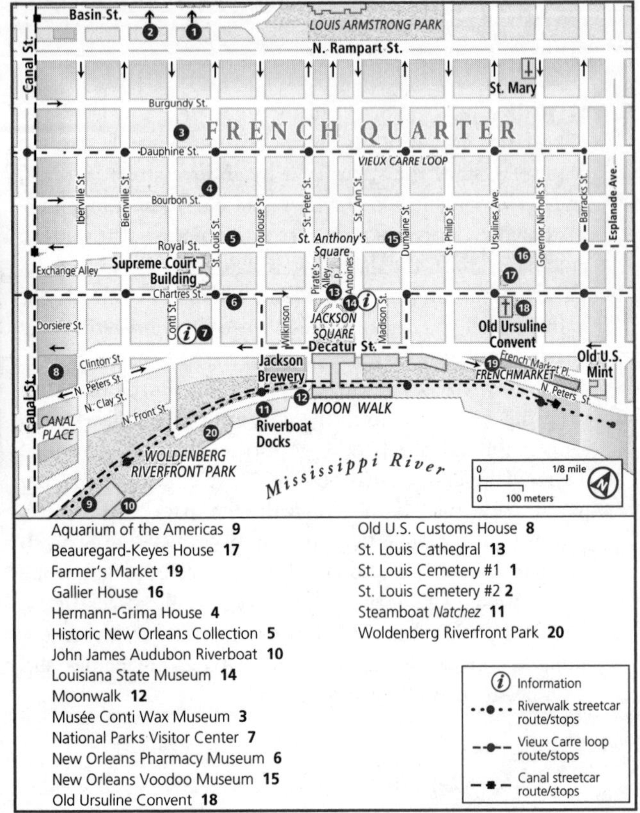

Aquarium of the Americas **9**
Beauregard-Keyes House **17**
Farmer's Market **19**
Gallier House **16**
Hermann-Grima House **4**
Historic New Orleans Collection **5**
John James Audubon Riverboat **10**
Louisiana State Museum **14**
Moonwalk **12**
Musée Conti Wax Museum **3**
National Parks Visitor Center **7**
New Orleans Pharmacy Museum **6**
New Orleans Voodoo Museum **15**
Old Ursuline Convent **18**
Old U.S. Customs House **8**
St. Louis Cathedral **13**
St. Louis Cemetery #1 **1**
St. Louis Cemetery #2 **2**
Steamboat *Natchez* **11**
Woldenberg Riverfront Park **20**

Map 12: Central Business District Diversions

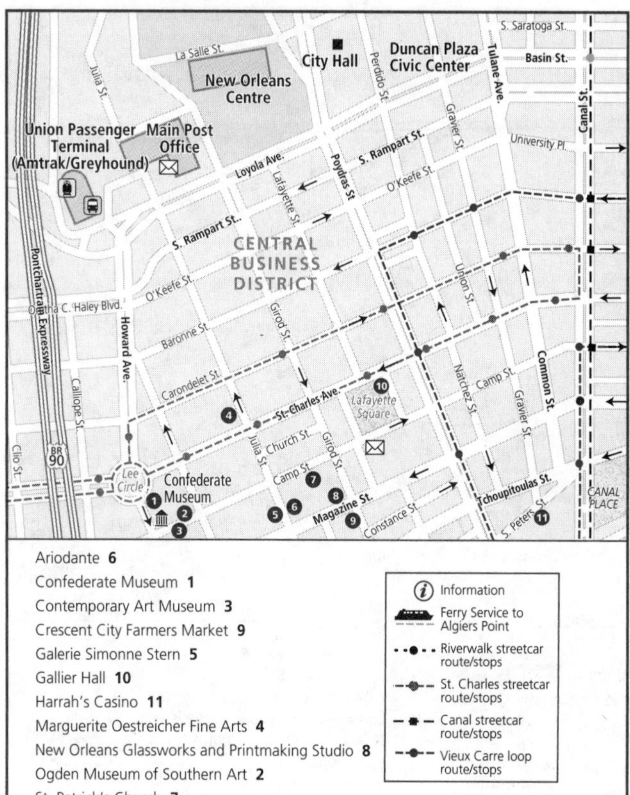

Ariodante **6**
Confederate Museum **1**
Contemporary Art Museum **3**
Crescent City Farmers Market **9**
Galerie Simonne Stern **5**
Gallier Hall **10**
Harrah's Casino **11**
Marguerite Oestreicher Fine Arts **4**
New Orleans Glassworks and Printmaking Studio **8**
Ogden Museum of Southern Art **2**
St. Patrick's Church **7**

Information
Ferry Service to Algiers Point
Riverwalk streetcar route/stops
St. Charles streetcar route/stops
Canal streetcar route/stops
Vieux Carre loop route/stops

Map 13: Mid-City Diversions

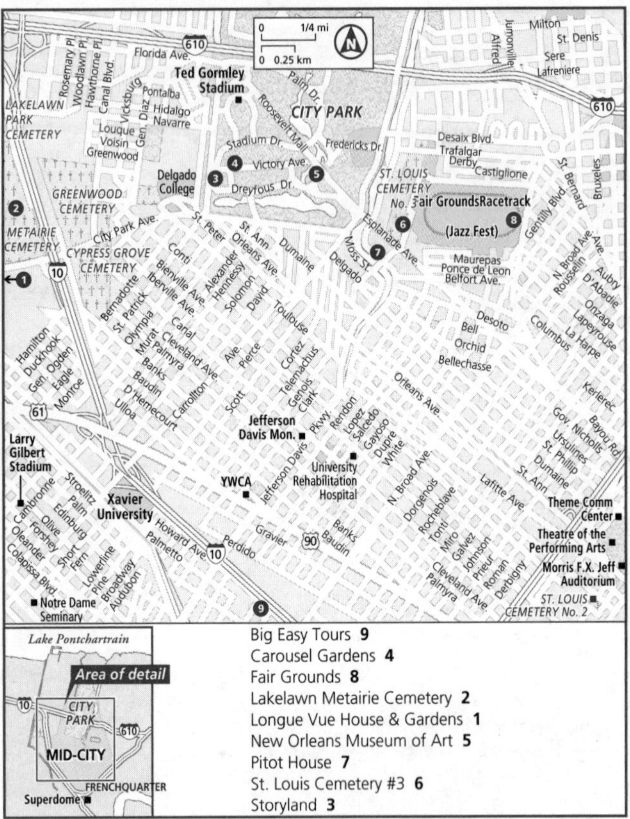

The Index

Aquarium of the Americas (p. 114) FRENCH QUARTER A lot of fishy business goes on in the Gulf of Mexico, Caribbean Reefs, Amazon Rain Forest, and Mississippi River/Gulf Shores exhibits, plus the giant IMAX theater in this watery place beside the Big Muddy.... *Tel 504/861-2537, 800/774-7394. www.audubon institute.org. Canal St. at the river, Woldenberg Riverfront Park. Sun–Thurs 9:30am–6pm, Fri–Sat 9:30am–7pm. Admission $14 adults, $10 seniors 65+, $6.50 children 2–12.*

See Map 11 on p. 132.

Ariodante (p. 130) WAREHOUSE/ARTS DISTRICT This small, chic gallery of contemporary crafts lies in the heart of Gallery Row in the Warehouse/Arts District. Most of the Warehouse District galleries show paintings, but Ariodante shows decorative pieces, such as pottery, small sculptures, lamps, and the like.... *Tel 504/ 524-3233. 535 Julia St. Tues–Sat 11am–6pm. Free admission.*

See Map 12 on p. 133.

Arthur Rogers Gallery (p. 130) WAREHOUSE/ARTS DISTRICT One of the city's most respected gallery owners, Arthur Rogers features contemporary art, and often showcases the work of well-known Orleanian George Dureau—jarring paintings, drawings, and sculptures.... *Tel 504/522-1999. 432 Julia St. Mon–Sat 10am–5pm. Free admission.*

See Map 10 on p. 102.

Audubon Louisiana Nature Center (p. 123) EAST NEW ORLEANS A planetarium, nature trails, and an interpretive center make up this educational flora and fauna haven. At the interpretive center you can learn about the diverse habitats in Louisiana, then later take a walk and experience them for yourself on the grounds.... *Tel 504/246-5672, 800/774-7394. 5601 Read Blvd., Joe W. Brown Memorial Park, E. New Orleans. Tues–Fri 9am–5pm, Sat 10am–5pm, Sun noon–5pm. Admission $5 adults, $4 seniors 65+, $3 children 2–12.*

See Map 10 on p. 102.

Audubon Park (p. 123) UPTOWN This 400-acre park features a jogging and biking path canopied by massive, moss-draped oaks, tennis courts, a golf course, a riding stable, children's playgrounds, a duck-filled lagoon, and the Audubon Zoo. Plus it's right on the streetcar line.... *Tel 504/861-2537, 800/774-7394. www.auduboninstitute.org. 6800 St. Charles Ave.*

Audubon Zoo (p. 114) UPTOWN On the river side of Audubon Park, the sister of the aquarium (see above) is a world-class zoo, where more than 1,800 creatures great and small laze around in simulated natural habitats. There is also a small playground and a glorious new endangered species carousel, where children can ride frogs and white tigers instead of horses. Friends of the Zoo operate a free shuttle from the St. Charles Streetcar stop in front of Tulane University. You can also walk from the streetcar through Audubon Park, or take the Magazine Street bus to the front entrance.... *Tel 504/861-2537, 800/774-7394. www.audubon institute.org. 6500 Magazine St. Daily 9:30am–5pm. Admission $10 adults, $6 seniors 65+, $5 children 2–12.*

Bally's New Orleans (p. 129) LAKE PONTCHARTRAIN This floating casino within Bally's Casino Lakeshore Resort has a whopping 1,200 or so slot machines and tables for blackjack, roulette, minibaccarat, and craps. There's also a bar with live music and a 400-seat showroom with live acts. The riverboat *New Orleans* docks on Lake Pontchartrain.... *Tel 800/57-BALLY. www.ballys. com. 1 Stars and Stripes Blvd. Daily 24 hours.*

See Map 10 on p. 102.

Bayou Barn (p. 125) WEST BANK At this funky little place—part Cajun dance hall (Sun 2–6pm), part souvenir shop, part cafe—you can rent canoes and hire a guide for paddling out on the ghostly beautiful wetlands. Be sure to ask them about the schedule for moonlight tours. Cross the Crescent City Connection and follow the West Bank Expressway (U.S. 90) to Barataria Blvd. (Rte. 45), where you turn left on Rte. 45 and watch for signs for the Barataria Unit, Jean Lafitte National Historical Park. Bayou Barn is across the street from it.... *Tel 504/689-2663, 800/TO-BAYOU. Intersection of Barataria Blvd. and Lafitte Larose Hwy., near Crown Point. Daily 10am–6pm, later when tours or dances are scheduled.*

See Map 10 on p. 102.

Beauregard-Keyes House (p. 126) FRENCH QUARTER Across the street from the Old Ursuline Convent in the lower Quarter, this hyphenated house with a Greek Revival portico was built in 1826 as a private residence. Once home to Confederate Gen. P. G. T. Beauregard, in the 1940s it was restored by novelist Frances Parkinson Keyes, whose study in the rear slave quarters is preserved.... *Tel 504/523-7257. 1113 Chartres St. Mon–Sat 10am–3pm; tours on the hour. Admission $5 adults, $2 children*

6–12, free for children under 6. Seniors and students with ID receive a $1 discount.

See Map 11 on p. 132.

Blaine Kern's Mardi Gras World (p. 114) WEST BANK If you miss the real deal, hop the Canal Street Ferry (see below) to Algiers, where a van waits to spirit you away to year-round Mardi Gras. Housed in a massive warehouse are floats galore made by the self-made King of Mardi Gras. It's a tame way to see the Greatest Free Show on Earth in the off season.... *Tel 504/361-7821. 233 Newton St. Daily 9:30am–4:30pm, with tours every hour on the hour. Admission $14 adults, $10 students and seniors 62+, $6.50 children 11 and under.*

See Map 10 on p. 102.

Boomtown Casino New Orleans (p. 129) WEST BANK This riverboat gambling den markets itself mainly to locals, but all are, of course, welcome. With 1,600 slots, scads of table games, and weekly tournaments, gamblers can keep very busy. And in a bold marketing stroke, they've even made it possible for you to bring the kids too! At the Fun Center kids can play video games and have birthday parties. Remember: The family that plays together, stays together!... *Tel 504/366-7711, 800/366-7711. www.boomtowncasinos.com. 4132 Peters Rd., in Harvey. Daily 24 hours.*

See Map 10 on p. 102.

***Cajun Queen* (p. 113)** FRENCH QUARTER Although she's less glamorous than either the *Creole Queen* or the Steamboat *Natchez,* the *Cajun Queen* nevertheless does her level best to imitate the old-fashioned 19th-century crafts that once plied the waters of the Mississippi. The boat cruises the river for an hour—enough time for a quick riverboat experience.... *Tel 504/529-4567, 800/445-4109. www.neworleanspaddlewheels.com. Departs from the Aquarium dock Fri–Sun at 11:30am, 1pm, 2:30pm, and 4pm. Admission $14 adults, $12 seniors 55+, $8 children 6–12.*

See Map 10 on p. 102.

Canal Street Ferry (p. 114) FRENCH QUARTER The ferry takes foot passengers and cars at the bottom of Canal Street for the run across to Algiers on the West Bank. The round-trip takes about 25 minutes, with about 20 minutes of that time devoted to loading and unloading. The boat leaves the West Bank at a quarter past and a quarter to the hour, and departs the East Bank on the hour and half-hour. It's the poor man's alternative to the fancy and pricey riverboats. Drivers note: When the country is on Orange Alert or higher, the ferry does not take cars.... *Tel 504/376-8114. Canal St. at the river. Operates daily, 5:45am–9:30pm. Free for pedestrians, toll of $1 for vehicles.*

See Map 10 on p. 102.

Carousel Gardens (p. 122) MID-CITY In City Park, adjacent to Storyland, you'll find a restored 1906 carousel, with delightful "Flying Horses," as the carved-wood critters are called by locals. Adults can ride, too.... *Tel 504/483-9356. www.neworleanscitypark.com. Victory Ave., in City Park. Hours vary seasonally. Check the Web or call for times. Admission $2 per person for entry. Rides $1 apiece.*

See Map 13 on p. 134.

City Park (p. 106) MID-CITY You can get lost for days within the park's 1,500 acres. You'll find four golf courses; a 39-court tennis center; children's playgrounds; a minitrain that tours the park; a delightful antique carousel (see above); softball diamonds; lagoons for pedal-boating, fishing, and canoeing; the New Orleans Museum of Art (see below); the Botanical Gardens—all sprawled beneath hundreds of live oaks swimming in Spanish moss.... *Tel 504/482-4888. 1 Palm Dr. Free admission to park. Pay separately for some attractions.*

See Map 13 on p. 134.

Confederate Museum (p. 124) WAREHOUSE/ARTS DISTRICT Opened in 1891, the museum displays scads of weapons, eight generals' uniforms, 150 battle flags, and a large collection of Jefferson Davis paraphernalia—plus thousands of other items pertaining to what some Southerners jokingly call the War of Northern Aggression.... *Tel 504/523-4522. 929 Camp St. Mon–Sat 10am–4pm. Admission $5 adults, $4 students and seniors 65+ with ID, $2 children 7–12, free for children under 7.*

See Map 12 on p. 133.

Contemporary Arts Center (p. 129) WAREHOUSE/ARTS DISTRICT This renovated warehouse holds several galleries and two theaters devoted to new art, be it traditional, avant-garde, or experimental. The modern exhibition space also houses a cybercafe, and is epicenter of the annual October Art for Art's Sake openings and parties and August White Linen Night.... *Tel 504/528-3800. www.cacno.org. 900 Camp St. Galleries open Tues–Sun 11am–5pm. Admission $5 non-members, $3 students and seniors, free for children under 12. Free entry for all on Thurs.*

See Map 12 on p. 133.

***Creole Queen* Paddle Wheeler (p. 113)** FRENCH QUARTER One of a handful of vintage boats at play on the Mississippi, the replica *Creole Queen* has all the requisite fittings of a 19th-century paddle wheeler. During the day, she heads downriver for 2½-hour tours of the Chalmette Battlefield (you can opt to go with or without lunch), and after the sun goes down she takes on food and a Dixieland band for an evening outing.... *Tel 504/529-4567, 800/445-4109. www.neworleanspaddlewheels.com. Departs from the Poydras St. Wharf, Riverwalk. Battlefield cruise operates daily at 10:30 am and 2pm. (But cruises will cancel if there are not* *enough patrons, so always call in advance.) With lunch $25, without lunch $19. Dinner cruise 8–10pm. Reservations required. $51 with dinner, $27 without.*

See Map 10 on p. 102.

Crescent City Farmer's Market (p. 121) WAREHOUSE/ARTS DISTRICT Here you can sample the best locally grown seasonal fruits and veggies along with handmade sausages and cheeses, baked goods, and fresh seafood. Local chefs hold cooking demos and there are often family-oriented activities going on as well. Though the marketplace moves to several locales around the city depending on the day of the week, the most accessible to visitors is the Warehouse District Saturday market.... *Tel 504/861-5898. www.crescentcityfarmersmarket.org. Corner of Magazine St. and Girod St. Sat 8am–noon. Free.*

See Map 12 on p. 133.

Delta Queen Steamboat Company (p. 114) FRENCH QUARTER No 3-hour tour for this outfit. The company's three 19th-century riverboat reproductions float at a lazy 8 miles an hour up and down the Mighty Miss for cruises lasting from 3 to 11 nights. Putting in at places like Natchez and St. Louis, it's the old school way to see the American Heartland.... *Tel 800/543-1949. www.deltaqueen.com. 30 Robin St., Wharf. Cruises $695–$7,135, with significant savings on advance bookings.*

Farmers' Market (p. 121) FRENCH QUARTER Area farmers and fishermen have been bringing their fresh produce and seafood to these open-air sheds for going on 200 years. It's open 24 hours a day, and crowded with locals (including famous New Orleans chefs) and visitors picking through the bins of fresh foodstuffs.... *Tel 504/596-3400. www.frenchmarket.org. Corner of Ursuline and N. Peters sts.*

See Map 11 on p. 132.

Galerie Simonne Stern (p. 129) WAREHOUSE/ARTS DISTRICT The oldest contemporary art gallery in the city, founded in 1965. Monthly changing exhibits of modern and contemporary art.... *Tel 504/529-1118. 518 Julia St. Tues–Sat 10am–5pm. Free admission.*

See Map 12 on p. 133.

Gallier Hall (p. 128) CBD Designed by New Orleans architect James Gallier, Sr., and completed about 1850, this handsome building has been hailed by the American Institute of Architects as the city's most brilliant extant example of Greek Revival architecture. Unfortunately, the facility is only used for private events, so visitors have to content themselves with the views from without.... *Tel 504/565-7457. 545 St. Charles Ave.*

See Map 12 on p. 133.

Gallier House (p. 126) FRENCH QUARTER This was the home of architect James Gallier, Jr., who designed and built it in 1857. The beautifully restored Creole town house features an indoor bathroom and kitchen, both rare for their day.... *Tel 504/525-5661. 1132 Royal St. Guided tours Mon–Fri 10am–3:30pm. Admission $6 adults; $5 seniors 65+, students, and children 8–18; free for children under 8.*

See Map 11 on p. 132.

Gray Line (p. 131) The old familiar bus tour does city orientation tours, plantation tours, Crescent City nights walking tours, and swamp tours, as well as combination land and Mississippi River tours.... *Tel 504/569-1401, 800/535-7786. www.graylineneworleans.com. Tours $18–$38 adults, less for children and groups of 10 or more.*

Harrah's Casino (p. 129) CBD Set in a 100,000-square-foot building, Harrah's is divided into five New Orleans–themed "courts"—such as a Smuggler's Court, a Court of the Mansion, and a Jazz Court. The casino boasts 2,500 slots and 100 table games, including a Blue Dog poker room (in honor of local artist George Rodrigue). There's plenty of food in the various courts, as well as music. They've even added fine dining so you'll never leave.... *Tel 504/533-6000, 800/HARRAHS. www.harrahs.com. Canal St. at the Mississippi River. Daily 24 hours. Free admission...if your luck holds out.*

See Map 12 on p. 133.

Heritage Tours (p. 130) This group offers a Tennessee Williams walk that is rich with anecdotes pertaining to "A Streetcar Named Desire." A general literary walk recounts tales of Williams, Lillian Hellman, Truman Capote, William Faulkner, and other 19th- and 20th-century literati who lived and hung out in New Orleans. Custom tours can also be designed for you around specific authors.... *Tel 504/949-9805. By appointment only. $20 per person, 3-person minimum.*

Hermann-Grima House (p. 126) FRENCH QUARTER One of three house museums in the Quarter, this one is a Federal-style town house built about 1831. Of particular interest are the formal dining room and the rear parterre gardens and outbuildings, where Creole cooking demonstrations take place on Thursdays from October until May.... *Tel 504/525-5661. 820 St. Louis St. Guided tours Mon–Fri 10am–3:30pm. Admission $6 adults; $5 seniors 65+, students, and children 8–18; free for children under 8.*

See Map 11 on p. 132.

Hidden Treasures Tours (p. 130) Minivans tool around the Garden District, while guides focus on women who have been influential in New Orleans. Groups are small, and tours are often customized to suit the crowd.... *Tel 504/529-4507. By appointment only. Tours $17–$25.*

Historic New Orleans Collection (p. 115) FRENCH QUARTER *The* place in the city to see historic papers and ephemera from this small city with a big past. Through changing and permanent exhibits of paintings and papers, visitors can learn about many facets of life in New Orleans from its sites, to its citizens, to actual events like the Louisiana Purchase. Local writers know to plant themselves in the research center—housed in a separate building on Chartres Street—where the helpful staff can produce material on anything from floor plans to Marie Laveau to famous floods.... *Tel 504/523-4662. www.hnoc.org. 533 Royal St. Tues–Sat 10am–4:30pm. Galleries free.*

See Map 11 on p. 132.

Honey Island Swamp Tours (p. 125) WEST PEARL RIVER Operated by wetland ecologist Dr. Paul Wagner, these riveting interpretive natural history tours take you through backwater bayous and secret sloughs where you can spy all manner of swamp life—including hungry gators and long-toothed nutria.... *Tel 504/242-5877 (in New Orleans), 985/641-1769 (in Slidell). www.honeyislandswamp.com. Crawford Landing, West Pearl River. Tours daily; times vary seasonally. Call for reservations and directions. $20 adults, $12 children 2–12. Hotel pick-up available for an extra cost.*

See Map 10 on p. 102.

Houmas House (p. 120) BURNSIDE The oldest section of this River Road plantation dates from the late 1700s and connects, by covered carriageway, to an 1840s Greek Revival mansion filled with period antiques. Costumed docents lead tours. Take I-10 west to Route 44 and head south toward Burnside, where signs point the way to the house.... *Tel 504/891-9494, 888/323-8314. 40136 Rte. 942, near Burnside. Daily 9am–5pm. Admission $20 adults, $15 teens 13–18, $10 children 6–12.*

Jean Lafitte National Historical Park and Preserve (p. 125) The park consists of six separate areas in South Louisiana, three of which are convenient for Crescent City visitors.

Barataria Preserve in Marrero: An outstanding place to learn about the natural and cultural aspects of the state's swamps and marshes. Take a hike along the more than 9 miles of trails and/or boardwalk. Or take a boat ride through more than 20 miles of waterways. And don't forget your insect repellent. (See the entry in Getting Outside.) *Tel 504/589-2330. LA Hwy. 45. Daily 9am–5pm. Free admission.*

Chalmette Battlefield and National Cemetery in Chalmette: History buffs never miss this place, the site of the Battle of New Orleans in 1815 and of the graves of soldiers who perished in wars ranging from the Civil War through Vietnam. There are daily talks on the battle and occasional living-history demonstrations.... *Tel 504/281-0510. St. Bernard Hwy. Daily 9am–5pm. Free admission.*

Visitor Center in the French Quarter: Come see exhibits pertaining to the state's and city's rich ethnic mix and a very good short film about the Mississippi River. This is also the kickoff spot for a free daily 9:30am walking tour conducted by park rangers of the French Quarter. Tickets are doled out, first come, first served, starting at 9am. *Tel 504/589-2636. 419 Decatur St. Daily 9am–5pm. Free admission.*

See Map 10 on p. 102.

***John James Audubon* Riverboat (p. 114)** FRENCH QUARTER Not as glitzy and architecturally retro as the other touring riverboats, the JJA nevertheless provides a great service for families: rides between the Aquarium and the Audubon Zoo. In fact, the JJA can be part of a fantastically fun day for the kids. If you're staying downtown, start at the Aquarium. Next, catch the JJA upriver to the zoo. After the zoo, catch the St. Charles Streetcar back downtown. If you are staying uptown, merely reverse the order. Packages for the zoo/aquarium/JJA are available, and the streetcar costs $1.25.... *Tel 504/586-8777, 800/233-BOAT. www.neworleanssteamboat.com. Daily departures from the aquarium at 10am, noon, 2pm, and 4pm; from the zoo at 11am, 1pm, 3pm, and 5pm. One-way cruises start at $13 for adults and $6.50 for kids 2–12, and prices go up from there depending on what permutation you want to book.*

See Map 11 on p. 132.

Lafayette Cemetery (p. 118) GARDEN DISTRICT This ancient walled City of the Dead is in the heart of the Garden District, across the street from Commander's Palace Restaurant. "Decorated" with elaborate aboveground tombs, its particular modern claim to fame is its role in *Interview with the Vampire.... No phone. Bounded by Washington Ave. and Coliseum, Prytania, and Sixth sts. Free admission.*

See Map 10 on p. 102.

Lakelawn Metairie Cemetery (p. 119) MID-CITY The great thing about this humongous Mid-City cemetery established in 1872 is that you never even have to get out of your car to enjoy it. At the entrance, you can borrow a free cassette tape that'll guide you through its more than 2,200 tombs, temples, and mausoleums, many of which feature elaborate statuary.... *Tel 504/486-6331. 5100 Pontchartrain Blvd. Daily 8:30am–5:30pm. Free admission.*

See Map 13 on p. 134.

Laura Plantation (p. 120) VACHERIE If you're suspicious of those perfect white columns and hoop-skirted guides who whoosh right past the tough questions of the antebellum South, then little old Laura is the place for you. The relatively modest Creole-style plantation and its 14 outbuildings date from 1805, and have been lovingly restored by a local family. The tour focuses on the women who ran Laura and the slaves who were technically their possessions, but also their partners. The legend of Br'er Rabbit is said to have been born here, amongst the West African slaves. Take I-10 west to I-310 and head south to cross the Veterans Memorial Bridge. Then veer right to Route 3127, and head toward Donaldsonville. Turn right on Route 20 and drive into Vacherie. When you come to Route 18 (River Rd.), turn right. The plantation is a few hundred yards away on the right.... *Tel 225/265-7690, 888/799-7090. www.lauraplantation.com. 2247 LA 18, Vacherie. Daily 9:30am–5pm. Closed major holidays. Admission $10 adults, $5 children 6–17, free for children under 6.*

See Map 10 on p. 102.

LeMieux Galleries (p. 130) WAREHOUSE/ARTS DISTRICT A restored warehouse is the setting for some exciting changing exhibits of contemporary art in multimedia.... *Tel 504/522-5988. 332 Julia St. Mon–Sat 10am–5:30pm. Free admission.*

See Map 10 on p. 102.

Le'Ob's Tours (p. 130) Knowledgeable guides conduct tours that take in sites and sights pertaining to the contributions African Americans have made to the city's culture and history. City tours, jazz tours, Garden District tours, plantation tours.... *Tel 504/288-3478. www.leobstours.com. 4635 Touro St. Office hours Mon–Sat 9am–9pm. Admission prices start at $45 for adults and $25 for children.*

Longue Vue House & Gardens (p. 126) MID-CITY The former home of local philanthropists Edgar and Edith Stern, this Classical Revival mansion offers 20 art- and antiques-ridden rooms to tour. Collections include cream- and pearlware, haute couture and ethnic costumes, and loads of porcelain. Rooms include spots that only stinking-rich people could dream up—like the wrapping room, used only for wrapping presents and opening mail. On a sunny day, no one should miss the 8 acres of manicured gardens outside. Families note: There are regularly scheduled events for children.... *Tel 504/488-5488. www.longuevue.com. 7 Bamboo Rd. Mon–Sat 10am–4:30pm, Sun 1–5pm (last house tour, 4pm). Admission $10 adults, $5 students and children.*

See Map 13 on p. 134.

Louisiana Children's Museum (p. 123) WAREHOUSE/ARTS DISTRICT Perfect for a rainy day, this hands-on educational indoor play spot had been busying local kids for years. Children can play and learn about everything from science to consumerism. There is also a great toddler spot, where the little ones can cut loose on padded tumbling toys, or with books and puzzles. The main drawback to the museum is its abysmal parking. Visitors can look for metered street parking (scant) or go to various lots in the Warehouse District (aggravating and not cheap).... *Tel 504/523-1357. www.lcm.org. 420 Julia St. Tues–Sat 9:30am–4:30pm, Sun noon–4:30pm. Admission $6 per person.*

See Map 10 on p. 102.

Louisiana State Museum (p. 115) FRENCH QUARTER The state museum is a complex of buildings, three of them on Jackson Square and one on the fringe of the French Quarter. The most important among them is the 18th-century Cabildo, where the Louisiana Purchase transfer papers were signed in 1803. The nearby Presbytère, from the same period, was built as a home for priests who served in the adjacent St. Louis Cathedral. The Cabildo houses changing exhibits, and the entire Presbytère is a wonderful Mardi Gras museum. The 1850 House, in the lower Pontalba Apartments, is done up just like a middle-class family from the period might have had it, right down to the domestic goods. The Old U.S. Mint on Esplanade Avenue, the only one to have minted both U.S. and Confederate coins, is home to a comprehensive jazz exhibit. Visit all of them and you will feel like a Big Easy expert.... *Tel 504/568-6968, 800/568-6968. Cabildo and Presbytere at 751 Chartres St. on Jackson Sq.; Old U.S. Mint at 400 Esplanade Ave. Tues–Sun 9am–5pm. Closed major holidays. Single building tickets are $5 adults; $4 seniors, students, and active military; free for children under 12.*

See Map 11 on p. 132.

Loyola University (p. 117) UPTOWN Across from Audubon Park and adjacent to Tulane University, Loyola University was incorporated in 1912.... *Tel 504/865-2011. 6363 St. Charles Ave.*

See Map 8 on p. 78.

Madewood Plantation (p. 121) NAPOLEONVILLE On the banks of Bayou Lafourche, this 21-room Greek Revival mansion welcomes overnighters to sleep in canopied beds and four-posters. Overnight stays include a wine-and-cheese cocktail hour, Southern meals in the candlelit dining rooms, coffee and liqueurs in the formal drawing room, and a full breakfast. Don't expect gourmet food; chat up the friendly staff, breathe deeply of the fresh country air, and remember that you were looking for a quiet retreat. The plantation is 74 miles from downtown New Orleans. Take I-10 west, head south on Route 70, cross the Sunshine Bridge, and follow the Bayou Plantation sign. Turn left on Spur 70 and left again on Route 308.... *Tel 985/369-7151, 800/375-7151. www.madewood.com. 4250 Rte. 308, near Napoleonville. Daily 10am–4pm for tours. Closed Thanksgiving Day, Christmas Eve, and Christmas Day. Admission charged.*

See Map 10 on p. 102.

Magic Walking Tours (p. 119) Guided tours walk you through St. Louis Cemetery No. 1, with histories of its creepy occupants, and the Garden District, with a stop at Lafayette cemetery. The Ghost Haunt Vampire tour carouses the Quarter pointing out haunted buildings and recounting freaky tales. Call for meeting spots.... *Tel 504/588-9693. St Louis tour leaves daily at 10:30am and 1:15pm, Garden District tour leaves daily at 10am and 12:30pm, Ghost Haunt tour leaves at 5pm and 8pm nightly. $18 adults, $15 students and seniors (60+), free for children under 6.*

Marguerite Oestreicher Fine Arts (p. 130) WAREHOUSE/ARTS DISTRICT Regional and national artists are represented in Oestreicher's gallery of contemporary sculpture, paintings, prints, and drawings.... *Tel 504/581-9253. 720–726 Julia St. Tues–Sat 10am–4:30pm. Free admission.*

See Map 12 on p. 133.

Moonwalk (p. 113) FRENCH QUARTER An open-air wooden promenade, lined with park benches, that stretches right alongside the Mississippi River, Moonwalk is a favorite Quarterite and tourist place for relaxing and watching the riverboats, tugs, and other traffic scudding by on the water.... *No phone. Alongside the Mississippi River, between St. Ann and Toulouse sts.*

See Map 11 on p. 132.

Musée Conti Wax Museum (p. 116) FRENCH QUARTER The wax figures in "Louisiana Legends" illustrate events from the late 17th century, with new "people" added from time to time. Cheesy for grown-ups, but a great way for kids to learn about Louisiana's and New Orleans's histories.... *Tel 504/525-2605, 800/233-5405. www.get-waxed.com. 917 Conti St. Mon–Sat 10am–5pm, Sun noon–5pm. Closed Mardi Gras and Christmas vacation. Admission $6.75 adults, $6.25 seniors, $5.75 children 4–17.*

See Map 11 on p. 132.

National D-Day Museum (p. 123) WAREHOUSE/ARTS DISTRICT Opened on June 6, 2000, with almost as much noise as the D-day invasion itself, this massive museum contains scads of artifacts, including a rebuilt Higgins boat, a Sherman tank, and a Spitfire airplane suspended from the ceiling. That's just the beginning: Enormous galleries include interactive exhibits, several oral history sections, a re-creation of an elaborate German bunker, exhibits detailing preparations for the invasion, a full-scale reconstruction of the aftermath of a glider landing, and a room-sized diorama of the air and sea armada. The museum has added a Pacific invasion area, with future plans to chronicle Asian and African invasions as well. There is also a theater, showing two World War II–related films with loads of never-before-seen footage.... *Tel 504/527-6012. www.ddaymuseum.org. 945 Magazine St. (entrance on Andrew Higgins Dr.). Daily*

9am–5pm. Admission $10 adults; $6 seniors 65+, students, and military with ID; $5 children 5–1; free for military in uniform.

See Map 10 on p. 102.

New Orleans Fair Grounds (p. 110) MID-CITY The fairgrounds does double duty as a thoroughbred racetrack and as the main hootin' and hollerin' place for the Jazz Fest. The racing season begins on Thanksgiving Day and runs, so to speak, until late March or early April. Hard on the heels of the horses, the Jazz Fest stomps off the last weekend in April and roars through the first weekend in May. (See Jazz Fest, p. 110.).... *Tel 504/943-2200, 800/262-7983. www.fgno.com. 1751 Gentilly Blvd. Mid-Nov to March, Wed–Sun, 1st post time 12:30pm. Jackets for men (no jeans or shorts). Reservations required for the clubhouse. Admission $4 clubhouse, $1 grandstand.*

See Map 13 on p. 134.

New Orleans Glassworks and Printmaking Studio (p. 130) WAREHOUSE/ARTS DISTRICT Working artists demonstrate architectural glassblowing, silversmithing, and other print and book arts at this combination gallery/studio. Incidentally, it's a sister school of the Louvre Museum in Paris.... *Tel 504/529-7277. www.neworleansglassworks.com, www.neworleansartworks.com. 727 Magazine St. Sept–May Mon–Sat 10am–5pm; June–Aug Mon–Fri 10am–5pm. Free admission.*

See Map 12 on p. 133.

New Orleans Historic Voodoo Museum (p. 119) FRENCH QUARTER A freaky, creaky old place, the museum displays gris-gris (voodoo charms), an altar, potions, artifacts, dolls, and such. A practitioner is on call for consultations, rituals, "or whatever is necessary".... *Tel 504/581-3824. www.voodoomuseum.com. 724 Dumaine St. Daily 10am–dusk. Admission $7 adults, $5.50 college students and seniors 62+, $4.50 high school students, $3.50 grade school students, free for children under 5.*

See Map 11 on p. 132.

New Orleans Museum of Art (p. 124) MID-CITY A white neoclassical building set in lush City Park, NOMA displays European paintings from the 17th through 19th centuries, Asian artworks, African tribal art, antique Louisiana furnishings, and a collection of Fabergé eggs, made by jeweler Peter Carl Fabergé for the royal Romanovs of czarist Russia.... *Tel 504/488-2631. www.noma.org. 1 Collins Diboll Circle, City Park. Tues–Sun 10am–5pm. Admission $8 adults, $7 seniors 65+ and students, $4 children 4–12, free for children 3 and under.*

See Map 13 on p. 134.

New Orleans Pharmacy Museum (p. 125) FRENCH QUARTER The apothecary shop of the nation's first licensed pharmacist, Louis J. Dufilho, Jr., has been converted into a museum of 19th-century pharmacy and medical artifacts. Cringe-worthy exhibits include Civil War surgical amputation kits, live leeches, old-time voodoo potions, and blood-letting instruments. You get the idea.... *Tel 504/565-8027. 514 Chartres St. Tues–Sun 10am–5pm. Admission $5 adults, $4 seniors 65+ and students, free for children under 5.*

See Map 11 on p. 132.

Ogden Museum of Southern Art (p. 124) WAREHOUSE/ARTS DISTRICT The recently opened Ogden houses the nation's largest space exclusively devoted to Southern decorative and fine arts. This Smithsonian affiliate features watercolors, paintings, prints, sculptures, and other work.... *Tel 504/539-9600. www.ogdenmuseum.org. 925 Camp St. Tues–Sun 9:30am–5:30pm, Thurs 'til 8:30pm. Admission $10 adults, $8 seniors and students, $5 children 5–17, free for children under 5.*

See Map 12 on p. 133.

Old U.S. Customs House (p. 124) CBD A gray chunk of granite occupying the entire 400 block of Canal Street. During the Civil War, the incomplete structure held more than 2,000 Confederate prisoners of war. Normal Customs activities are still carried out in part of the building, though it is currently under major construction and not open to the public. In an "only in New Orleans" combo, a massive Insectarium is slated to share the building with U.S. Customs starting in 2005.... *Tel 504/670-2000. 423 Canal St. Mon–Fri 8am–4pm, though currently closed to the public due to construction.*

See Map 11 on p. 132.

Old Ursuline Convent (p. 116) FRENCH QUARTER Guided tours take you through the oldest structure in the lower Mississippi Valley, where you can see the ancient cypress spiral staircase from an even earlier 18th-century convent on this site, and displays of 18th-century furniture, religious iconography, and documents pertaining to the building's history.... *Tel 504/529-3040. 1100 Chartres St. Tours given Tues–Fri at 10am, 11am, 1pm, 2pm, and 3pm; Sat–Sun at 11:15am, 1pm, and 2pm. Admission $5 adults, $4 seniors 65+, $2 students.*

See Map 11 on p. 132.

Pitot House (p. 127) MID-CITY Dating from about 1799, this West Indies–style house decked with galleries and jalousies is a great place to get a glimpse of how the early planters lived. Located on Bayou St. John.... *Tel 504/482-0312. www.pitothouse.org. 1440 Moss St. Wed–Sat 10am–3pm; last tour at 2pm. Admission $5 general, $4 seniors 60+, $2 children under 12.*

See Map 13 on p. 134.

Preservation Resource Center (p. 130) WAREHOUSE/ARTS DISTRICT Just as the name may suggest, this is the administrative office for the city's strong preservationist movement. The PRC spearheaded the drive to renovate the Warehouse District, in which its offices are located, and works diligently on programs such as Operation Comeback and Rebuilding Together in the Lower Garden District. From time to time, PRC does worthwhile architectural tours. Call or check their website to see what's coming up.... *Tel 504/581-7032. www.prcno.org. 923 Tchoupitoulas St. Office hours Mon–Fri 9:30am–4pm. Admission charge for tours.*

See Map 10 on p. 102.

St. Louis Cathedral (p. 127) FRENCH QUARTER Relatively small as cathedrals go, this white-stone church, with its three steeples and shingled roof, dates from 1794; it's the third church to occupy this site. The large mural over the high altar, depicting Louis IX announcing the Seventh Crusade, as well as the ceiling frescoes, were painted in 1872 by Erafme Humbrecht. Mass is conducted daily, and guided tours of the cathedral are conducted irregularly during the day, except during church services.... *Tel 504/525-9585. 615 Pere Antoine's Alley. Tours Mon–Sat 9am–5pm, Sun 1:30–5pm. Free admission.*

See Map 11 on p. 132.

St. Louis Cemeteries (p. 118) Creepy though they are, these three aboveground cemeteries are often near the top of visitors' must-see lists. The oldest of the city's cemeteries is St. Louis Cemetery No. 1, established in 1789 (Basin St. at St. Louis St.). St. Louis No. 2 is at North Claiborne Avenue and Bienville Street. St. Louis No. 3, the largest and the youngest of the three, is at 3421 Esplanade Ave., not far from City Park.... *Tel 504/596-3050. Guided tours conducted by Save Our Cemeteries (tel 504/525–3377) or Magic Walking Tours (tel 504/588–9693).*

See Map 11 on p. 132.
See Map 13 on p. 134.

St. Patrick's Church (p. 127) WAREHOUSE/ARTS DISTRICT Built as a house of worship for the Irish Catholics who settled in the American sector, this gray Gothic church was designed in 1833 by Irishmen James and Charles Dakin; the interior was the work of James Gallier, Sr. The church is famous for the dramatic murals over the altar, painted in 1841 by Leon Pomerade.... *Tel 504/525-4413. 724 Camp St. Mon–Fri 10am–4pm, Sat noon–6pm, Sun 7:30am–5:30pm. Free admission.*

See Map 12 on p. 133.

Save Our Cemeteries (p. 119) Tours conducted by this group walk you through Lafayette Cemetery and St. Louis Cemetery No. 1, and all proceeds go toward preservation of the "cities of the dead." St. Louis tours begin Sunday mornings at The Royal Blend Coffee Shop in the Quarter, where you can have your croissants and coffee before ambling to the graveyards.... *Tel 504/525-3377, 888/721-7493. www.saveourcemeteries.org. St. Louis cemetery tours meet at The Royal Blend Coffee Shop, 621 Royal*

St., French Quarter. Sun only, 10am. Admission $12 adults, $10 seniors 65+, $6 students 12–18, free for children under 12. Lafayette Cemetery No. 1 tours leave from the main gates of the cemetery at 1400 Washington Ave. Mon, Wed, Fri, Sat 10:30am. Admission $6 adults, $5 seniors 65+ and students 12–18, free for children under 12.

Six Flags New Orleans (p. 122) EAST NEW ORLEANS As if Bourbon Street were not enough of a thrill ride, now the Big Easy can boast its own amusement park. This newish 140-acre theme park is choked with hair-raising rides that will drop, throw, and speed you around 'til you can't take it anymore. There's also a kiddie area with activities for wee ones, a large picnic area, shops, and all kinds of diversions. To reach the park, take I-10 east to the intersection with I-510, exit 246A to Lake Forest Boulevard east.... *Tel 504/253-8100. www.sixflags.com/parks/neworleans. 12301 Lake Forest Blvd., New Orleans. March–Oct: weekends only during spring and fall, daily during the summer. Visit the website for exact days and hours. Admission $35 for those 48 inches and taller, $22 for those shorter than 48 inches, free for children 2 and under, $22 seniors 65+ and visitors with disabilities.*

See Map 10 on p. 102.

Steamboat *Natchez* (p. 113) FRENCH QUARTER This gingerbready replica of a 19th-century paddle wheeler does 2-hour harbor cruise and evening dinner-with-jazz outings replete with a Creole buffet and the Dukes of Dixieland tooting their horns for you.... *Tel 504/586-8777, 800/233-BOAT. www.steamboatnatchez.com. Board at the Toulouse St. Wharf, behind the Jax Brewery. Reservations required for night cruises. Day cruises at 11:30am and 2:30pm, with an optional lunch. Admission $19 adults, $9.25 kids 6–12. Evening cruise departs at 7pm. Admission with dinner $51 adults, $26 kids 6–12; admission without dinner $30 adults, $15 kids 6–12. Free for children under 6.*

See Map 11 on p. 132.

Storyland (p. 122) MID-CITY A pint-sized amusement park in City Park, ideal for the very young.... *Tel 504/483-9382. Victory Ave., City Park. Wed–Fri 10am–12:30pm, weekends 10am–4:30pm. Admission charged.*

See Map 13 on p. 134.

Tours by Isabelle (p. 130) Orientation tours of the city, plus outings to plantation country (with lunch at Madewood Plantation) and swamps are done in 13-passenger minibuses. Guides are multilingual (on request) and tours run half- and full days.... *Tel 504/391-3544, 888/223-2093. www.toursbyisabelle.com. Call for times and availability. Hotel pickups available. Prices from $49.*

Treasure Chest Casino (p. 129) LAKE PONTCHARTRAIN Docked across from the Pontchartrain Center in Kenner, this replica of a 19th-century paddle wheeler is a three-decker with 19,000 square feet in which you can place your bets or put your coins. Live entertainment, fine dining at Bobby G's, a snack bar, and an all-you-can-eat buffet are other *divertissements*.... *Tel 504/443-8000, 800/298-0711. www.treasurechestcasino.com. 5050 Williams Blvd., Kenner; docked on Lake Pontchartrain across from the Pontchartrain Center. Free admission.*

See Map 10 on p. 102.

Tulane University (p. 131) UPTOWN Named for philanthropist Paul Tulane, this is Louisiana's largest private university, with a student body of more than 12,000. The hundred-acre oak- and azalea-studded campus is located in the uptown section of New Orleans.... *Tel 504/865-5000. 6823 St. Charles Ave.*

See Map 8 on p. 78.

Vietnamese Market (p. 122) EAST NEW ORLEANS This open-air market makes you feel like you've been dropped off in Saigon—live rabbits, ducks and chickens; buckets of fish and shrimp; bushels of cilantro, basil, and lemon grass. And everyone is wearing those traditional conical straw hats. Don't forget to pick up one of the Vietnamese po'boys for a snack! *No phone, no website. Take Chef Menteur Hwy. to Alcee Fortier Blvd. in New Orleans E. Make a left, and the Versailles Arms Apartments will be down the road on the right.*

See Map 10 on p. 102.

Woldenberg Riverfront Park (p. 113) FRENCH QUARTER This 13-acre park, locally adored, is landscaped with shade trees and plenty of green spaces and park benches scattered here and there. It stretches along the Mississippi from the Aquarium of the Americas up to Jax Brewery.... *Tel 504/861-2537 (Audubon Institute, which administers the park).*

See Map 11 on p. 132.

GETTING

OUTSIDE

Map 14: Getting Outside in New Orleans

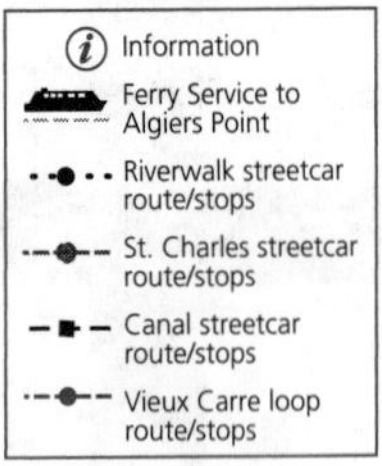

(i) Information

Ferry Service to Algiers Point

Riverwalk streetcar route/stops

St. Charles streetcar route/stops

Canal streetcar route/stops

Vieux Carre loop route/stops

Audubon Louisiana Nature Center **10**
Audubon Park **1**
Bicycle Michael's **7**
City Park **8**
Downtown Fitness Center **5**
Elmwood Fitness Center **3**

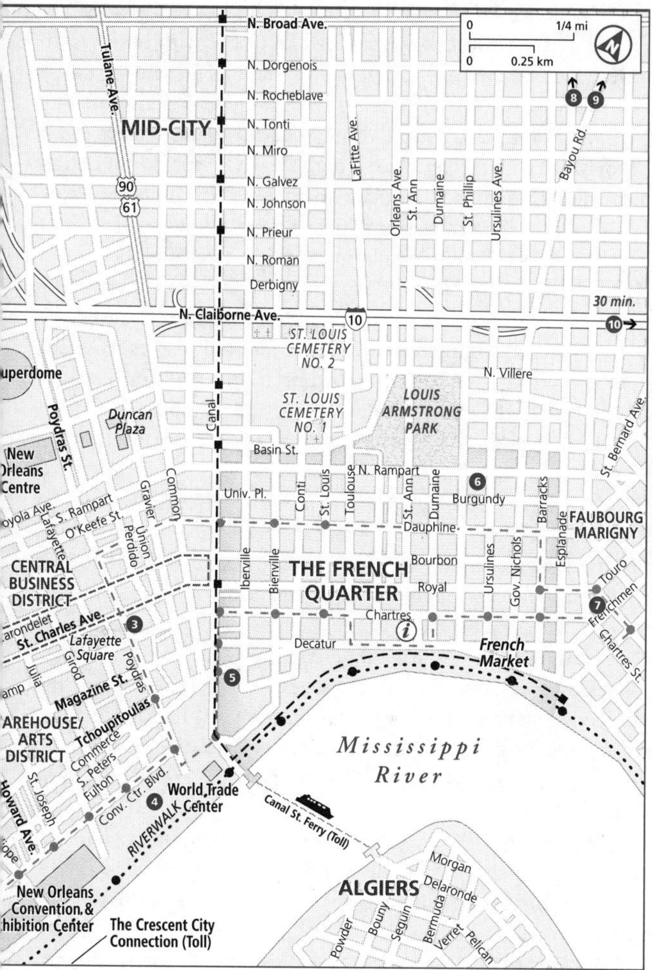

0
1/4 mi
0
0.25 km
N
N. Broad Ave.
N. Dorgenois
N. Rocheblave
N. Tonti
N. Miro
N. Galvez
N. Johnson
N. Prieur
N. Roman
Derbigny
N. Claiborne Ave.
Tulane Ave.
MID-CITY
90
61
LaFitte Ave.
Orleans Ave.
St. Ann
Dumaine
St. Phillip
Ursulines Ave.
Bayou Rd.
8
9
30 min.
10
ST. LOUIS CEMETERY NO. 2
ST. LOUIS CEMETERY NO. 1
LOUIS ARMSTRONG PARK
N. Villere
St. Bernard Ave.
Superdome
Duncan Plaza
Poydras St.
New Orleans Centre
Canal
Basin St.
N. Rampart
Univ. Pl.
Conti
St. Louis
Toulouse
St. Ann
Dumaine
6
Burgundy
Barracks
Esplanade
FAUBOURG MARIGNY
Dauphine
Bourbon
Royal
Chartres
Decatur
Iberville
Bienville
THE FRENCH QUARTER
Ursulines
Gov. Nichols
Touro
Frenchmen
7
Chartres St.
French Market
Loyola Ave.
S. Rampart
O'Keefe St.
Lafayette
Gravier
Union
Perdido
Common
CENTRAL BUSINESS DISTRICT
Carondelet
St. Charles Ave.
3
Lafayette Square
Girod
Julia
Camp
Poydras
Magazine St.
Tchoupitoulas
WAREHOUSE/ ARTS DISTRICT
Commerce
S. Peters
Fulton
Conv. Ctr. Blvd.
St. Joseph
Howard Ave.
Hope
5
4
World Trade Center
RIVERWALK
Mississippi River
Canal St. Ferry (Toll)
Morgan
Delaronde
ALGIERS
Powder
Bouny
Seguin
Bermuda
Verret
Pelican
New Orleans Convention & Exhibition Center
The Crescent City Connection (Toll)

Fairgrounds Racetrack **9**
Fishhunter Guide Service, Inc. **6**
Joe Bartholomew Golf Course **10**
Rivercenter Racquet and Health Club **4**
Mackie Shilstone's Pro Spa **2**

Lake Pontchartrain
CITY PARK
10
610
10
Area of detail
Superdome

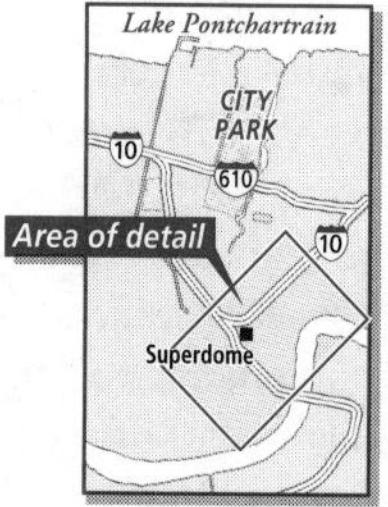

Basic Stuff

If you've ever lived in places like Honolulu, Los Angeles, or San Francisco, then you know what it's like to live with health-and-fitness True Believers. Jogging, Pilates, aerobics—these are things that many people out West actually build their lives around.

Not so in Louisiana. Sure, license plates claim it's a "Sportsman's Paradise," but when they say sports here they mean shooting guns at animals or catching fish on hooks. And let's face it, having muscular trigger fingers or shapely forearms hardly counts as being "fit" in most people's vocabularies.

Frighteningly, New Orleans may well be the flab capital of this fleshy state. Before it went bankrupt, the local McKenzie's Bakery had a commercial on television touting its fantastic pound cake. It ended with the exhortation, "And for a special treat, try it fried!" And there was a picture of that yellow cake, famous for containing a full pound of butter, being fried up on a greasy griddle.

Or what about Chef Paul Prudhomme—himself once so fat he could not walk unassisted—and his deep-fried po'boy? Those tasty sandwiches aren't naughty enough stuffed with mayo and fried seafood? Now he's dipping them in batter and throwing them in the deep fat fryer! In the Crescent City, it seems, everything improves with a little plunge in the peanut oil.

Alas, we may be losing our touch. In the mid-nineties the Big Easy ranked tops as America's Fattest City. In 2003, a *Men's Fitness* magazine poll informed us we had been demoted to an ignominious 11th. And for 2004, people were appalled to hear we'd plummeted to 22nd.

But all that fat might not be entirely our fault. For one thing, our topography hardly supports tight quads and hearty lungs. In this flat city in a mostly flat state, we've got nary a hill to bike or a mountain to climb. And unlike our cool Western cousins, we have no waves to surf or currents to swim—just swamps teeming with alligators, not the most supportive of training partners. Also, let's not forget that even the fittest person trying to exercise outside in the summer here may well end up in the E.R. with a nasty heatstroke. So, we have a few natural deterrents to health. And let's not even consider all the unnatural ones—Mardi Gras, Abita beer, fried shrimp, to name a few.

Nonetheless, the city does have a few True Believers, though most of them are tourists or transplants. And thanks to them, we do have some comfortable, picturesque places to run, stretch, or unblock your *qi.* So if you just can't live without your workout, read on.

The Lowdown

Walk in the park... In the northeast part of the city, a 10-minute drive up Esplanade Avenue from the Quarter, **City Park,** 1 Palm Dr. (tel 504/482-4888 park headquarters), is one of the nation's largest urban parks, with 1,500 acres of trails, gardens, and lagoons, and hundreds of majestic live oaks. This place is huge. Lope along the meandering pathways, or head for the **City Park Track,** a 400m polyurethane track just outside Tad Gormley Stadium, on Roosevelt Mall (tel 504/482-4888; daily dawn–dusk). There's an identical track inside the stadium, too, which was built for and used during the 1992 Olympic track and field trials.

A 15-minute drive in another direction from the Quarter, out through the Garden District, 400-acre **Audubon Park** at 6800 St. Charles Ave., across from Tulane and Loyola universities (tel 504/861-2537), can be reached via the St. Charles Streetcar. Shaded by giant live oaks whose ancient boughs bend and scrape the ground, it's got a 1.5-mile paved track around its lagoon, which you can extend to 2.5 miles by crossing Magazine Street and following the road up past the zoo and along the river. If you really want to go crazy, the park also has a par course. Running through a bucolic area where ducks and geese cruise on a sleepy lagoon, you can stop along the way at 18 exercise stations (chin-up bars and the like—don't expect Nautilus equipment). ***Bikers and bladers note:*** There's a bike lane to the right of the jogging/walking path, though you may have to circle the park many times to feel like you got a workout.

Some New Orleanians like to beat their feet beside the **Mississippi River,** taking in great views of the riverboats and the skyline, especially along the levee. One of the most popular stretches is around Riverbend, the little pocket neighborhood where the river makes a spectacular bend, and where St. Charles Avenue dead-ends at Carrollton Avenue. Take the St. Charles Streetcar and get off at Carrollton Avenue to walk up on the levee, where you can stroll, run, jog, or fly a kite to your heart's content. The city recently finished work on an excellent paved path that you can bike or blade all the way to Jefferson Parish. It's a fabulous improvement and a fun trip if you've got the time. Out in eastern New Orleans, about 20 minutes from the

Quarter, the **Audubon Louisiana Nature Center,** Joe Brown Memorial Park, 5601 Read Blvd. (tel 504/246-5672, 800/774-7394; closed Mon; $5 adults, $4 seniors, $3 for children 3–12) offers easygoing nature trails lacing through an 86-acre preserve of bottomland hardwood forest. But it's hardly fitness central; we're talking leisurely strolls through nature.

Run, baby, run... If you'd rather run with the pack and if your timing is right, you can sign up for the **Crescent City Classic,** P.O. Box 13587, 70185 (tel 504/861-8686; www.ccc10k.com), held the Saturday of Easter weekend. Some 18,000 runners head from Jackson Square along Esplanade to City Park, and in typical New Orleans style, there's plenty of jazz and food and beer to spirit them along. Check also with the **New Orleans Track Club,** P.O. Box 52003, 70152 (tel 504/482-6682), which has its foot in about 45 club races annually; or **Southern Runner Productions,** 6112 Magazine St., 70118 (tel 504/891-9999; daily 10am–6pm, Sat to 5pm). If you're up for a fun run for a good cause and you're in town in mid-October, sign up for the **WRBH Light in the Dark Moonlight Run** (tel 504/899-1144), a 5K coed race to support WRBH (88.3), the only 24-hour news station in the world that airs nonstop reading for the blind. Runners show up at night for the "race" decked in outlandish costumes, and most wind up imbibing right there on the street or at whichever downtown hotel is hosting seasonal festivities.

Tennis, anyone?... For most active sports, the slickest venue for visitors is the **Rivercenter Racquet and Health Club** at the Hilton Riverside, 2 Poydras St. (tel 504/556-3742). It's right here in the CBD and is just about always open (Mon–Fri 5:30am–9pm, Sat 7am–7pm, Sun 7am–5pm). The only catch is the $11 fee, and the four indoor tennis courts may be all booked up. There are also three squash courts, three racquetball courts, and tennis instruction. A 10-minute drive away from the French Quarter, the **City Park Tennis Center,** 1 Palm Dr., City Park (tel 504/483-9383; Mon–Thurs 7am–10pm, Fri–Sun 7am–7pm), has many more courts—34 lighted rubico and Laykold courts, shaded by oaks and cypress trees—as well as equipment rentals and individual and group lessons by USPTA pros. Fees start at $6.50, but you usually don't need to reserve ahead to get on a court. There are also 10 clay courts in **Audubon Park** near the zoo at Henry Clay and Tchoupitoulas streets (tel 504/895-1042), where you can usually drop by and get on a court with no fuss. They open at 8am and usually don't close until it's too dark to see the ball.

Par for the course... You can play golf year-round down here, and as a result there's a good supply of courses, though most are pretty flat. There's usually no problem getting tee times on the public courses—just call. Visiting golfers often head for City Park's **Bayou Oaks Golf Courses,** 1040 Filmore Dr. (tel 504/483-9396; non-resident greens fees $13–$22, cart rental $20), where there are four—count 'em, four—18-holers, not to mention a 100-tee double-decker driving range, lit at night. Uptown, the **Audubon Park Course** (tel 504/212-5290; Mon–Fri $27 to walk, $38 to ride; Sat and Sun $35 to walk, $46 to ride; daily 7am–dusk) was recently and beautifully renovated. It's now a par-62 course that most consider short but challenging. The new clubhouse is pretty spiffy, too. Out in eastern New Orleans's Pontchartrain Park, about half an hour from the Quarter, the par-72 **Joe Bartholomew Golf Course,** 6514 Congress Dr. (tel 504/288-0928; greens fees $8, cart rental $20), is worth the trek if you like long courses—it's 6,700 yards for men, 5,970 for women. Over on the West Bank of the river, the public courses are the par-70 **Brechtel,** 3700 Behrman Place (tel 504/362-4761; greens fees $7.75–$10, cart rental $18); and the par-71 **Bayou Barriere Golf Course,** 7427 Hwy. 23, Belle Chase (tel 504/394-9500; greens fees $35–$45 including cart), which has 27 holes (three 9-hole courses), so you can vary the layout.

If you're a dedicated golfer—and that's often a redundant term—you might want to drive into the instep of this boot-shaped state to play the area's best course, designed by Arnold Palmer, at **The Bluffs on Thompson Creek,** Route 965, 6 miles east of U.S. 61 (tel 225/634-5551; www.thebluffs.com; greens fees $57–$67, includes cart). Its signature hole, number 17, is a stunning par-3 atop one of the high bluffs (with 60 ft. of elevation) that give the club its name. The par-72 course is wildly popular with St. Francisville duffers, but it's not impossible to get a tee time—non-members can call 6 days in advance (starting Thurs morning for weekend times) and reserve any times not already booked by members. To really make sure you can get on the course, reserve a room at the attached **Lodge at the Bluffs** (tel 225/634-3410, 888/634-3410), which has 37 fairly plush one-bedroom suites and two two-bedroom suites; lodge guests are guaranteed tee times and get discounts on the greens fee. Considering the 3-hour drive from New Orleans, staying over's not a bad idea anyway.

On a bicycle built for one... There are no hills to slow you down in this horizontal town, so pumping is easy; the humidity, however, can really get to you. At **Bicycle Michael's,** 622 Frenchmen St., Faubourg Marigny (tel 504/945-9505; daily at 10am), you can rent two wheels. If you want to do more than just putter around in the city parks, Bicycle Michael himself, Mike Ferrand, recommends this 25-mile route: From the French Quarter, head up Esplanade Avenue to City Park, loop along Lakeshore Drive, come back into Mid-City, and spin through Audubon Park and the Tulane campus; then go along the levee at Riverbend, down through the Garden District and along St. Charles Avenue back to the Quarter. If you're moving fast, it'll take about an hour and a half; cruisin', you'll be pedaling for about 3½ hours.

Back in the saddle... There is no place in the city where you can rent a horse and bolt off on your own. However, you can take a guided trail ride at **Cascade Stables,** 700 East Dr. near the zoo (tel 504/891-2246; Tues–Sun 9am–5pm, closed Mon; last trail ride leaves at 4pm; $20 per horse). You'll only ride for about an hour, but the guide leads you through some of the prettiest areas of the park. No trail rides are offered at **City Park Stables,** 1001 Filmore Ave. (tel 504/483-9398; daily 8am–5pm; $35 for first lesson), but you can take lessons and attend an occasional horse show.

Though they no longer do rides on horseback, the best nature experience in these parts is the guided safari at the **Global Wildlife Center,** across Lake Pontchartrain, Route 40 East, just outside of Folsom (tel 985/624-WILD; www.globalwildlife.com; daily 8:30am–5pm; admission $8–$10; call for tour availability). One of only three such wildlife facilities in the country, the 900-acre center is a protected area for scores of endangered species. The animals roam free, while humans are the ones cooped up in tractor-pulled covered wagons. You can get remarkably close to nature. Friendly giraffes, camels, zebras, llamas, bison, and antelopes (to name a few) go about their business, while visitors snap pictures like mad and feed them tidbits provided by the tour guides. The countryside is lovely, all green and lush with ponds and wooded groves. To reach the Global Wildlife Center, take the Lake Pontchartrain Causeway to I-12 West, turn right at the town of Robert (exit 47) onto Route 445 North, and drive 10½ miles to Route 40 East; turn right and drive for 1 mile.

Gone fishin'... The main fish in these parts are speckled trout, redfish, and bass. Former TV weatherman Nash Roberts will run you out into the coastal marshes year-round through **Fishhunter Guide Service, Inc.,** 1040 N. Rampart St., 70116 (tel 504/837-0703, 800/887-1385), which provides everything you need for light tackle fishing. He will even pick you up at your hotel.

You'll need your own wheels for our other two options. **Co Co Marina,** 106 Pier 56, Chauvin, LA 70344 (tel 985/594-6626, 800/648-2626), offers charter service for fishing, and has its feet smack in the Gulf of Mexico. The drive down, about an hour from New Orleans, is splendid, especially in the spring, when colorfully decorated shrimp boats line the bayous. Take U.S. 90 south from New Orleans and hitch up with Route 56 (take Rte. 57 for the return drive). It goes without saying that this is really not the place to be when hurricanes sweep up through the Gulf. **Capt. Phil's Saltwater Guide Service,** 4775 Jean Lafitte Blvd., Lafitte, LA 70067 (tel 504/689-2006; www.rodnreel.com/captphil), is operated by Captain Phil Robichaux, a familiar face to many Orleanians from a local fishing show hosted by sportsfisherman and TV personality Frank Davis. Equipment and artificial bait are provided. Captain Phil's five boats prowl the coastal marshes, setting off from the Lafitte Harbor Marina near the Barataria Unit of the Jean Lafitte National Historical Park. The park is about an hour's drive from downtown New Orleans. Follow Decatur Street across Canal Street, where it becomes Magazine Street, then cross the Crescent City Connection and take the West Bank Expressway (U.S. 90) to Barataria Boulevard (Rte. 45). Turn left on Route 45 and watch for the Barataria Unit signs.

On the Bayou... If you're at all inclined toward outdoorsy things, you really should not leave this area without visiting the aforementioned **Barataria Unit of the Jean Lafitte National Historical Park,** Highway 45/Barataria Boulevard near the town of Jean Lafitte (tel 504/589-2330; www.nps.gov/jela; free admission; hours are seasonal), a 20,000-acre preserve about an hour southwest of the city. Eight miles of paved and dirt nature trails, as well as boardwalk trails, wind through the wetlands, where you can see egrets, all sorts of slithery critters (including the occasional gator), and those really hideous nutria—they're the giant web-footed rodents you've read about that are eating up the coastal wetlands. (Keep in mind what the rangers tell us: It's their home, not ours. We're the ones trespassing.) You can strike out on your own (ever mindful of whose home this is) or hook up with a ranger-guided tour. Trails lead through a hardwood forest and a picture-postcard Louisiana swamp with spectacular scenery and great bird-watching.

At the nearby **Bayou Barn,** 7145 Barataria Blvd. in Crown Point (tel 504/689-2663, 800/TO-BAYOU; www.bayoubarn.com; daily 10am–6pm), you can rent a canoe, either on your own or with a guide, and paddle off among the moss-draped cypresses that jut out of the water—eerily beautiful. Be sure to ask about the schedule for moonlight canoeing, which usually happens about once a month. The Bayou Barn also serves up pretty fair gumbo and jambalaya and has Sunday fais-do-do (Cajun dances), when the friendly staff will show you how to jig and two-step.

Boating and fishing for urban wimps... If you'd just as soon forgo the nutria and gators, you can get some peaceful **pedal-boating** done in City Park at the end of Roosevelt Mall (tel 504/482-4888; March–Oct, Sat–Sun 10am–3pm, $5 per person per hour). Graceful white swans, ducks, and geese glide along 11 miles of artificial lagoons in a romantic setting of ancient oak trees. The lagoons are stocked with bass, catfish, and perch, who haven't a clue in the world that they're fair game. You'll have to bring your own fishing gear and fish from the shore, not in the boats. You can get the required City Park fishing permits in the Timken Center (tel 504/483-9475), formerly known as the Casino Building (though there's not a trace of gambling in the building anymore).

Not really getting outside: indoor fitness... The best health club in town available to visitors is the **Rivercenter Racquet and Health Club** at the New Orleans Hilton Riverside Hotel, 2 Poydras St., CBD (tel 504/556-3742; $10 for hotel guests, $12 for others), the same place we recommended above for tennis and racquetball. The exercise room here is stellar, too, with state-of-the-art Nautilus equipment and Universal gym stuff, as well as Bally computerized Lifecycles, free weights, and a rowing machine. There's also a room for aerobics, yoga, and Pilates. For those who prefer their fitness to be passive, there are saunas, whirlpools, a masseur, a full-service unisex salon, and a tanning bed.

Many a famed sports figure, including Brett Butler, Ozzie Smith, Will Clark, Riddick Bowe, and Michael Spinks has been toned, trimmed, and trained by New Orleanian Mackie Shilstone. The well-equipped **Mackie Shilstone's Pro Spa,** 2111 St. Charles Ave. in the Garden District (tel 504/679-7691; www.mackieshilstone.com; $9 per day), in the Avenue Plaza Hotel, has a slew of treadmills, stair-climbers, rowing machines, saunas, massages, herbal wraps, and whirlpools, as well as trainers and supervisors.

Shilstone is on the staff of the **Elmwood Fitness Center,** 701 Poydras St. in the CBD (tel 504/588-1600; www.elmwoodfitness.com; $10 per day or $35 per week non-members), which is, in turn, affiliated with the Ochsner Medical Foundation. In addition to a full array of Icarian gear, there are racquetball courts, a one-on-one basketball court, spinning, aerobics, massages, trainers, a sauna, and a whirlpool. They also have a huge facility at 1200 South Clearview Pkwy. (tel 504/733-1600) with multiple pools and 160,000 square feet of "gym." At the Clearview facility, there's a "Kidsports" program and a child-care center.

Downtown Fitness Center, Canal Place, CBD (tel 504/525-2956; www.downtownfitnesscenter.com; $12 per day), is conveniently located just past the popcorn and candy concessions at the Canal Place Cinemas. Along with the Nautilus and Cybex stuff, there are yoga, aerobics, sauna, a tanning bed, and trainers to help you along the way.

SHOP

PING

5

Map 15: New Orleans Shopping Orientation

ah-ha **3**
Adler's **14**
Antiques and Things **5**
Big Fisherman **2**
Blackamoor **11**
Broadway Bound **22**
Canal Place **16**
Charbonnet & Charbonnet **6**
Creole Delicacies **19**
Deville Books and Prints **13**
Funky Monkey **1**
Garden District Bookshop **7**

Judys at the Rink **7**
Kohlmaier and Kohlmaier **4**
Louisiana Products **10**
Masks and Make Believe **20**
Meyer the Hatter **15**
MGM Costumes **9**
Mignon Faget **17**
New Orleans Centre **12**
RHINO Gallery **18**
Riverwalk **21**
Trashy Diva **8**

Basic Stuff

Never doubt that New Orleans is a two-faced city—just look at the French Quarter, where ritzy, world-class antiques stores and art galleries sit cheek-by-jowl with some of the world's raunchiest T-shirt stands. Naturally, because it is the tourist center, the Quarter has an overabundance of really tacky souvenir shops. You won't have any trouble at all finding miniature alligator heads, naughty Mardi Gras beads, or take-home Hurricane glasses. On the other hand, you won't have trouble finding that rare gilded Napoleon III desk, either. This is not a hot retail clothing market; there are plenty of clothing stores, of course, to serve style-conscious locals—you'll find Lord & Taylor, Saks Fifth Avenue, and Macy's—but no one comes to New Orleans from, say, New York or L.A. or even Dallas on a clothes-buying spree. Unless it's for vintage clothes, which we seem to have in abundance. The big-ticket items are to be found in antiques stores, but there are also wonderful little gift shops, boutiques, bookstores, and record shops.

What to Buy

Rare is the person who leaves this town without buying at least one box of **pralines** (say "praw-leens")—those teeth-crackingly sweet candy patties made of sugar, butter, and pecans. They're sold in gift shops all over town, but Orleanians themselves like to pop into the Old Town Praline Shop on Royal Street to satisfy their sweet tooth. **Carnival masks** are also enormously popular souvenirs and gifts. Some are those horrible little ceramic harlequin masks you can buy anywhere, but others are handmade works of art—and they are not cheap. In addition to the masks, local crafts include marvelous **handmade dolls**—some of them of the antique persuasion, which makes them too expensive to play with. **Wembley Tabasco ties** are also a fun keepsake. Splashy Mardi Gras and Jazz Fest **posters** are popular take-home items. The sounds of New Orleans's world-class musicians sing out on **records, CDs,** and **tapes** at places like the Louisiana Music Factory and the retail outlet of the GHB Jazz Foundation; they'll carry some recordings you couldn't hope to find in most other cities. There are even places that package **New Orleans food,** either to take with you or have shipped. Speaking of which, **cookbooks** abound with regional recipes, and most of the top local chefs have produced at least one cookbook, including Emeril Lagasse, Paul Prudhomme, and Alex Patout (see "Really Cooking," below).

Target Zones

In the city proper (in other words, not Metairie or the West Bank), the largest concentration of malls, stores, and shops lies in the **French Quarter** and the **Central Business District (CBD).** There's at least one shop on almost all of the Quarter's 96 blocks, hunkering for the most part in those charming little 19th-century buildings, town houses, and cottages. The great majority of the shops we list below are in the Quarter. The stroll-through **French Market,** a 200-year-old restored marketplace, is a seven-block collection of pastel-painted low stone buildings containing open-air cafes and shops selling clothes, candy, T-shirts, and the like; it stretches from St. Ann Street to Barracks Street. It's full of tourists, simply by virtue of being in the Quarter, but it isn't glitzy and the atmosphere is authentically New Orleans. The century-old **Café du Monde** (see Dining, p. 83) is traditionally considered the upriver anchor (at St. Ann St., though there's been a recent addition of a Visitor Information Center at Washington Artillery Park); at the Barracks Street end are the ramshackle **Old Farmers' Market** and **Community Flea Market,** two completely ungentrified shopping areas where locals go for produce and bargain items. The Jackson Brewery Corporation (locally called Jax Brewery) has three indoor marketplaces, which you can bet means they're tourist-oriented, geared mostly to sell food, entertainment, fashion, and impulse items: **Jax Brewery** is in the restored 1891 Jackson Brewery and houses a mammoth **Virgin Records;** walkways connect it to its sister, the **Millhouse;** and two blocks toward Canal Street is the third Jax mall, the **Marketplace.** Though they have less New Orleans color than the French Quarter shops, the stores in the CBD are where Orleanians themselves go for their high-end shopping. Maison Blanche, which had stood on Canal Street since the 19th century, is no more. The building was converted to a luxury Ritz-Carlton Hotel, which opened in 2000. The coming of the ritzy hotel meant a bon voyage for Mr. Bingle. In an ages-old tradition, Mr. Bingle—a giant white effigy of a snowman, based on a puppet from an ancient TV kiddie show—appeared on the handsome cast-iron facade of the Maison Blanche building, heralding the start of the Christmas season. Toward the river, **Canal Place** is a tony pedestrian mall set in a three-story marble and travertine atrium, starring Saks Fifth Avenue, BCBG, Brooks Brothers, Williams-Sonoma, and Gucci, along with 40 or so other stores. **Riverwalk,** with 200 shops, restaurants, and a food court, is another festival marketplace alongside the river,

> **Learn the Lingo**
> *If the baker tosses in one extra doughnut to make it 13, he's given you a baker's dozen. In New Orleans that little something extra is called* **lagniappe** *(roughly pronounced lan-yap), though the term is not nearly as prevalent as it used to be.* **Makin' groceries** *means going to the grocery store. The root of this ubiquitous phrase is the French word faire, which means "to do" or "to make." But Orleanians never "do" groceries. They say, "I gotta make groceries today...." You'll hear* **praline** *pronounced pray-leen a lot, but that's because the city is full of Yankees who don't know any better. It's prah-leen.*

with a plastic atmosphere not unlike the other Rouse Company developments in New York and Baltimore. The mix of tenants includes national chains (Banana Republic, The Disney Store, The Sharper Image) and local upscale shops (Cajun Clothing and Street Scenes). However, it's probably less famous for its shopping than for the fact that around Christmastime in 1996, a 763-foot-long Liberian freighter loaded with 56,000 tons of corn lost control on the river and rammed right into the mall, tearing away a huge chunk of it. The mall was busy with holiday shoppers, but miraculously no one was killed. The event is memorialized in a big book of news clippings under the stairs on one of the lower levels. Or if you want, a fascinating website (http://virtualpet.com/bright) gives a very detailed description of the accident along with photos and a clip from CNN of the crash. The **New Orleans Centre** is a sleek, characterless atrium mall connected by walkways to the adjacent Superdome and Hyatt Regency Hotel. Leading lights here are Lord & Taylor and Macy's, but there are dozens of other chains, as well as a large food court.

The place to head for contemporary artworks is **Gallery Row,** on Julia Street (and some of its cross streets as well) in the Warehouse/Arts District, in which old abandoned warehouses have been converted into galleries, apartments, and restaurants. Julia Street between St. Charles Avenue and the convention center is the hot stretch, so it's fairly convenient to CBD hotels. The first Saturday of every month is the night for openings—the biggest two being White Linen Night in August and Art For Art's Sake in October. Call the Contemporary Arts Center at 504/523-1216 for information about openings; see "SoHo in NoLa..." in Diversions for a rundown of the best/trendiest/most interesting places. There are 6 miles or so of shops lining **Magazine Street,** which stretches upriver from Canal Street all the way to the Audubon Zoo.

The entire street has been on the rise—retailwise—for the last decade and now sports same fantastic local clothing boutiques, jewelry makers, pottery, contemporary furniture, and loads of antiques, as well as great eats. The street runs in strips, though: a row of shops followed by a long row of houses. You can ride the Magazine Street bus all the way up, stopping along the way, if you want to do it yourself. Or you could engage **Macon Riddle** for a half- or full-day shopping expedition. A shopping consultant with a special interest in antiques, she keeps up to speed on what's where and how much it costs. **Riverbend** is a small pocket of shops tucked in beside the Uptown great bend in the river. You can reach it on the St. Charles Streetcar—get off where the streetcar turns off St. Charles Avenue onto Carrollton Avenue. A toy store, a vintage clothier, and a mask shop—among others—are tucked into Creole cottages scattered on tree-lined streets. It's a good place to wander in conjunction with a trip to the wildly popular Camellia Grill.

Good Reads

Anne Rice's fictional multi-volume Vampire Chronicles are set in New Orleans and in her former Garden District homes. Fans of Anne Rice will love ***Haunted City: An Unauthorized Guide to the Magical, Magnificent New Orleans of Anne Rice*** *by Joy Dickinson. Other fiction set in New Orleans:* ***In the Land of Dreamy Dreams*** *by Ellen Gilchrist and* ***The Moviegoer*** *by Walker Percy. New Orleans dialects are done to a T in John Kennedy Toole's riotous Pulitzer Prize–winning* ***A Confederacy of Dunces.*** *Julie Smith, not an Orleanian, has written five books based here, most recently 1997's* ***Kindness of Strangers.*** *And homegrown novelist Nancy Lemann has captured the city in her* ***Lives of the Saints*** *and* ***Ritz of the Bayou.*** *For nonfiction, Lyle Saxon's* ***Fabulous New Orleans*** *is, well, fabulous; it was written long before 1936, when the preservationists began their rescue of the French Quarter, and gives you an entirely different view of the old city. Saxon collaborated with Robert Tallant and Edward Dreyer for* ***Gumbo Ya Ya,*** *a collection of old folk tales. Voodoo is revealed by Robert Tallant in* ***Voodoo in New Orleans.*** *John Churchill Chase's* ***Frenchmen, Desire, Good Children*** *has some fun insider stuff.*

Trading with the Natives

What with an annual onslaught of about nine million visitors, New Orleans's merchants are accustomed to packing and mailing. Don't expect such service from the vendors in the Community Flea Market, that jumble of stalls behind the Old Farmers' Market in the French Quarter, but many other places will ship. Haggling is often an option here—especially at the Flea Market. But don't sell yourself short with the antiques dealers either. A discreet, "Is this your best price?" will signal your interest and if the retailer isn't into bargaining, you'll know right away.

Hours of Business

Almost all shops downtown in the French Quarter and the CBD are open daily, but many shops uptown—in the Garden District, in Riverbend, and on Magazine Street—are closed on Sunday. As a very general rule, New Orleans shops open around 9 or 10am and close at 5:30 or 6pm, but in the Quarter opening hours can depend on how hung over the owner is and closing hours can depend upon how heavy the foot traffic is. Shops in the malls keep more reliable hours.

Sales Tax

The combined state and local tax comes to a whopping 9%. Louisiana's Tax-Free Shopping program helps, if you happen to be visiting from another country. The program applies to international visitors with valid passports and return tickets, and is available in stores that display the LTFS insignia. It works like this: When making a purchase, show your passport and request a refund voucher for the sales tax. You'll be charged full price, including sales tax. Keep your sales slip and refund voucher. When you arrive at the airport for your departure, go to the LTFS refund center and present the sales slip, tax refund voucher, your passport, and your return ticket. Refunds under $500 will be made in cash; amounts over $500 will be sent by check to your home address. A handling fee of $5 to $10 is deducted from your refund.

The Lowdown

Antiquities... Many of the antiques stores on Royal Street are age-old establishments, most of them operated by a third or fourth generation of the founders, and accustomed to working with similarly venerable dealers in Europe and in this country. Obviously, there are different items in every store on the street, but they're all—usually—top quality. If you're an antiques lover, you'll want to browse the whole strip. Expect prices to be high. The oldest on the street is

Waldhorn & Adler, established in 1881 by Moise Waldhorn, and now owned and run by fourth-generation Adlers. Stop here for the amazing display of antique and Art Deco estate jewelry. The owners of **Moss Antiques, Keil's Antiques,** and **Royal Antiques** are all related, having descended from founders of The Royal Company, founded in 1899, and their stocks are also similar—precious old French and English furnishings and jewelry, with Royal tending a bit more toward country-style stuff. The **French Antique Shop** is the best place for Tiffany and Baccarat crystal chandeliers. **M. S. Rau,** begun in 1912 by Mendel Rau and his wife, Fanny, is operated now by their grandson and specializes in 19th-century American antiques, including lots of Victorian cut glass. One of the largest stores on Royal Street is **Dixon & Harris,** owned by civic leader Arthur Harris and art dealer David Dixon, who travels throughout Europe buying estate jewels; collections of French, English, and Dutch furnishings; oil paintings; and Persian rugs. Look in prestigious **Rothchild's Antiques** for fine custom-made jewelry and elegant 18th- and 19th-century French and English furnishings. **Ida Manheim Antiques,** opened in 1910 and currently run by the second-generation owner, occupies a 19th-century bank building. The gallery has also sewn up the local market on delicate porcelain Boehm Birds. Patrick Dunne's **Lucullus** (which is not on Royal, but on Chartres with a branch on Magazine St.) is a very posh place to purchase 17th- to 19th-century cookware, furnishings, and paintings. Also on Chartres is another shop worthy of reflection. **Mirror, Mirror** has an outstanding collection of "looking glass" artwork, from the 18th century to Art Deco. Men's gifts and accessories are the specialty at **Jack Sutton.** You'll want to detour from Royal Street and head Uptown to see the outstanding antique furniture reproductions at **Kohlmaier and Kohlmaier,** off Magazine Street. And speaking of Magazine Street, a few other dealers up there definitely give the Royal Street merchants a run for their money. **Jon Antiques,** which occupies a historic 19th-century house, directly imports some very fine 18th- and 19th-century English and French furniture and furnishings. **Antiques and Things** is a good place to go for objets d'art from the 1950s and 1960s. **Blackamoor,** which handles furniture as well as porcelain and Asian art, has a shop on Julia Street.

Collectibles... You can brush up on military history while chatting up the knowledgeable folks at **Le Petit Soldier Shop,** which has 2-inch-tall toy soldiers all lined up in rows. Look for a miniature Napoleon, an Eisenhower, both Lee and Grant, and even a Mussolini. The **Brass Monkey** absolutely shines with all its brass lamps, and ceiling fans. Collectors should make a beeline for the Limoges porcelain boxes and walking sticks. A third-generation owner operates **James H. Cohen & Sons,** a huge antiques store that has everything from Civil War cannonballs to Confederate money, Frederic Remington bronco-busters, rare coins, antique firearms, and flags. While George Rodrigue's Blue Dog paintings aren't collectibles in the purest sense, people who love them tend to own more than one. **Rodrigue Studios** is heaven for those who love the mournful little bayou pooch.

Crafty things... At **The Idea Factory,** a marvelous and affordable place owned and run by the friendly Kenny Ford family, you can watch them carve adorable tiny toys out of wood—and they'll carve your name on that toy airplane, or whatever else you buy. For whimsical works and unique blown-glass pieces, head to **Judy at the Rink** in the Garden District. Check in at **RHINO,** a big, modern, well-lit store in Canal Place, for upscale handcrafted jewelry and artworks by regional artisans. Visit **Crafty Louisianians** to see pottery, hand-crafted animals, wood-turned bowls, and jewelry by local artists. And for those who want the *Architectural Digest* look, there are some splendid high-priced garden ornaments—statuary and fountains of carved granite and marble—set out in the peaceful courtyard of **Coghlan Galleries.** At **Charbonnet & Charbonnet,** a Magazine Street store, the scent of sawdust hits you as soon as you walk in the door—the in-house cabinet shop custom-produces furnishings from relics of razed houses and buildings. Even if you're not in the market for furnishings, it's fascinating to witness this urban archaeology in action.

Diamonds are a girl's best friend... On the very upper end of the scale, Orleanian **Mignon Faget** creates elegant designs of bronze d'or and silver, inspired by local architecture and nature—look for motifs such as banana leaves, palm fronds, and even sea creatures. For fine jewelry that doesn't necessarily show its Louisiana roots, try **Adler's,** an old-line CBD jeweler selling pricey baubles. Among the antiques stores, **Waldhorn & Adler's** specializes in remarkable estate and modern jewelry. Newcomer **Wellington & Company** also sells older gems, with particular emphasis on shiny stuff from the Victorian, Edwardian, and Art Deco periods. If all you want are cheap trinkets, of course, there's always the **Community Flea Market.**

Masking for Mardi Gras... While you can buy cheesy souvenir masks at gift shops throughout the Quarter, high-quality Carnival masks—which can cost anywhere from $20 to $3,000—are sold at these stores. Master maskmaker Ann Guccione's **Little Shop of Fantasy** may look like a hole in the wall, but inside it's brightened by fantastic leather and feather masks lining the walls and counters. More than 100 regional artists make the fabulous creations at **Rumors,** a more upscale store that sells jewelry as well as masks. For a Cajun spin on things, check out the Mardi Gras masks by Acadian artist Cathy Judice at **Crafty Louisianians**—her Masks of Mamou, made from painted window screens, resemble those worn by Cajun horsemen in the **Courir du Mardi Gras,** an ages-old race where masked riders gallop on horseback through the Cajun Country countryside. At **Riverwalk,** you can buy elaborate masks made of everything from ceramic to rubber, in a small shop called **Masks & Make Believe.**

Incredible edibles... Do as all the tourists do, and stop by **Aunt Sally's Praline Shop** on Decatur Street to watch the praline making and browse through the cookbooks, aprons, and things. The pralines aren't bad either. **Creole Delicacies** also boasts of its pralines, which are perfectly fine, but the reason to come here is for one-stop shopping on gift packages of spices, rémoulade sauce, and hot sauces. Cooking demonstrations (and tastings) are offered by the **New Orleans School of Cooking.** You won't get your hands all greasy and doughy, since the classes are not hands-on. NOSC has a retail outlet as well: the **Louisiana General Store,** where you can buy a variety of New Orleans and regional food items. **Gumbo Ya Ya** has gift baskets of Louisiana foods, as does **Louisiana Products.** In the Garden District, stop by the **Big Fisherman**—a corner fish market where neighborhood folk go for their seafood—to order fresh fish for shipping.

Flea and vintage... Locals love to hang out at the **Community Flea Market** at the Old Farmers' Market, where tables and bins are loaded with all manner of items for sale. You can pick up Mardi Gras beads and doubloons (aluminum coins tossed from Carnival floats); jazz records, CDs, and tapes; stuffed toys; houseplants; maybe a fringed lampshade or even a fringed flapper dress from somebody's attic. The **Old Farmers' Market** itself is in rickety open-air sheds, where farmers have been bringing just-picked produce and fruit for about 200 years.

If you prefer fashion to fresh fruit and antiques, you should check out the city's vintage shops. Most of them are spread out on Magazine Street, and they provide a respite for fashionistas underwhelmed by the couture at Lord & Taylor and Macy's. You'll find accessories, jewelry, and all manner of clothing from the '20s through the '80s. **Retro Active** is packed with chic accessories and dresses from the '30s through the '60s. **Funky Monkey** sells '50s to '80s stuff to cool college students. You can find more upscale wear at **Miss Claudia's**, including '40s and '50s ballgowns, suits, and tuxedos—some straight from the (old) racks and never worn. **Trashy Diva** lives up to its name with vintage, "new vintage" (newly made from retro fabrics), and a special array of fancy corsets, which we're guessing are not conducive to dining on po'boys and banana Fosters. Most of these shops are also handy for Halloween and Mardi Gras.

Exotic and erotic... You won't have any trouble at all finding the erotic. Just walk down Bourbon Street and look at all the X-rated undies and unmentionables displayed in shop windows. What you see is what you get—all are of the same sleazy quality, and the shop owners are used to tittering tourists who gawk at the merchandise but never buy. **Second Skin Leather** is a bit off the beaten track (though still in the Quarter), but it delivers its exotica—leather, latex, and "sexual hardware"—with a welcome glint of humor.

The sounds of music... You can't talk about where to buy New Orleans music without first discussing where to hear it. Of course the clubs are the best place. But you can also listen to it all day long on the city's own **WWOZ FM 90.7.** It's *the* local jazz and heritage station and it will turn you on to so much more than you'll hear in a club on a single night. If you really want to expose yourself to New Orleans's astonishing collection of artists—besides Jazz Fest—this is the best way. Virtually everything that plays on 'OZ, as locals lovingly call the station, is sold at the **Louisiana Music Factory,** a divey old shop in the Quarter. The Music Factory especially rocks during Jazz Fest, when jam sessions are a featured attraction. The **Palm Court Jazz Café,** owned by George and Nina Buck, is a great place for dinner accompanied by live traditional jazz (see Dining). George is the founder of GHB Records and several other labels, all of which carry a formidable roster of jazz artists playing a variety of jazz sub-genres. His website, **www.jazzology.com,** is a thrill to look at, especially when you see some of the ancient recordings he has and realize you can actually purchase them on CD. Do not miss George's stuff. If you stop by **Preservation Hall** to hear the music, you'll probably have to wait in the carriageway, the whole purpose of which is to encourage you to browse through the bins for records and tapes of all the jazz legends who perform, or have performed, here. If you can't find what you're looking for in the local stores, all is certainly not lost. **Virgin Megastore** and **Tower Records & Video** both have mammoth outlets in the French Quarter.

Book nooks... In the Quarter, **Beckham's Bookshop** has been going strong for more than 25 years, its shelves sagging with thousands of used books. The **Librairiè** is a branch of Beckham's that just stays open a little later. Both are generally crowded with shoppers thumbing through old treasures, some of which sell for only a buck or two. Another great stop for used books is **Crescent City Books,** which specializes in scholarly and antiquarian books. With two stories for book browsing, it has a trove of high-quality art and philosophy tomes, including a Petrarch from 1550. Their fiction section is not bad either. Perhaps the city's most atmospheric bookstore is **Faulkner House Books,** on the ground floor of the apartment building in which William Faulkner wrote his first novel, *A Soldier's Pay;* green shutters open on to the cracked flagstones of

Pirate's Alley. The staff here is helpful, knowledgeable, and tactful enough to let you browse for hours undisturbed. Uptown, the **Maple Street Book Shop, DeVille Books and Prints,** and the **Garden District Book Shop** are all locally owned. Maple Street's Rhoda Faust is a veritable guru among local book lovers, known for helping readers locate hard-to-find books. The Garden District Book Shop's owner Britton Trice publishes his own limited editions of prominent local writers, including Anne Rice and Richard Ford.

Dolls to ooh and aah over... If you're a collector—and collectible dolls are a big thing down here—there are three places to head for. At **Oh, Susannah,** the exquisite dolls are too pricey to play with, but the play dolls won't break the bank. About 45-minutes out of the city, in lovely old Ponchatoula, is **Boyer Antiques & Doll Shop,** which is a doll museum but also sells exceptional antique items and restored dolls and dollhouses. You could really set aside a day to spend cruising Ponchatoula's main street, which is filled with fabulous shops carrying all manner of antiques and vintage items. Back in town, doll lovers never miss **The Ginja Jar,** known for its wonderful bisque dolls. The **Little Toy Shoppe**—which, despite its name, is a large toy store—includes in its wide selection some lovely porcelain dolls and creations by name dollmakers Madame Alexander and Peggy Nisbet.

A tip of the hat... Folks down here tend to wear hats a lot, especially Panama hats. Custom-made ladies' hats—the sort Princess Di wore so well, with ribbons, bows, and frilly froufrous—can be found at **Yvonne LaFleur,** a Riverbend shop that also carries sportswear, formal gowns, and bridal gowns. The same kinds of smart chapeaux, in the shop windows at **Fleur de Paris,** practically stop traffic on Royal Street. Local hatmakers make clever little novelty hats for women that you can find at the **Little Shop of Fantasy,** a pocket-sized boutique in the French Quarter. In-the-know Orleanian men go straight to long-established **Meyer the Hatter** in the CBD.

For your voodoo to-do... Do not be fooled by films such as *Angel Heart*—you're unlikely to run across any blood-letting voodoo rites down here. There are an estimated

20,000 voodoo practitioners in New Orleans, but they consider it a religion and not a black magic cult. (Occasionally someone will stage a cleansing ritual to publicly chase out bad spirits, but you can bet that's done as much for the P.R. value as anything else.) Several shops in town cater to the tourists' curiosity about voodoo (or hoodoo, as it's sometimes called)—foremost among them is the **New Orleans Historic Voodoo Museum,** which takes itself (and the tourist dollar) very seriously indeed. It displays and sells gris-gris (pronounced gree-gree, and meaning voodoo charms) and various potions and powders. **Sideshow** doesn't deal in voodoo, but it has an offbeat theme: freaks. The store carries and purveys the strange and the curious, from taxidermied animals and unicorn skulls to tarot cards and ouija boards. Go and discover your inner weirdo.

Picking up the scent... New Orleans is home to a couple of very old-line perfumers, the oldest being **Bourbon French Parfum.** This tiny place will sell you a fragrance or custom-blend one just for you. Let them anoint you with a sample of Kus Kus, the very first scent created when the store was founded in 1843. A mere babe compared to Bourbon French Parfum—and with a much less friendly staff—**Hové Parfumeur** is the retail outlet for a New Orleans–based mail-order company that was founded in 1931. Although it's in a historic 19th-century Creole house, the place has about as much character as—well, as a mail-order catalog.

Really cooking... Almost all of the top-name chefs have produced a cookbook or two, among them Paul Prudhomme, Emeril Lagasse, and Alex Patout. There are tables full of local cookbooks at gift shops like **Aunt Sally's Praline Shop,** as well as at the **Maple Street Book Shop** uptown, and the **Garden District Book Shop.**

Dressed to the nines... In a city where "costume" is a verb and cross-dressing an art form, you don't have to wait for Carnival to don outrageous garb. Only the tourists will do double-takes; we natives are accustomed to the costumed characters who roam around the Quarter. The clothes, hats, and bags at **Violets** are delicious copies of those from the Twenties and Thirties—fringed dresses, beaded bags, and such. For fun, trendy finds from tees to sunglasses, head to **ah-ha** on Magazine Street. And if you want to look like a million bucks (and have a million bucks), hit the ritzy **Angelique** boutique. At **Fifi Mahony's** you can shop for Urban Decay and Ben Nye makeup, and find a fabulous wig. **MGM Costume Rentals** and **Broadway Bound** sell as well as rent costumes, ranging from ape suits to Scarlett O'Hara–style gowns.

Map 16: French Quarter Shopping

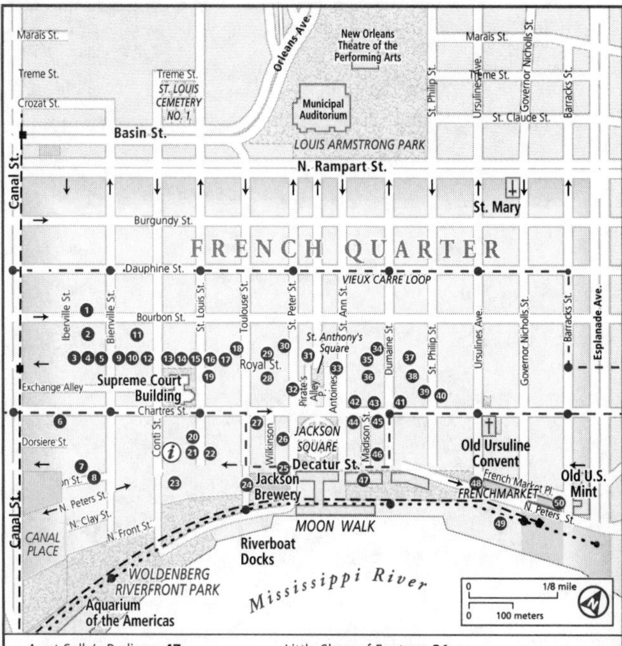

Aunt Sally's Pralines **47**
Beckham's Bookshop **8**
Bourbon French Parfums **42**
Brass Monkey **4**
Coghlan Galleries **18**
Community Flea Market **50**
Crafty Louisianians **40**
Crescent City Books **6**
Dixon & Harris **5**
Faulkner House Books **32**
Fifi Mahony's **38**
Fleur de Paris **33**
French Antique Shop **3**
French Market **49**
The Ginja Jar **29**
Gumbo Ya Ya **1**
Hove Parfumeur **36**
Ida Manheim Antiques **14**
The Idea Factory **45**
Jack Sutton **10**
Jackson Brewery **24**
James H. Cohen & Sons **15**
Keil's Antiques **12**
Le Petit Soldier Shop **19**
Librairie **35**
Little Shop of Fantasy **21**
Little Toy Shoppe **46**
Louisiana General Store **22**
Louisiana Music Factory **7**
Lucullus **27**
M.S. Rau **28**
Mirror Mirror **37**
Moss Antiques **13**
New Orleans Historic Voodoo Museum **34**
New Orelans School of Cooking **20**
Oh, Susannah **26**
Old Farmer's Market **48**
Preservation Hall **30**
Rodrigue Studios **31**
Rothchild's Antiques **2**
Royal Antiques **9**
Rumors **17**
Second Skin Leather **39**
Sideshow **41**
Tower Records **23**
Trashy Diva **43**
Violet's **44**
Virgin Megastore **25**
Waldhorn & Adler **11**
Wellington & Co. **16**

(i) Information
Riverwalk streetcar route/stops
Vieux Carre loop route/stops
Canal streetcar route/stops

Map 17: Uptown Shopping

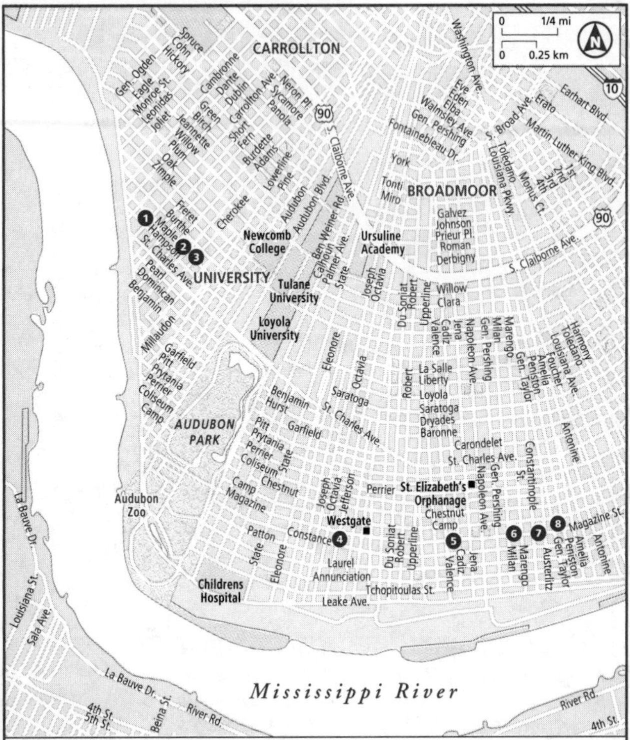

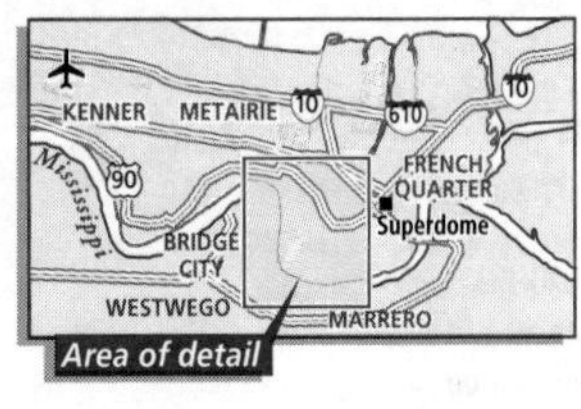

Angelique/Victoria's **2**
Jon Antiques **5**
Lucullus **7**
Maple St. Books **3**
Mignon Faget **8**
Miss Claudia's **6**
Retro Active **4**
Yvonne LaFleur **1**

The Index

Adler's (p. 174) CBD In business since 1898, this elegant jewelry store glitters with diamonds, emeralds, and other expensive gems.... *Tel 504/523-5292, 800/925-7912. www.adlersjewelry.com. 722 Canal St. Mon–Sat 10am–5:30pm.*

See Map 15 on p. 166.

ah-ha (p. 180) UPTOWN If you like Urban Outfitters, you'll be at home in this trendy teens' and women's boutique. Its recently renovated and expanded space is a major improvement from its formerly minuscule digs.... *Tel 504/269-2442. 3119 Magazine St. Mon–Sat 11am–6pm.*

See Map 15 on p. 166.

Angelique (p. 180) UPTOWN A recent addition to the upscale scene, this self-declared "shabby chic" boutique carries everything from T-shirts to dressy duds. They share space with Victoria's, a shoe place, for one-stop shopping. Even if you can't afford the clothes, don't miss the tents that double as dressing rooms.... *Tel 504/866-1092. 7725 Maple St. Mon–Sat 10am–6pm.*

See Map 17 on p. 182.

Antiques and Things (p. 173) UPTOWN Come here for imported mid-20th-century modern vintage furnishings, art, lighting, and prints.... *Tel 504/897-9466. 2855 Magazine St. Mon–Sat 10am–5pm.*

See Map 15 on p. 166.

Aunt Sally's Praline Shop (p. 175) FRENCH QUARTER You can watch the candymakers stirring up batches of pralines and buy boxes to take home. The shop has all sorts of souvenir items, including chicory-laced New Orleans coffee and beignet mix.... *Tel 504/524-3373. www.auntsallys.com. 810 Decatur St. Daily 8am–8pm.*

See Map 16 on p. 181.

Beckham's Bookshop (p. 177) FRENCH QUARTER This creaky old three-story bookstore, a French Quarter fixture for more than 25 years, overflows with secondhand and rare books.... *Tel 504/522-9875. 228 Decatur St. Daily 10am–6pm.*

See Map 16 on p. 181.

Big Fisherman (p. 175) UPTOWN This corner fish market prepares very fresh Louisiana seafood to go—shrimp, crawfish, blue crabs, speckled trout, whatever's in season—at reasonable prices.... *Tel 504/897-9907. www.bigfishermanseafood.com. 3301 Magazine St. Mon–Thurs 10am–7pm, Fri 10am–7:30pm, Sat 10am–7pm, Sun 10am–6pm.*

See Map 15 on p. 166.

Blackamoor (p. 173) WAREHOUSE/ARTS DISTRICT The stock here includes antique furniture and porcelain, as well as Asian art and antiques.... *Tel 504/523-7786. www.blackamoor.com. 600 Julia St. Mon–Sat 10:30am–4:30pm and by appointment.*

See Map 15 on p. 166.

Bourbon French Parfums (p. 179) FRENCH QUARTER Your wildest perfume dreams can be fulfilled in this tiny shop carrying scores of fragrances with seductive names. The shop was founded in 1843 (on Bourbon St., hence the name).... *Tel 504/522-4480. www.neworleansperfume.com. 815 Royal St. Daily 9am–7pm.*

See Map 16 on p. 181.

Boyer Antiques & Doll Shop (p. 178) PONCHATOULA Toy lovers will adore the antique dolls, doll restorations, and small antiques to be found here. There's even an impressive antique doll museum for connoisseurs.... *Tel 985/370-0804, 800/522-4513. 157 W. Pine St., Ponchatoula, LA 70454. Mon–Fri 10am–5pm. Hours vary on weekends; call ahead.*

Brass Monkey (p. 174) FRENCH QUARTER The focus here is on brass and brass-trimmed items. Limoges porcelain boxes and antique walking sticks are specialties.... *Tel 504/561-0688. 235 Royal St., French Quarter. Daily 9am–5pm.*

See Map 16 on p. 181.

Broadway Bound (p. 180) CBD If MGM Costume Rentals (see below) is fresh out of fangs and capes, or low on boas, tiaras, and scepters, dance on over to Broadway Bound, this costume-loving city's second-tier rent-a-costume emporium. Browsing is a kick, even if you don't buy anything.... *Tel 504/821-1000. 2737 Canal St. Mon–Sat 9:30am–5pm.*

See Map 15 on p. 166.

Canal Place (p. 169) FRENCH QUARTER This tiny downtown mall has three levels of stores: Saks Fifth Avenue, Laura Ashley, Gucci, Ann Taylor, Williams-Sonoma, and Brooks Brothers, and about 40 other upscale tenants. The third level has a food court; four first-run, art house movie theaters; and the Southern Rep Theatre (see Entertainment).... *Tel 504/522-9200. www.theshopsatcanalplace.com. 333 Canal St. Mall open Mon–Sat 10am–7pm, Sun noon–6pm.*

See Map 15 on p. 166.

Charbonnet & Charbonnet (p. 174) UPTOWN As well as selling English and Irish country antiques, this store has an in-house cabinet shop for making customized furnishings using components from razed houses and buildings.... *Tel 504/891-9948. www.charbonnetantiques.com. 2728 Magazine St. Mon–Sat 9am–5pm.*

See Map 15 on p. 166.

Coghlan Galleries (p. 174) FRENCH QUARTER Statuary, fountains, and charming garden ornaments—winged cherubs, tiny lambs, gargoyles, all carved by regional artisans—are displayed in a peaceful courtyard.... *Tel 504/525-8550. 710 Toulouse St. Daily 11am–5pm.*

See Map 16 on p. 181.

Community Flea Market (p. 169) FRENCH QUARTER Clothes, books, records, jewelry, and trinkets, as well as furniture, are sold by vendors in this outdoor flea market spread beside the Old Farmers' Market.... *Tel 504/596-3420. 1235 N. Peters St. Daily 7am–7pm.*

See Map 16 on p. 181.

Crafty Louisianians (p. 174) FRENCH QUARTER You'll find an assortment of Louisiana handicrafts here, including lots of folk-art dolls.... *Tel 504/528-3094. www.craftylousianians.com. 613 St. Philip St. Daily 11am–5:30pm.*

See Map 16 on p. 181.

Creole Delicacies (p. 175) FRENCH QUARTER/CBD The main draw is the pralines, but gift packages of spices, rémoulade sauce, and hot sauces are sold here, too. The Cookin' Cajun Cooking School (you should pardon the redundancy) is conducted at the company's Riverwalk outlet.... *French Quarter: Tel 525-9508; www.cookincajun.com; 533 St. Ann St.; daily 9am–5pm. CBD: Tel 504/523-6425; Branch 1 Poydras St., 116 Riverwalk; Mon–Sat 10am–9pm, Sun 9:30am–7pm.*

See Map 15 on p. 166.

Crescent City Books (p. 177) FRENCH QUARTER This two-story haven for antiquarian books is known for its high-quality stock, from leaves of an illuminated medieval book of hours to a tome penned by Petrarch in 1550. The store offers hours of riveting browsing.... *Tel 504/524-4997. 204 Chartres St. Mon–Wed 10am–6:30pm, Thurs–Sat 10am–7:30pm, Sun 11am–5pm.*

See Map 16 on p. 181.

DeVille Books and Prints (p. 178) CBD This locally owned shop carries regional books, guidebooks, cookbooks, maps, posters, and prints.... *Tel 504/525-1846. www.devillebooksandprints.com. 344 Carondelet St. Mon–Fri 9:30am–5:30pm.*

See Map 15 on p. 166.

Dixon & Harris (p. 173) FRENCH QUARTER All 20,000 square feet of this huge emporium are filled with antiques from the 18th to 19th centuries, estate jewelry, antique rugs, and European oil paintings.... *Tel 504/524-0282, 800/848-5148. 237 Royal St. Mon–Sat 9am–5:30pm, Sun 10am–5pm.*

See Map 16 on p. 181.

Faulkner House Books (p. 177) FRENCH QUARTER Located in the building in which William Faulkner wrote his first book, this shop specializes in that author's works and in books by other Southern writers.... *Tel 504/524-2940. 624 Pirate's Alley. Daily 10am–6pm.*

See Map 16 on p. 181.

Fifi Mahony's (p. 180) FRENCH QUARTER A trendy place indeed, this little shop has the very latest in false eyelashes and green wigs, plus cosmetics by Urban Decay, Ben Nye, Tony & Tina, and others.... *Tel 504/525-4343. www.fifi-mahony.com. 934 Royal St. Sun–Fri noon–6pm, Sat 11am–7pm.*

See Map 16 on p. 181.

Fleur de Paris (p. 178) FRENCH QUARTER One of the city's most elegant haute couture boutiques—with haute prices to match—Fleur de Paris features its own private label collection of fine women's streetwear, tailored suits, cocktail dresses, formal gowns, and hats.... *Tel 504/525-1899. 712 Royal St. Daily 10am–6pm.*

See Map 16 on p. 181.

French Antique Shop (p. 173) FRENCH QUARTER Among the fine 18th- and 19th-century French and Continental furnishings in this lovely store are chandeliers, mirrors, marble mantels, porcelains, and bronze statues.... *Tel 504/524-9861. www.gofrenchantiques.com. 225 Royal St. Mon–Fri 9am–4:45pm, Sat 9:30am–4:30pm.*

See Map 16 on p. 181.

French Market (p. 169) FRENCH QUARTER A former Native American trading post, this restored seven-block complex of shops, restaurants, and open-air cafes includes the long-popular hangout Café du Monde and the Old Farmers' Market (see below), both of which are open 24 hours.... *Tel 504/522-2621. www.frenchmarket.org. 1008 N. Peters St. Daily 9am–6pm. F & M Produce and Café du Monde open 24 hours.*

See Map 16 on p. 181.

Funky Monkey (p. 176) FRENCH QUARTER College-age hipsters, male and female, flock to this zooey little spot on Magazine. Nothing earlier than the '50s; '60s go-go dresses, '70s hippie garb, '80s band shirts, too. During Halloween and Mardi Gras you can get costumes, makeup and wigs here.... *Tel 504/899-5587. 3127 Magazine St. Mon–Sat 11am–6pm, Sun 11am–5pm.*

See Map 15 on p. 166.

Garden District Book Shop (p. 178) UPTOWN Britton Trice and company have encyclopedic knowledge about book-related subjects, especially regional and hard-to-find volumes. The store is tucked into The Rink, a small mall in the Garden District.... *Tel 504/895-2266. 2727 Prytania St. Mon–Sat 10am–6pm, Sun 11am–5pm.*

See Map 15 on p. 166.

The Ginja Jar (p. 178) FRENCH QUARTER The bisque dolls here are top-quality, handcrafted by national and local artists. They have some marvelous dollhouses, antique walking sticks, and much more.... *Tel 504/523-7643, 800/259-7643. 611 Royal St. Daily 10am–5pm.*

See Map 16 on p. 181.

Gumbo Ya Ya (p. 175) FRENCH QUARTER Pralines, fudge, spices, and homemade sauces are among the take-home items at this singular Cajun food store.... *Tel 504/522-7484, 800/GUMBO. www.gumboyaya.com. 219 Bourbon St. Daily 9am–midnight.*

See Map 16 on p. 181.

Hové Parfumeur (p. 179) FRENCH QUARTER This manufacturer's retail outlet, flagship of a long-established catalog company (what kind of people shop for perfume by mail?), is a bit sterile; expect scented soaps, sachets, and perfumes with names such as Kiss in the Dark and Pirate's Gold.... *Tel 504/525-7827. www.hoveparfumeur.com. 824 Royal St. Mon–Sat 10am–5pm.*

See Map 16 on p. 181.

Ida Manheim Antiques (p. 173) FRENCH QUARTER The local agent for Boehm Birds, Ida Manheim Antiques also has an extensive selection of antique European and Oriental furnishings and decorative art; 17th- and 18th-century English, French, and Continental furniture; and fine 18th- and 19th-century paintings and porcelains.... *Tel 504/568-1901, 888/627-5969. www.idamanheimantiques.com. 409 Royal St. Mon–Sat 9am–5pm.*

See Map 16 on p. 181.

The Idea Factory (p. 174) FRENCH QUARTER Kenny Ford carves wonderful wooden jewelry boxes, paddle wheelers, alligators, roadster convertibles, signs, toy dump trucks and fire engines, miniature working mantel clocks, and scores of other items, from the large to the little.... *Tel 504/524-5195, 800/524–IDEA. www.ideafactoryneworleans.com. 838 Chartres St. Mon–Sat 10am–6pm, Sun 10am–5pm.*

See Map 16 on p. 181.

Jack Sutton Antique and Jewelry Company (p. 173) FRENCH QUARTER Men's gift items like vintage tools and nautical instruments are the specialty at this elegant antiques store, but there are also glass cases lined with silver boxes and inkwells, as well as small, intricately carved ivory figures and fine jewelry.... *Tel 504/522-0555. 315 Royal St. Mon–Sat 10am–5:30pm, Sun 11am–5pm.*

See Map 16 on p. 181.

Jackson Brewery (p. 169) FRENCH QUARTER Three large indoor pedestrian malls in the French Quarter are run by the Jackson Brewery Corporation. The flagship Jax Brewery mall occupies a historic 19th-century building where Jax beer was once brewed. A three-level Virgin Megastore is all that remains. Adjacent is the Millhouse with tourist shops and a food court. Two blocks toward Canal St. (400 block of N. Peters St., between St. Louis and Conti sts.), the Marketplace contains Tower Records and Video, the Hard Rock Cafe, and not much else.... *Tel 504/566-7601. www.jacksonbrewery.com. 600 Decatur St. Mon–Sat 9am–8pm, Sun 10am–7pm.*

See Map 16 on p. 181.

James H. Cohen & Sons (p. 174) FRENCH QUARTER A wooden Indian guards the front door of this large, fascinating store, open since 1898. Antique weapons and flags hang on the walls, and glass cases are filled with rare Confederate currency, Frederic Remington bronzes, Civil War cannonballs, and much, much more.... *Tel 504/522-3305, 800/535-1853. 437 Royal St. Daily 9:30am–5:30pm.*

See Map 16 on p. 181.

Jon Antiques (p. 173) UPTOWN Well deserving its fine reputation, Mrs. Jon Strauss's antiques shop deals in 18th- and 19th-century English, French, and Continental furniture, books, mirrors, lamps, porcelains, and tea caddies.... *Tel 504/899-4482. www.jonantiques.com. 4605 Magazine St. Mon–Sat 10am–5pm.*

See Map 17 on p. 182.

Judy at the Rink (p. 174) GARDEN DISTRICT You'll smile just walking into this whimsical, bright gift shop. Lamps in crazy colors and designs are an icon here (the nun is a personal favorite), along with pottery, metalwork, and blown-glass pieces which add to the artsy flair.... *Tel 504/891-7018. 2727 Prytania St. Mon–Sat 10am–5pm.*

See Map 15 on p. 166.

Keil's Antiques (p. 173) FRENCH QUARTER Since 1899, Keil's has specialized in French and English antiques, including jewelry, marble mantels, gold-leaf mirrors, and chandeliers.... *Tel 504/522-4552. www.keilsantiques.com. 325 Royal St. Mon–Sat 9am–5pm.*

See Map 16 on p. 181.

Kohlmaier and Kohlmaier (p. 173) UPTOWN Antique furniture reproductions and custom upholstery are the specialties. Ruppert Kohlmaier, Jr.'s cabinetmakers create the period furnishings sold here.... *Tel 504/895-6394. 1018 Harmony St. Mon–Fri 8am–5pm, Sat 8:30am–12:30pm.*

See Map 15 on p. 166.

Le Petit Soldier Shop (p. 174) FRENCH QUARTER You'll marvel at the miniature toy soldiers here, with fine detailing in uniforms, weapons, and horses.... *Tel 504/523-7741. www.lepetitsoldier shop.com. 528 Royal St. Mon–Sat 10am–4pm.*

See Map 16 on p. 181.

Librairiè (p. 177) FRENCH QUARTER A branch of the venerable Beckham's Bookshop (see above), this, too, is a big, musty old place with racks, stacks, and shelves of used books. The small staff will not exactly overwhelm you with offers of assistance, but with time and patience you may find some old postcards and out-of-print treasures.... *Tel 504/525-4837. 823 Chartres St. Daily 10am–6pm.*

See Map 16 on p. 181.

Little Shop of Fantasy (p. 175) FRENCH QUARTER Artist-owned and operated, this small store features exotic handmade masks of leather, papier-mâché, feathers, you name it. If you're playing dress-up, they've got costume hats, boas, tiaras, and cloaks galore.... *Tel 504/529-4243. www.littleshopoffantasy.com. 517 St. Louis St. Mon–Tues and Thurs–Sat 11am–6pm; Sun 1–6pm.*

See Map 16 on p. 181.

Little Toy Shoppe (p. 178) FRENCH QUARTER This large store is the place to go for toys of all types—tops, puzzles, kites, toy airplanes, and blocks—and it has an exceptional collection of porcelain bisque dolls, dressed in organdy, velvets, and lace.... *Tel 504/522-6588, 800/432-7080. 900 Decatur St. Sun–Thurs 9am–7pm, Fri–Sat 9am–8pm.*

See Map 16 on p. 181.

Louisiana General Store (p. 175) FRENCH QUARTER The retail outlet at the New Orleans School of Cooking is full of south Louisiana condiments, Cajun spices, rice, cookbooks, T-shirts, and aprons.... *Tel 504/525-2665. www.nosoc.com. 524 St. Louis St. Mon–Fri 10am–5pm.*

See Map 16 on p. 181.

Louisiana Music Factory (p. 177) FRENCH QUARTER The focus here is on jazz, Cajun, zydeco, R&B, and other south Louisiana sounds.... *Tel 504/586-1094. www.louisianamusicfactory.com. 210 Decatur St. Mon–Sat 10am–7pm, Sun 11am–7pm.*

See Map 16 on p. 181.

Louisiana Products (p. 175) CBD True to its name, this shop carries a plethora of gift baskets filled with chicory coffee, beignet mix, Cajun spices, and other goodies.... *Tel 504/529-1666. 618 Julia St., near Lafayette Sq. Mon–Fri 7:15am–5:30pm.*

See Map 15 on p. 166.

Lucullus (p. 173) FRENCH QUARTER/UPTOWN Proprietor Patrick Dunne named his gallery for Lucius Licinius Lucullus, who was a wealthy Roman general famous for his lavish banquets. The feast here includes 17th-, 18th-, and 19th-century culinary antiques, including cookware, silverware, china, furnishings, and objets d'art.... *French Quarter: Tel 504/528-9620; 610 Chartres St.; June–Aug, Mon–Sat 9:30am–5pm. Uptown: Tel 504/894-0500; 3932 Magazine St.; June–Aug, Mon–Sat 10am–5pm.*

See Map 16 on p. 181.
See Map 17 on p. 182.

Macon Riddle (p. 171) She's a shopping consultant whose business motto is "Let's Go Antiquing," and can be engaged for half- and full-day antiquing excursions replete with expert, up-to-the-minute advice and commentary.... *Tel 504/899-3027. www.neworleansantiquing.com. By appointment.*

Maple Street Book Shop (p. 178) UPTOWN Owned by Orleanian Rhoda Faust, there's the original store on Maple Street and a fine children's bookstore next door. These well-stocked stores are funky, fun, and, well—literary.... *Tel 504/866-4916. www.maplestreetbookshop.com. 7523 Maple St. Mon–Sat 9am–9pm, Sun 10am–6pm.*

See Map 17 on p. 182.

Masks & Make Believe (p. 175) CBD The vivid creations here range from specialty Mardi Gras beads to small ceramic wall decorations to feathery eye-masks to rubber full-face masks of George W. Bush.... *Tel 504/522-6473. www.masksandmakebelieve.com. 1 Poydras St., #122 Riverwalk. Mon–Sat 10am–9pm, Sun 11am–7pm.*

See Map 15 on p. 166.

Meyer the Hatter (p. 178) CBD In business since 1894, the Hatter has Panama straws, Western Stetsons, fine men's headwear, Kangol caps, and even major league baseball caps.... *Tel 504/525-1048, 800/882-HATS. www.meyerthehatter.com. 120 St. Charles Ave. Mon–Sat 10am–5:45pm.*

See Map 15 on p. 166.

MGM Costume Rentals (p. 180) LOWER GARDEN DISTRICT A favorite stop for locals who wish to be incognito, it has thousands of costumes from the old MGM studio.... *Tel 504/581-3999. 1617 St. Charles Ave. Tues, Wed, and Fri 9:30am–5pm; Sat until 5pm.*

See Map 15 on p. 166.

Mignon Faget (p. 174) CBD/UPTOWN Mignon Faget finds inspiration in her native New Orleans for the jewelry she makes of 14K gold, silver, and bronze d'or—imaginative earrings, cuff links, tie clasps, and bracelets.... *CBD: Tel 504/524-2973; www.mignonfaget.com; Canal Place, 1st level; Mon–Sat 10am–7pm, Sun* *noon–6pm. Uptown: Tel 504/891-2005; 3801 Magazine St.; Mon–Sat 10am–6pm.*

See Map 15 on p. 166.
See Map 17 on p. 182.

Mirror, Mirror (p. 173) FRENCH QUARTER The mother and daughter-in-law team of Betty and Ellie Fowler are out to convince the world that these looking glasses are artistic as much as they are functional. They've even got mirrors made of architectural pieces like church windows and transoms. Every unique piece in the store is made of—well, what the name says.... *Tel 504/ 566-1990. www.mirrorx2.com. 933 Royal St. Mon–Sat 10am–5pm, Sun noon–5pm.*

See Map 16 on p. 181.

Miss Claudia's Vintage Clothing and Costumes (p. 176) FRENCH QUARTER Miss Claudia deals in vintage, some already worn, some bought from other stores' racks that were never worn. They have clothes from Garden District doyennes, '40s to '50s ball gowns and suits worn only once, tuxes and dinner jackets. Also, '60s to '80s stuff, a few things from '10s and '20s, a large men's section, Halloween and Mardi Gras costumes, plus accessories—hankies, gloves, hats, bow ties, and cuff links.... *Tel 504/897-6310. 4204 Magazine St. Mon–Sat 10am–5pm, Sun noon–5pm.*

See Map 17 on p. 182.

Moss Antiques (p. 173) FRENCH QUARTER Top-of-the-line antique jewelry, crystal chandeliers, and decorative arts are showcased in this handsome store.... *Tel 504/522-3981. 411 Royal St. Mon–Sat 9:30am–5pm.*

See Map 16 on p. 181.

M. S. Rau (p. 173) FRENCH QUARTER Royal Street's venerable antiques store specializes in American antiques, jewelry, music boxes, silver, porcelain, and glass.... *Tel 504/523-5660, 800/ 544-9440. www.rauantiques.com. 630 Royal St. Daily Mon–Sat 9am–5pm.*

See Map 16 on p. 181.

New Orleans Centre (p. 170) CBD Adjacent to the Superdome and the Hyatt Regency Hotel, this large and rambling modern mall's two biggest tenants are Macy's and Lord & Taylor. There are dozens of other shops (Gap, Foot Locker, and other national chains), as well as restaurants and a food court.... *Tel 504/ 568-0000. 1400 Poydras St. Mon–Sat 10am–8pm, Sun noon–6pm.*

See Map 15 on p. 166.

New Orleans Historic Voodoo Museum (p. 179) FRENCH QUARTER In the cramped front room of this only-in-New-Orleans institution, studiedly spooky-looking folk will chat to you about their religion and then sell you various powders, potions, and charms to ward off evil spirits, bring you true love, or make an enemy dead.... *Tel 504/581-3824. www.voodoomuseum.com. 724 Dumaine St. Daily 10am–dusk.*

See Map 16 on p. 181.

New Orleans School of Cooking (p. 175) FRENCH QUARTER Cooking demonstrations are held here; reservations are advised, and when you call, ask what's to be prepared—it may be an étouffée, jambalaya, shrimp Creole, or some other dish for which Louisiana is famous.... *Tel 504/525-2665, 800/237-4841. www.nosoc.com. 524 St. Louis St. Cooking demonstrations Mon–Sun 10am–1pm, Mon–Sat 2–4pm.*

See Map 16 on p. 181.

Oh, Susannah (p. 178) FRENCH QUARTER The shop's exquisite collection of one-of-a-kind old-fashioned dolls, as well as African American, Asian, and baby dolls, are all dressed in beautifully crafted clothing.... *Tel 504/586-8701. 518 St. Peter St. on Jackson Sq. Mon–Sat 10am–5:30pm, Sun 11am–5pm.*

See Map 16 on p. 181.

Old Farmers' Market (p. 169) FRENCH QUARTER Tumbledown open-air sheds house this almost always crowded fruit and vegetable market at the downriver end of the French Market (see above). Farmers have been bringing fresh produce here for around 200 years.... *Tel 504/596-3400. www.frenchmarket.org. 1235 N. Peter St. F & M Produce open 24 hours.*

See Map 16 on p. 181.

Preservation Hall (p. 177) FRENCH QUARTER Only open at night when the bands are playing, the Hall has several bins of records for sale by Preservation Hall veteran recording stars.... *Tel 504/522-2841, 800/946-JAZZ. www.preservationhall.com. 726 St. Peter St. Daily 8pm–midnight. Cover $5.*

See Map 16 on p. 181.

Retro Active (p. 176) CBD/FRENCH QUARTER Lotsa accessories: bakelite bangles, hats, purses. Mostly '30s to '60s stuff but other eras as well, plus women's gowns and men's jackets. Very small cramped space, but so tightly packed you could spend days here. Owner doesn't like you pawing all the stuff but can be helpful if you engage him and respect the merchandise.... *Tel 504/895-5054. 5418 Magazine St. 11am–6pm. Closed Sun, Wed.*

See Map 17 on p. 182.

RHINO (p. 174) CBD/FRENCH QUARTER The acronym stands for "Right Here In New Orleans," and all of the crafts in this nonprofit shop are indeed made right here. More than 80 artists create the furnishings, paintings, apparel, and decorative items. A very upscale place.... *CBD: Tel 504/523-7945; www.rhinocrafts.com; Canal Place, 333 Canal St.; Mon–Sat 10am–7pm, Sun noon–6pm.*

French Quarter: Tel 504/569-8191; 927 Royal St.; Mon–Sat 10am–6pm, Sun 11am–6pm.

See Map 15 on p. 166.

Riverwalk (p. 169) CBD A riverside mall that stretches from the foot of Poydras Street upriver to Julia Street, the Convention Center, and the Warehouse District, this complex has 200 or so shops and restaurants including Abercrombie & Fitch, Banana Republic, and The Sharper Image, as well as local stores like Yvonne LaFleur and Street Scenes, and a huge food court.... *Tel 504/522-1555. www.riverwalkmarketplace.com. 1 Poydras St. Mon–Sat 10am–9pm, Sun 11am–7pm.*

See Map 15 on p. 166.

Rodrigue Studios (p. 174) FRENCH QUARTER George Rodrigue's claim to great fame and immense fortune is his late terrier, immortalized by the Acadian painter as a mournful-looking, royal-blue dog with staring yellow eyes. Thousands of Blue Dogs have been sold worldwide, and several of them stare wistfully through the windows of this gallery.... *Tel 504/581-4244. www.georgerodrigue.com. 721 Royal St. Mon–Sat 10am–6pm, Sun noon–5pm.*

See Map 16 on p. 181.

Rothschild's Antiques (p. 173) FRENCH QUARTER This prestigious store handles antique English and French furniture, estate jewelry, crystal chandeliers, marble mantels, silver, and porcelain.... *Tel 504/523-5816. www.rothschildsantiques.com. 241 and 321 Royal St. 241 Royal St. open Mon–Sat 9:30am–5pm. 321 Royal St., variable hours; call ahead.*

See Map 16 on p. 181.

Royal Antiques (p. 173) Since 1899, this store has carried unusually high-quality 18th- and 19th-century traditional and country French and English furnishings, chandeliers, and brass and copper accessories.... *Tel 504/524-7033. www.royalantiques.com. 307–09 Royal St. Mon–Sat 9am–5pm.*

See Map 16 on p. 181.

Rumors (p. 175) FRENCH QUARTER Using leather, feathers, beads, and sequins, more than 30 artists create the delightful, very fantastical masks, silver, and hand-blown glass jewelry here.... *Tel 504/525-0292. www.rumorsno.com. 513 Royal St. Daily 9:30am–6pm.*

See Map 16 on p. 181.

Second Skin Leather (p. 176) FRENCH QUARTER "Purveyors of leather, latex, sexual hardware, and erotica for men and women," the shop proclaims, and it lives up to its claims in this Quarter side-street sexual emporium.... *Tel 504/561-8167. 521 St. Philip St. Mon–Sat 10am–10pm, Sun 10am–8pm.*

See Map 16 on p. 181.

Sideshow **(p. 179)** FRENCH QUARTER An homage to the old-fashioned, crazy, kitschy sideshow, this shop celebrates freaks in all their incarnations. Taxidermied two-headed ducks, a jack-a-lope, and unicorn skulls, along with sideshow canvases and posters, are on the block here. You'll find magic tricks, tarot cards, and other curios as well. Owned by former Night Court judge and local resident Harry Anderson and his wife Elizabeth.... *Tel 504/581-2012. 901 Chartres St. Thurs–Mon 11am–5:30pm.*

See Map 16 on p. 181.

Tower Records & Video **(p. 177)** FRENCH QUARTER Big, noisy, and bustling—what more needs to be said? Oh, except that their impressive stock of records, CDs, and stuff primarily includes New Orleans and regional artists.... *Tel 504/529-4411. The Marketplace, 408 N. Peters St. Daily 9am–midnight.*

See Map 16 on p. 181.

Trashy Diva **(p. 176)** FRENCH QUARTER This pair of boutiques started out as vintage only, but now sells vintage and new-vintage (designed by the owners in retro styles and fabrics). They also specialize in corsets, which brings them a wide and weird clientele. A bit pricey.... *829 Chartres St.: Tel 504/581-4555; daily 12-6pm; www.trashydiva.com. 2048 Magazine St.: Tel 504/299-8777; Mon–Sat 12–6pm, Sun 1–5pm.*

See Map 15 on p. 166.
See Map 16 on p. 181.

Violet's **(p. 179)** FRENCH QUARTER There are outfits here to swoon over. The clothing isn't vintage, but the reproductions of '20s and '30s embroidered gowns, befringed flapper outfits, and hand-beaded bags and shawls are simply wonderful. Violet's II and Jackie's are their teen components (tel 504/588-9894, 507 St. Anne St.; tel 504/588-9575, 528 St. Anne St.), where funky pants, cowboy hats, and jewels are the name of the game.... *Tel 504/569-0088. 808 Chartres St. Mon–Sun 10am–6pm.*

See Map 16 on p. 181.

Virgin Megastore **(p. 169)** FRENCH QUARTER It's here—and it's huge! Don't expect much in the way of character; it's all that's left of the mall. But, what? You were planning to marry the store? It's like a warehouse, full of records, tapes, CDs, books. Lots of stuff.... *Tel 504/671-8100. Jax Brewery. 620 Decatur St. Tues–Sat 10am–midnight, Mon 10am–12:30am.*

See Map 16 on p. 181.

Waldhorn & Adler **(p. 173)** FRENCH QUARTER The oldest store on Royal Street, Waldhorn's was established in 1881 and has been going strong ever since, selling an extensive collection of antique Art Deco jewelry and silver, and 18th- and 19th-century French and English furnishings.... *Tel 504/581-6379. www.waldhornadlers.com. 343 Royal St. Mon–Sat 10am–5pm.*

See Map 16 on p. 181.

Wellington & Company **(p. 175)** FRENCH QUARTER Large collections of antique, estate, and contemporary fine jewelry with a particular emphasis on Victorian, Edwardian, and Art Deco periods. They also have an excellent collection of framed paintings, etchings, antiques, and gifts.... *Tel 504/525-4855. 505 Royal St. Tues–Sat 9:30am–5pm, Sun 10am–4pm.*

See Map 16 on p. 181.

Yvonne LaFleur **(p. 178)** RIVERBEND New Orleans fashion-plate LaFleur carries a line of upmarket women's ready-to-wear; she also custom-designs hats, casualwear, party dresses, and wedding gowns. Nothing in this boutique is cheap, in any sense of the word.... *Tel 504/866-9666. www.yvonnelafleur.com. 8131 Hampson St. Mon–Sat 10am–6pm, Thurs until 8pm.*

See Map 17 on p. 182.

NIGH

TLIFE

6

Map 18: New Orleans Nightlife Orientation

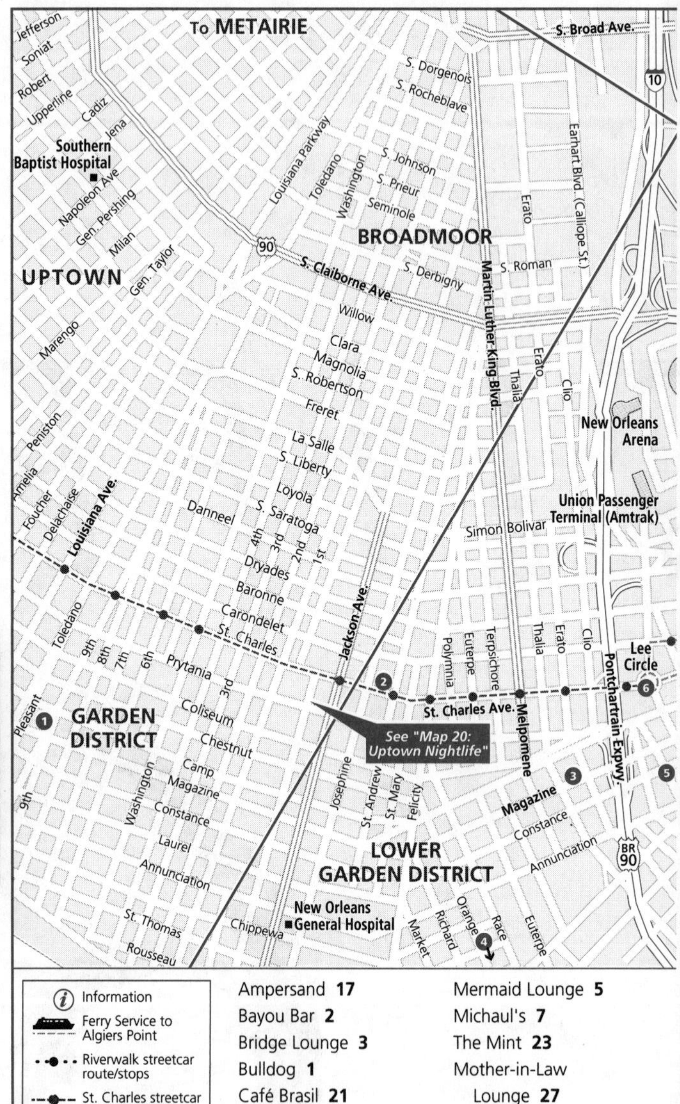

(i)	Information
	Ferry Service to Algiers Point
• - • -	Riverwalk streetcar route/stops
- - • - -	St. Charles streetcar route/stops
— ■ —	Canal streetcar route/stops
- - • - -	Vieux Carre loop route/stops

Ampersand **17**
Bayou Bar **2**
Bridge Lounge **3**
Bulldog **1**
Café Brasil **21**
Circle Bar **6**
Creole Queen **14**
dba **19**
The Howlin' Wolf **10**
Loft 523 **15**
Mermaid Lounge **5**
Michaul's **7**
The Mint **23**
Mother-in-Law Lounge **27**
Mulate's **11**
The Phoenix Bar **24**
Praline Connection **9**
R Bar **18**
Saturn Bar **26**

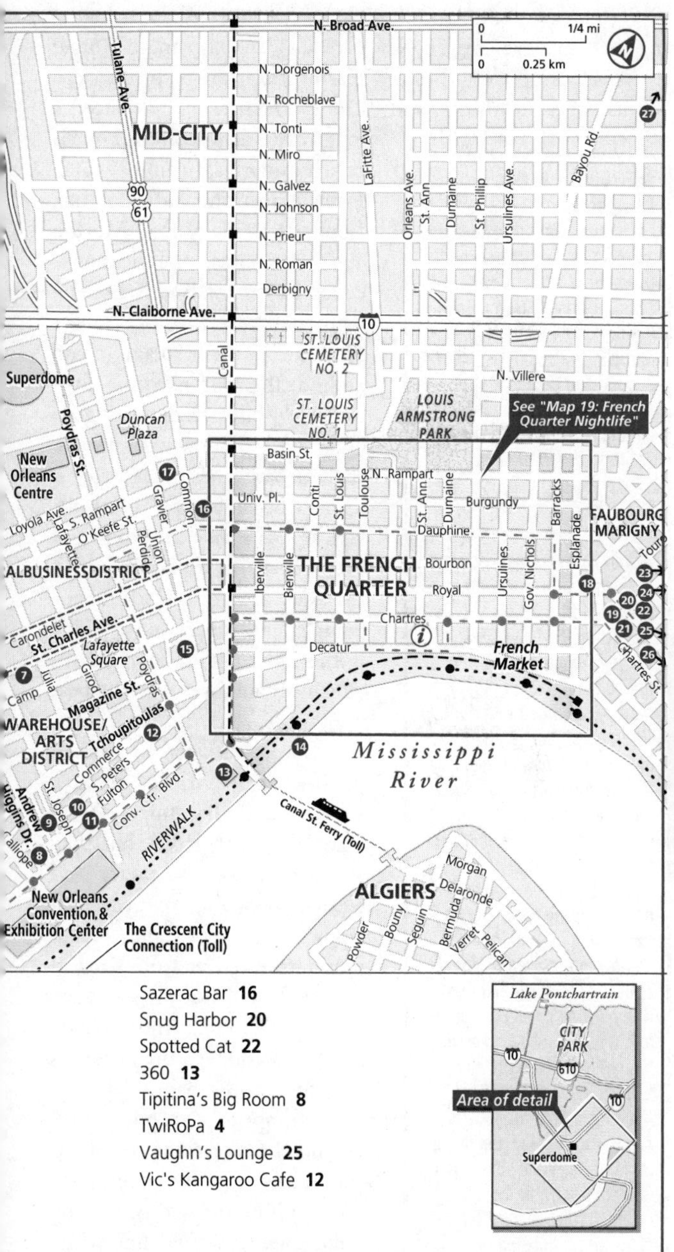

N. Broad Ave.
0 1/4 mi
0 0.25 km
N. Dorgenois
N. Rocheblave
N. Tonti
N. Miro
N. Galvez
N. Johnson
N. Prieur
N. Roman
Derbigny
N. Claiborne Ave.
Tulane Ave.
MID-CITY
90
61
10
LaFitte Ave.
Orleans Ave.
St. Ann
Dumaine
St. Phillip
Ursulines Ave.
Bayou Rd.
Canal
ST. LOUIS CEMETERY NO. 2
ST. LOUIS CEMETERY NO. 1
LOUIS ARMSTRONG PARK
N. Villere
See "Map 19: French Quarter Nightlife"
Superdome
Duncan Plaza
Poydras St.
New Orleans Centre
Basin St.
N. Rampart
Univ. Pl.
Conti
St. Louis
Toulouse
Burgundy
Dauphine
Barracks
Esplanade
FAUBOURG MARIGNY
Touro
Common
Gravier
Loyola Ave.
S. Rampart
O'Keefe St.
Lafayette
Perdido
Union
ALBUSINESSDISTRICT
Iberville
Bienville
THE FRENCH QUARTER
Bourbon
Royal
Ursulines
Gov. Nichols
Chartres
Decatur
French Market
Chartres St.
Carondelet
St. Charles Ave.
Lafayette Square
Camp
Julia
Girod
Poydras
Magazine St.
Tchoupitoulas
WAREHOUSE/ ARTS DISTRICT
Commerce
S. Peters
Fulton
Conv. Ctr. Blvd.
St. Joseph
Andrew Higgins Dr.
Calliope
RIVERWALK
Mississippi River
Canal St. Ferry (Toll)
New Orleans Convention & Exhibition Center
The Crescent City Connection (Toll)
ALGIERS
Morgan
Delaronde
Powder
Bouny
Seguin
Bermuda
Verret
Pelican
Sazerac Bar 16
Snug Harbor 20
Spotted Cat 22
360 13
Tipitina's Big Room 8
TwiRoPa 4
Vaughn's Lounge 25
Vic's Kangaroo Cafe 12
Lake Pontchartrain
CITY PARK
610
Area of detail
Superdome

Basic Stuff

One thing's for sure: You won't leave this town without knowing that jazz was born in New Orleans. No way can you forget it. Music is all over the city, blaring from dingy dives, sleek rooms, frilly riverboats, and casinos. The city has produced a long roster of world-class musical luminaries, among them Louis Armstrong, Fats Domino, Louis Prima, Jelly Roll Morton and, of course, the acknowledged originator, Buddy Bolden, who trilled the first riffs in the genre a century or so ago in and around the bordellos of Storyville. While jazzologists generally agree on how it all started, they debate the exact year it actually became "jazz." (Just like Orleanians—they love to bicker and split hairs, especially about the exact dates of historical happenings and superlatives: which is the oldest building in town, which restaurant serves the best rémoulade, etc.)

Locals also get all worked up over New Orleans funk, a sultry sound that mixes Afro-Caribbean with R&B, but they also get their clocks pretty well cleaned boogying to zydeco, a zippy soul mate of Cajun. Cajun music itself ranges from languid waltzes to red-hot jigs—zydeco is just red-hotter. And second-lining is second-nature here. (At jazz funerals, a hand-clapping, foot-stomping "second line" behind the musicians celebrates the release of the deceased's soul.) It is entirely possible, even preferable, to second-line without a funeral.

Storyville & the Blue Book

Local lore has it that in 1744 a French officer complained—or was that applauded?—that there were not 10 women of blameless character to be found in the colony. By most accounts, it seems that prostitution began to flourish almost as soon as the French settlers settled. Various means were employed to control it, all to no avail. Then, in 1897, a city alderman named Sidney Story introduced an ordinance that would restrict bordellos to a 20-block area behind the French Quarter. The legislation passed and, to the horror of the alderman, the neighborhood was dubbed "Storyville." Stories about the old red-light district abound in this legend-loving city—about the "sporting houses," the jazz musicians who played in the parlors (notably, Jelly Roll Morton), and the spasm bands (ragtag bands, often kids, using makeshift instruments) that played on the street corners. The Blue Book was a listing of all the houses and the girls who worked in them. Today, it's a pricey collector's item, selling in antiques stores for upward of $150. It's the only remaining trace of Storyville—the district was shut down in 1917 on orders of the United States Navy, and a housing project now sprawls over the site.

You may have heard of Bourbon Street. If not, welcome to the planet. The city's most famous street is virtually riddled with funky hole-in-the-wall music clubs where you can hear everything from karaoke to bagpipes. And jazz, of course. They're all lined up in a row, some of them with carny-type barkers out front drumming up trade. Sure, it's overrun with tourists, but Bourbon runs through a neighborhood—the French Quarter—which has some 5,000 residents, local people who work and play and cross-dress and belly up to bars, too. Neighborhood entertainers have names like the Neville Brothers, the Iguanas, Walter "Wolfman" Washington, Marva Wright, Charmaine Neville, the Meters, and Li'l Queenie, and you're damn right locals turn out to hear them. Outside the Quarter the music scene is not as concentrated. Except for a couple of pockets, notably in the Marigny, the Warehouse District, and the University area, you'll have to do your bar-hopping on wheels—streetcar or cab wheels, please. Sad to say, many locals think nothing of driving with a few drinks under their belts; all the more reason tourists should let someone else do the navigating.

The French Quarter has a highly visible gay community, with a pack of hopping bars to support the scene. The annual gay costume competition on Burgundy Street is a dazzling affair on Fat Tuesday. And you'll know you're not in Kansas anymore if you're anywhere in the French Quarter during Southern Decadence weekend—still known in other places as Labor Day weekend. The drag parade will knock your socks smack off your feet, and gay bars like Café Lafitte in Exile and the Golden Lantern have outrageous Easter Bonnet Contests.

You may question this city's reputation as a laid-back kind of town once you get a load of the locals working up a lather on a dime-sized dance floor. Orleanians are big on grungy dives, the grungier the better. The trick is to avoid slipping on all the "glow" dripping off faces onto the floor.

Of course, virtually none of the rules apply during Mardi Gras or Jazz Fest. During those events, thousands of people pour into New Orleans, a goodly portion of them headed for the French Quarter. Hours expand, prices skyrocket, and schedules change as the entire city gears up for the onslaught.

Sources

The editors of ***Gambit,*** a weekly newspaper, keep up to speed on the music scene. The paper is free and can be picked up at newsstands, grocery stores, and bookstores, as well as in some hotels and restaurants. ***Offbeat*** magazine, another freebie, offers news, views, and reviews of the hot and the not on the music and nightclub scene. Friday's ***Times-Picayune*** carries "Lagniappe," a tabloid section detailing the weekend's best bets, including a thorough listing of what's doing around town. And ***Ambush*** is a free, adults-only publication with news about gay and lesbian happenings. Tune in, too, to **WWOZ-90.7 FM,** a radio station devoted to playing local music and broadcasting local music calendars. In fact, "O-Z" as it's lovingly called by locals, should be your soundtrack whenever you're near a radio in the Big Easy. It is one sure way to get your fill of all the wonderful tunes and genres the city has to offer and it plays 24/7. It's a New Orleans institution.

By the way, schedules can change between the time the printed calendars are put together and the times of the performances, so always call ahead to double-check. And one more rule of thumb: At nearly all the clubs, you should add one hour to whatever time they say the band will take the stage, especially if it's not the first band in the lineup.

Liquor Laws & Drinking Hours

New Orleans's nightlife happens around the clock. There are no legal closing hours and no curfews; many bars have no locks on their front doors because they never shut. If there are closing hours, they often depend upon the flow of traffic, especially on Bourbon Street. Before you hit a Bourbon Street dive, ask about the minimum and the cover charge—there's often a two-drink minimum per set.

You can buy liquor in grocery stores and drugstores, and you may do so whenever the doors are open for business, even on Sundays and election days.

And if you think it's easy to buy liquor here, wait 'til you hear how easy it is to drink it: The Big Easy has open container laws here that allow you to walk around in broad daylight with a drink in hand. If you're a certain type of tourist, the little plastic "go-cup" may well become your constant companion. Yes, you can walk around town with a Cosmo in your hand as long as it's in a plastic cup—no glass, no cans. Speaking of open containers, get this: Under state law, passengers in a car are also allowed to drink. Many drivers subvert this by handing their drinks to their passengers if they get pulled over. But don't bust open that Bud yet. Many parishes—Orleans and Jefferson among them—have enacted stricter drink/drive laws, so you're going to have to take a road trip to feel the wind of the open road in your hair and that fizzy beer in your throat simultaneously. Just to confuse things though, there is a loophole for all those drive-in daiquiri shops you see around town: As long as the top of the cup has not been pierced with a straw, you're okay. We can think of about three ways to subvert *that* rule—not that we're recommending it....

It took time to settle, but the legal drinking age is 21. In typical Louisiana fashion, less than a decade ago, the law was so unclear that cops didn't even know how to enforce it. We think it went something like this (though few have yet to conclusively figure it out): If you were 18 to 20 you could drink alcohol, but you could not legally purchase it. So you had to get a 21-year-old to buy it for you, but after that you were free and clear to drink it. Apparently, though, those Federal highway funds eventually became more important to our politicians than keeping voters under 21 happy.

Locals love their beer, here: Abita is the brew of choice for many. It comes in a variety of flavors with clever names like Turbodog and Purple Haze. Abita's brewery and brewpub is across the lake in Abita Springs and is worth a trip if you like to imbibe in a more bucolic setting. Dixie is also a popular choice, but only when you're slumming it. New Orleans's best-known adult beverage (that few locals actually drink) is the Hurricane, a potently sweet concoction of rum and fruit juices. The Sazerac (which some locals actually do drink) is made with bourbon and bitters and served in a glass coated with ersatz absinthe. Both beverages should be approached with caution and plenty of respect.

The Lowdown

Only in New Orleans... Touristy though it is, **Preservation Hall** can be a fun stop. The "hall" is really a single boxlike room. The name is a throwback to the turn of the century, when early jazz bands played around town in halls that had names like Funky Butts, the Odd Fellows, and Perseverance Hall. In the early 1960s, the late Allen Jaffe, a jazz buff and tuba player from Pennsylvania—a man much loved and highly respected among musicians—set up Preservation Hall in order to replicate those old music halls, to preserve the tradition of jazz bands, and to give the old-time legends a regular place to play. The small, dingy, cramped room has no creature comforts, only a few hard benches and some filthy cushions scattered on the floor, where you can sit at the feet of the musicians. If you're standing in the back, as you'll probably have to, you won't be able to see the musicians unless you're tall. You won't have any trouble hearing them, however, even though there's no sound system, because the hall is so small. The band plays 35-minute sets, then takes a break while a hawker comes in to hawk records. Many people leave after the first set, either because they're uncomfortable or because they think they have to. In fact, you don't have to leave until the place closes at midnight. Those in the back who opt to stay can then move forward, aiming for the hard benches. After you've been standing awhile, those benches look real cozy. Admission is $5, and you can stay for 10 minutes or 4 hours, depending upon your physical stamina. Best advice: If you don't like traditional jazz, stay away. It is touristy—locals avoid it because there's no bar or dance floor—but $5 for 4 hours doth not a trap make. Another veritable institution is funky-as-they-come **Tipitina's.** Tips, as locals call it, is perched on a random corner Uptown, catty-corner from the Sav-A-Center, the better to keep away posers. This place is REAL—with bare bones decor and a bust of Professor Longhair greeting you at the door. Heck, they only put in air-conditioning a couple years ago. People come here to get down with New Orleans funk, R&B, reggae, rock, and even some Cajun. Down in the Quarter, **Lafitte's Blacksmith Shop** packs in peeps who love a sing-along. The piano player tickles the ivories while people of all walks warble along, privy to the secret that a night of drinkin' and singin' does wonders for the soul. Just ask former First Mistress Gennifer Flowers who opened up **Gennifer Flowers' Kelsto Club** in the Vieux Carré not too long ago. There the woman who can tell you all about Bill's technique belts out vintage love songs and chats up guests between sets. If has-been celebs are your bag, then you definitely should consider a field trip to **Ernie K-Doe's Mother-in-Law Lounge,** which is perched under a freeway overpass in a slightly ominous part of town. Old schoolers may remember K-Doe's number-one hit "Mother-in-Law" which he rode to fame in the early '60s. Though he kept making music after that, the number-one hits stopped—but not K-Doe. His outrageous hair and clothes and his fabulously inflated sense of self (he referred to himself as Emperor of the Universe) kept him going year after year, decade after decade, making him a much-loved icon in the Crescent City. When K-Doe died in 2001, his jazz funeral was one of the great spectacles of recent memory. His name and spirit—along with his widow Antoinette—live on at the lounge. (Don't miss his website, a great fun read: www.k-doe.com.) Another fabulous slice of reality in N'awlins is **Vaughn's,** a bar in the Bywater. (Take cabs to and fro, please.) Most Thursday nights, beloved local trumpeter Kermit Ruffins plays with his group the Barbecue Swingers—Ruffins not only plays, but between sets he cooks up free barbecue for hungry patrons! Of course there's no absinthe at **Tony Moran's Old Absinthe House** anymore, but it sure is old—as is its clientele. Go there for the daiquiris, or try **Mango Mango,** which has three locations on Bourbon Street, lest you miss one.

Isn't it romantic?... If troths be still plighted, a splendid place for doing so is the **Victorian Lounge,** with its wood-burning fireplace, pressed-tin ceiling, velvet-covered chairs, and wood paneling. Many people swoon over the **Napoleon House,** though the place is all but falling apart at the seams. There's just something about the candlelight flickering off those sepia walls and the opera on the sound system. George and Nina Buck's **Palm Court Jazz Café** is another place that can put you in the mood. Traditional jazz is played out in an airy cafe-style space. Sit at the bar, away from the fray, and hear the house band play dreamy melodies like Sidney Bechet's "Petit Fleur."

Hipster scenes... David Pirner of Soul Asylum has been known to do acoustic performances at **dba,** an industrial-looking bar in the Marigny featuring a mixed bag of music and patronized by the dreads and piercings set. **Loft 523**'s bar features cast-iron columns original to the building (it was once a carriage and dry goods warehouse), wide plank flooring, pressed tin ceilings, and a polished crowd. It also has a beguilingly named "grotto room" where the über fabulous can hang out in private. Another place that harnesses the mojo of its former life is **TwiRoPa,** once a twine, rope, and paper warehouse, now a 67,000-square-foot entertainment biosphere that features six separate staging areas, eight bars, and six dance floors. Hipsters like to slum it at the **Saturn Bar.** The life-sized mummy dangling from the ceiling is a bit the worse for wear. It has, after all, probably been contributing to the atmosphere there for more than 50 years, beneath the astonishing ceiling depiction of the solar system, the tinsel, and the neon chandeliers. Deep in "Yat Country" (as in the ubiquitous greeting, "Hey man, where're y'at?"), the Saturn is an institution, with a hard-drinking, hard-core clientele, the majority of whom probably never heard the term New Age, let alone Women's Lib. On the other side of the spectrum is the CBD's **Ampersand,** owned by Billy Blatty, whose father wrote *The Exorcist* (yikes). There they can down Red Bulls and dance to DJs 'til 5am. **360** is another hot spot for dancing; parked atop the unfortunately named World Trade Center, it's the only dance club that literally spins for revolving views of the city. Two hipster havens that may be fading into oblivion are **El Matador** (owned by director Taylor Hackford's son Rio) and the **Mermaid Lounge.** At press time, Rio had been run out of the Matador by magician/former "Night Court" star Harry Anderson who bought the building to turn it into a performance space for himself. No word on where/when/if Hackford will relocate El Mat. The Mermaid, meanwhile, was also having lease issues and threatening to close. Coolios all over New Orleans were flippin' their dope lids over the 411. Many of them will take refuge at the **Circle Bar** not coincidentally located on Lee Circle.

Where the locals go... Locals go anyplace that has good music. Young uptowners flood **Carrollton Station,** a small spot with a BIG beer selection. The music ranges from acoustic/singer/songwriter stuff to full-blown Nola jazz. It's also located across the street from **Jimmy's Club,** which

O. Henry Was Born in a Bar

The pen names "Mark Twain" and "O. Henry" were both adopted in New Orleans when the two writers were working in the city as journalists. As a riverboat pilot, Samuel Clemens spent a lot of time in New Orleans. He first wrote under the name Mark Twain in 1857, in a piece he wrote for the New Orleans Crescent. *And in 1896, William S. Porter lived here and wrote for the* New Orleans Item. *According to local lore, he was nursing a drink in a bar when someone summoned the bartender—"Oh, Henry"—and the name O. Henry was born.*

only features bands during Mardi Gras and Jazz Fest. Up at the top end of Tchoupitoulas St. sits **Dos Jefes** with pool, cigars, and all manner of live music. **Tipitina's** Uptown is a bastion for die-hard music lovers. They've also opened two locations downtown—in the Warehouse and in the Quarter. Another Uptowner, this one on Oak Street, is the **Maple Leaf Bar,** which rocks with a host of genres from Cajun Beausoleil to the rollicking ReBirth Brass Band. Incidentally, the ReBirth has a standing gig on Tuesday nights that often sees musicians and patrons jamming and dancing 'til dawn. Another place that pumps 'til late is **Café Brasil** in the Marigny. The New Orleans home of world music—meaning a cornucopia of genres including Klezmer, salsa, and reggae—the fervent, dancing crowd often spills out onto the street. In the Warehouse District, try **Howlin' Wolf** for alternative and punk music. Without a doubt the least-publicized place in all New Orleans, the grungy, shoebox-sized **Dungeon** draws locals in-the-know, plus every with-it celebrity who comes to town. Maybe it's the Friday morning, 1am to 4am, three-for-one drink special. The only music they have comes to you canned. It's almost hidden between **Molly's** and the **Tropical Isle** on Toulouse Street, and it doesn't open until midnight, but things keep on till the early morning. **Donna's Bar & Grill,** which showcases brass bands, is grungy enough to appeal to local tastes. The photos of neighborhood dogs at the **Bridge Lounge** attest to the place's local draw. Wine-lovers take note: They serve more than 20 vintages by the glass. Uptown locals head to **St. Joe's Bar,** which has one of the most exquisite patios in the city, lit by billowing red silk lanterns and serviced by bodacious bartenders. New Orleans's sizeable Irish population—very much in evidence during the city's three St. Patrick's Day parades—tosses back stout and shakes its legs to Celtic rock/folk at **O'Flaherty's Irish** pub. When local journalists want to talk politics and drink at the same time, they head to **Molly's**. The **House of Blues,** aka The House of Rules, is the place the locals love to hate—but they go anyway. HOB is expensive, polished, and heavy on logoed merchandise. But it also consistently books excellent bands and has great sound. Whatcha gonna do? And now they have created the Parish Room upstairs featuring local acts, giving critics even less to complain about. Farther down the river in the Marigny are the **R-Bar,** where tattooed, pierced regulars knock 'em back, and **The Spotted Cat**, a little hole in the wall that plays stellar jazz every night of the week.

Where the locals don't go... There's plenty of great music even at the tourist traps. **Storyville Jazz Parlor,** a cavernous club that opened in late 1999 right on Bourbon Street, features, well, uh, jazz. Farther down Bourbon, and much older, the **Cat's Meow** attracts a few locals, as well as crowds of tourists. **Chris Owens Club** plays primarily for the tourist trade, as does the **Famous Door** just down the street. Locals rarely darken the door of **Preservation Hall,** and the only ones that frequent **Pat O'Brien's** are college kids. (O'Brien's invented the Hurricane cocktail and serves it up in 26-oz. glasses shaped like hurricane lamps, which countless tourists have bought to take home.) The **Cajun Cabin** is another Bourbon Street trap, where drinks with names like Swamp Water and Cajun Sunrise come in 16-ounce souvenir cups. **Tropical Isle Bourbon, Funky Pirate,** and **Tropical Isle Toulouse** are all after-hours clubs that are pretty touristy but can really zing during Jazz Fest. The **Maison Bourbon,** the **Krazy Korner,** and the **Hard Rock Cafe** are loaded with tourists, and usually avoided by locals. And, far be it from an Orleanian to go cruising off on the *Creole Queen* riverboat or the **Steamboat** ***Natchez.*** Orleanians love the Mississippi, but they tend to take it for granted, along with the boats that float on it.

Cajun and zydeco dancing... Across the street from the Convention Center, **Mulate's** is an old-fashioned dance hall where feet fly to beat the band. Nearby, **Michaul's Live Cajun Music Restaurant** is pretty much what the name says, with instructors on hand for free two-stepping lessons. A lot of fun—so what if it's loaded with tourists and conventioneers? Same goes for the **Cajun Cabin** on Bourbon where they feature live Cajun—bands like Mitch Cormier and the Can't Hardly Playboys—7 nights a week. On Thursdays, tromp over for a bowl and a boogie to **Mid-City Bowling Lanes Rock 'n' Bowl,** where it's zydeco night. And finish out the weekend at the Sunday night fais-do-dos at **Tipitina's.**

Music and munchies... In addition to Preservation Hall, the **Palm Court Jazz Cafe** does great traditional jazz. But at the Palm Court, you can eat good local food, drink booze, *and* sit on real chairs, all in the comfort of a smart cafe. Soul food is super at the cavernous **Praline Connection Gospel & Blues Hall** in the Warehouse District. The **House of Blues** serves up surprisingly great local-influenced food, and at their gospel brunch you can dine and dance at the same time. **Jimmy Buffett's Margaritaville** is a lively spot in the lower Quarter, where the food pays tribute to Key West (Key lime pie, conch fritters, cheeseburgers, and the like). There are great burgers at **Snug Harbor,** though the jazz and food are served up in separate sections. The city is packed with dive-y spots that are chiefly concerned with excellent music, but that happen to serve victuals as well. Among them: **Vaughn's, Donna's Bar & Grill,** and the **Funky Butt.**

Where to pick up someone else's spouse... Hotel lounges seem to provide the right aura for possibly illicit behavior, maybe because both parties know that, should matters progress, there are bedrooms available not so far away. At any rate, the Fairmont Hotel's darkly romantic **Sazerac Bar,** with its long wooden bar and handsome murals, is a fine place to pull up a barstool and chat up your fellow imbiber. The **Esplanade Lounge** in the marbled halls of the Royal Orleans Hotel has soft piano music, delicious desserts, and a cozy ambience. Uptowners and guests at the Pontchartrain Hotel love to hang out at the hotel's **Bayou Bar** and listen to the piano. And if it's newer and sleeker you crave, head over to **FQB** at the Ritz-Carlton where the handsome Jeremy Davenport croons and women tend to flock.

The college scene... Kids from Tulane and Loyola, among several other local colleges, are all over the place. Uptown, check out the **Maple Leaf Bar, Jimmy's Club, Tipitina's, The Bulldog,** and **Carrollton Station,** among others. In the Warehouse District, young people don't seem to mind the crowds and cramped quarters at **Howlin' Wolf,** for alternative music, and **Vic's Kangaroo Cafe,** for blues blaring from a jazz jukebox. And college kids seem impervious to the general theory that **Pat O'Brien's** is just for tourists—they belly up for the Hurricanes there, too. When coeds (and high schoolers, but we're *sure* management has *no* idea) want to dance in the Quarter, they'll hit **735**, which is also a gay hangout.

The gay scene... New Orleans is a rainbow flag kinda town, with a long history of welcoming gays and lesbians. The oldest and most famous (Tennessee Williams used to visit) of the men's gay bars is **Café Lafitte in Exile,** so named because the late owner felt "exiled" after losing **Lafitte's Blacksmith Shop,** a mostly straight bar just down the street. **Bourbon Pub/Parade** is another hot spot where the Sunday tea dances are an institution. Leather lovers head over to **Rawhide,** where they have tough-guy events like "Tattoos and Tequila" night and Bare Chest contests. If you really just gotta dance, then you'll be traipsing over to **Oz** where Thursday is Calendar Boy Night and Sunday is Disco Night, even though disco is dead—again. The **Golden Lantern** does determinedly outrageous drag shows, scheduled and unscheduled. It's also the starting point for the fabulous Southern Decadence parade the Sunday before Labor Day. The area's only predominantly lesbian bar, **The Mint,** is just slightly off the beaten track in the Faubourg Marigny. Also in the Marigny is **Phoenix Bar,** which draws a real local crowd and is a big scene during Southern Decadence and Mardi Gras.

Map 19: French Quarter Nightlife

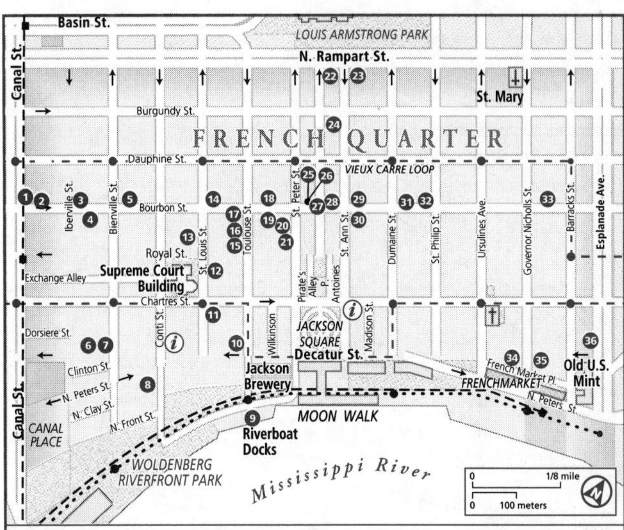

Bourbon Pub/Parade **29**
Café Lafitte in Exile **31**
Cajun Cabin **14**
Cat's Meow **25**
Chris Owens Club **14**
Donna's **23**
The Dungeon **15**
El Matador **36**
Esplanade Lounge **12**
Famous Door **5**
FBQ **1**
Funky Butt **22**
Funky Pirate **26**
Gennifer Flowers' Kelsto Club **13**
Golden Lantern **33**
Hard Rock Cafe **8**
House of Blues **6**
Jazz Parlor at Storyville **2**
Jimmy Buffet's Margaritaville **34**
Krazy Korner **19**
Lafitte's Blacksmith Bar **32**
Maison Bourbon **18**
Mango Mango **3**
Molly's **16**
Napoleon House **11**
O'Flaherty's **10**
Oz **30**
Palm Court Jazz Cafe **35**
Pat O'Brien's **21**
Preservation Hall **20**
Rawhide **24**
735 **28**
Steamboat Natchez **9**
Tipitina's French Quarter **7**
Tony Moran's Absinthe House **4**
Tropical Isle Bourbon **27**
Tropical Isle Toulouse **17**
Utopia **4**

Map 20: Uptown Nightlife

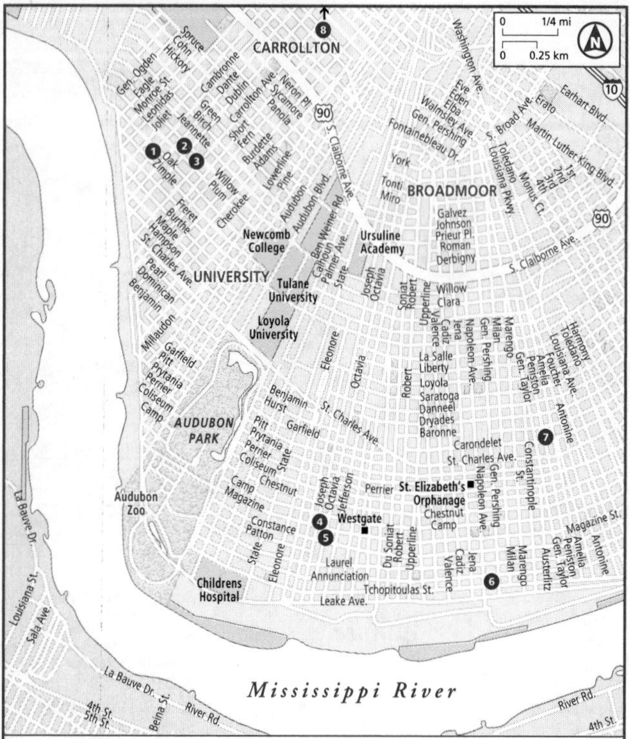

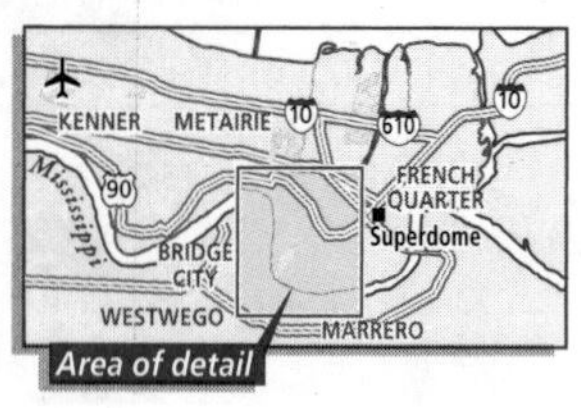

Carrollton Station **3**
Dos Jefe's **5**
Jimmy's Club **2**
Maple Leaf **1**
Mid-City Bowling Lanes **8**
St. Joe's Bar **4**
Tipitina's **6**
Victorian Lounge **7**

The Index

Ampersand (p. 206) CBD Where the trendoids meet to drink and dance. International DJ's, $1 Cosmos and champagne (sometimes), and even free sushi, reel in hot babes and studs and that's just the way GM Billy Blatty wants it.... *Tel 504/587-3737. www.clubampersand.com. 1100 Tulane Ave. AE, DISC, MC, V. Fri 10pm–3am, Sat 10pm–7am, closed for private parties Sun–Thurs. Cover $5–$10.*

See Map 18 on p. 198.

Bayou Bar (p. 209) GARDEN DISTRICT Uptowners and celeb guests of the Pontchartrain frequent this sophisticated piano bar with fabric sofas, murals of the bayou, and windows that open onto the street.... *Tel 504/524-0581. Pontchartrain Hotel, 2031 St. Charles Ave. AE, DC, DISC, MC, V. Mon–Thurs 5–11pm, Fri 5pm–2am, Sat 11am–2am, Sun 11am–11pm. No cover.*

See Map 18 on p. 198.

Bourbon Pub/Parade (p. 210) FRENCH QUARTER A popular gay men's club, the Parade has lasers, videos, a good dance floor, and a decorous tea dance every Sunday afternoon.... *Tel 504/529-2107. www.bourbonpub.com. 801 Bourbon St. No credit cards. Daily 24 hours. Fri after 10pm $5 cover; Sat after 10pm $10 cover.*

See Map 19 on p. 211.

Bridge Lounge (p. 207) LOWER GARDEN DISTRICT "Swanky, not skanky" is the motto here, lest you confuse the bar with its former identity as a strip joint. Drinks are served to an artsy crowd atop a 45-foot-long limestone bar (with matching tables scattered throughout), and the Thursday-night wine tastings are good enough to take your mind off the black-and-white photos of neighborhood dogs that line the walls.... *Tel 504/299-1888. 1201 Magazine St. AE, DC, DISC, MC, V. Daily 4pm–closing. No cover.*

See Map 18 on p. 198.

The Bulldog (p. 209) UPTOWN The beer selection at this uptown watering hole is, well, animalistic—about 250 varieties between tap and bottles. Think English pub that dishes out Tex-Mex food, add the requisite Guinness mirrors and picnic-table outdoor seating, and you're here in spirit.... *Tel 504/891-1516. www.draftfreak.com. 3236 Magazine St. AE, DISC, MC, V. Mon–Thurs 2pm–closing. Fri–Sun 12pm–closing. No cover.*

See Map 18 on p. 198.

Café Brasil (p. 207) FAUBOURG MARIGNY There are no tables inside—just dancing and hanging out—and the crowd collapsed over the sidewalk tables nursing espressos and liqueurs is young and Bohemian. Rare is the tourist who wanders in here.... *Tel 504/949-0851. 2100 Chartres St. No credit cards. Daily from 8pm. Call ahead for cover information.*

See Map 18 on p. 198.

Café Lafitte in Exile (p. 210) FRENCH QUARTER Headquarters for the annual Gay Pride Day festivities, this has been a popular gay men's bar since the early '50s. Unsuspecting passersby on Bourbon are sometimes startled by the hoots emanating from enthusiastic revelers hanging over the second-floor balcony.... *Tel 504/522-8397. www.lafittes.com. 901 Bourbon St. MC, V. Daily 24 hours. Cover for special events only.*

See Map 19 on p. 211.

Cajun Cabin (p. 208) FRENCH QUARTER Tops with tourists, who think they've died and gone to Acadiana, the rollicking Cabin opens its doors wide and spills its little heart right out onto Bourbon. The music is live every night; the chef cooks Cajun, and the food's not bad at all.... *Tel 504/529-4256. www.patoutscajuncabin.com. 501 Bourbon St. AE, DC, DISC, MC, V. Daily 11pm–closing. 1 drink minimum.*

See Map 19 on p. 211.

Carrollton Station (p. 206) UPTOWN A snug little joint that rocks till very late. Monday night's open acoustic mic is a big hit with locals, who come in all ages and descriptions.... *Tel 504/861-9718. www.carrolltonstation.com. 8140 Willow St. AE, DC, DISC, MC, V. Daily 3pm–closing. Call ahead for cover information.*

See Map 20 on p. 212.

Cat's Meow (p. 208) FRENCH QUARTER On one of the loudest corners of the Quarter, locals mix it up with tourists in this busy place, where the activity is upstairs and down. There's a karaoke bar, videos, and stuff like hokey-pokey and hand jive.... *Tel 504/523-2788. 701 Bourbon St. AE, DC, DISC, MC, V. Open Mon-Fri 4pm–closing, Sat–Sun 2pm–closing. $5 cover Fri and Sat if under 21.*

See Map 19 on p. 211.

Chris Owens Club (p. 208) FRENCH QUARTER Ms. Owens is a legend on Bourbon Street, which mainly means she's been around for a spell. All a-shimmer and a-glitter, she performs a one-woman variety show, singing and dancing renditions of Top 40, show tunes, blues, and a little Latin stuff.... *Tel 504/523-6400. www.chrisowensclub.com. 500 Bourbon St. AE, DC, DISC, MC, V. Mon–Thurs 6pm–4am, Fri–Sat noon–5am. Cover Thurs–Sat $11 includes 1 cocktail.*

See Map 19 on p. 211.

Circle Bar (p. 206) WAREHOUSE/ARTS DISTRICT This eensy weensy club, right on Lee Circle, is a magnet for locals on the cool side. Twenty- and thirty-somethings belly up to the bar, while bands ranging from punk to funk and way beyond play nearly every night of the week starting at around 10:30pm.... *Tel 504/588-2616. 1032 St. Charles Ave. No credit cards. Daily 4pm–4am. No cover.*

See Map 18 on p. 198.

***Creole Queen* (p. 208)** FRENCH QUARTER The various cruises of the great white riverboat include "Dinner on the River & All That Jazz"—a nice outing if you're looking for something the whole family can enjoy.... *Tel 504/524-0814. www.neworleanspaddle wheels.com. Canal St. Wharf. AE, DC, DISC, MC, V. Boarding buffet begins at 7pm; cruise 8–10pm. Admission $51 with dinner, $27 without.*

See Map 18 on p. 198.

dba (p. 205) FAUBOURG MARIGNY A mixed bag of live music 6 nights a week, coupled with a pool table and video games, is draw enough. But what seals the deal is the recent addition of a webcam that connects you from the Big Easy to the Big Apple (they have a sister bar in NYC). If a long-distance toast doesn't lure you, Dave Pirner of Soul Asylum has been known to do acoustic shows here.... *Tel 504/942-3731. www.drinkgoodstuff.com. 618 Frenchmen St. Daily 4pm–closing. AE, DISC, MC, V. No cover.*

See Map 18 on p. 198.

Donna's Bar & Grill (p. 209) FRENCH QUARTER A strictly no-frills (and no tourists) bar devoted solely to brass bands. The best of them play here—the Rebirth, the Chosen Few, the Little Rascals, the Soul Rebels. It's on the fringe of the Quarter.... *Tel 504/596-6914. www.donnasbarandgrill.com. 800 N. Rampart St. AE, DC, DISC, MC, V. Thurs–Mon 8:30pm–closing. Thurs–Sun $5 cover, Mon $10, includes BBQ chicken, red beans and rice, and seating.*

See Map 19 on p. 211.

Dos Jefes (p. 207) UPTOWN A cigar smoking bar–cum–pool hall–cum–live music venue 7 nights a week, Dos Jefes covers all.... *Tel 504/891-8500. 5535 Tchoupitoulas St. AE, DC, DISC, MC, V. Daily 5pm–closing. No cover.*

See Map 20 on p. 212.

Dungeon (p. 207) FRENCH QUARTER If you're wondering where the Rolling Stones and other superstars hang out after the concert, this is it. Hard-core grunge decor; don't expect elbow room. The entrance is squeezed between Molly's and the Tropical Isle.... *Tel 504/523-5530. www.originaldungeon.com. About 738 Toulouse St. Opens at midnight. $3 cover on Fri and Sat.*

See Map 19 on p. 211.

El Matador (p. 206) FRENCH QUARTER New Orleans groovesters gravitate to El Mat like, well, like bulls to a red cape. A selection of cool bands, strong drinks, and guest bartenders the likes of Vince Vaughn (thanks to owner Rio Hackford's Hollywood cred) make it a must on the list for barflies with a little savoir-faire.... *Tel 504/569-8361. 504 Esplanade Ave. No credit cards. Mon–Thurs 9pm–closing, Fri–Sat 4pm–closing. Cover varies; call ahead.*

See Map 19 on p. 211.

Esplanade Lounge (p. 209) FRENCH QUARTER Marble floors, Oriental carpets, and cushy drawing-room seating add up to a swell place to wind down. Desserts and coffee are served to the tune of the grand piano.... *Tel 504/529-5333. Omni Royal Orleans Hotel, 621 St. Louis St. AE, DC, DISC, MC, V. Daily 4pm–midnight. No cover.*

See Map 19 on p. 211.

Famous Door (p. 208) FRENCH QUARTER The French Quarter was little more than a run-down slum when the doors opened on this club in 1934. The decor is rinky-dink, tables are minuscule, and music is loud—R&B and traditional jazz are on tap.... *Tel 504/598-4334. 339 Bourbon St. AE, DC, DISC, MC, V. Mon–Wed 3pm–closing, Thurs–Sat midnight–closing. Cover for major events only.*

See Map 19 on p. 211.

FQB (French Quarter Bar) (p. 209) FRENCH QUARTER Popular with locals and tourists alike, mostly because handsome crooner Jeremy Davenport sings and plays trumpet several nights a week. Can be quite the yuppie pickup scene... *Tel 504/524-1331. 921 Canal St. AE, DC, DISC, MC, V. Weds–Mon, 11am–1am.*

See Map 19 on p. 211.

Funky Butt (p. 209) FRENCH QUARTER In a relatively short amount of time the Funky Butt has distinguished itself as one of the best places in the city to hear some of the best musicians in the city. Winton Marsalis, Henry Butler, Nicholas Payton, Marva Wright, and many others have played the Butt. And like all the good places, it's in a sketchy 'hood at the outskirts of the Quarter. You can also eat here: fried seafood, pastas, po'boys, and New

Orleans classics like jambalaya and étouffée.... *Tel 504/558-0872. www.funkybutt.com. 714 N. Rampart St. No credit cards. Daily 7pm–2am. Early acts 7:30–9:30pm. Feature acts at 10pm and midnight. Cover after 10pm, $5–$10.*

See Map 19 on p. 211.

Funky Pirate (p. 208) FRENCH QUARTER What's in a name? At this quaint, cozy blues club which draws a European crowd, the funk factor kicks in with the house drinks. And you'd probably have to be a pirate (or the president) to stake out a spot in the tiny courtyard out back.... *Tel 504/523-1960. www.tropicalisle.com. 727 Bourbon St. AE, DC, DISC, MC, V. Mon–Thurs 5pm–2am, Fri–Sat 5pm–3:30am, Sun 5pm–1am. No cover.*

See Map 19 on p. 211.

Gennifer Flowers' Kelsto Club (p. 204) FRENCH QUARTER Yes, it's that Gennifer Flowers. And, yes, she sings. Torch songs. Not too badly either. She took some time off for her Broadway debut in *Boobs, The Musical,* but she's back now, safely ensconced in her dark, tiny bar and under the protective eye of her husband.... *Tel 504/524-1111. 720 St. Louis St. AE, DISC, MC, V. Daily 5pm–closing. No cover.*

See Map 19 on p. 211.

Golden Lantern (p. 210) FRENCH QUARTER The Quarter's second-oldest gay men's bar, the GL is one of the main drags, so to speak, for the annual Southern Decadence Day doings. Drag shows every other Saturday and twice-daily happy hours (4am–9am and 4–9pm) are among the draws.... *Tel 504/529-2860. 1239 Royal St. No credit cards. Daily 24 hours. No cover.*

See Map 19 on p. 211.

Hard Rock Cafe (p. 208) FRENCH QUARTER The big bar is guitar-shaped, and the de rigueur rock and pop iconography is on display.... *Tel 504/529-5617. 418 N. Peters St. AE, DC, DISC, MC, V. Sun–Thurs 11am–11pm, Fri–Sat 11am–midnight. No cover.*

See Map 19 on p. 211.

House of Blues (p. 207) FRENCH QUARTER The very best that $7 million can buy, HOB is a rambling high-tech place with standing room for 1,100 in the cavernous concert hall, done up with an overkill of folk art. The restaurant seats 175, and Sunday gospel brunches on the second-floor balcony are worth inquiring about. Top names and local talent take the stage.... *Tel 504/529-2624. www.hob.com. 225 Decatur St. Credit cards accepted at ticket window. Call for show times and prices.*

See Map 19 on p. 211.

Howlin' Wolf (p. 207) WAREHOUSE/ARTS DISTRICT Alternative, rock, country, and Latin jazz dominate and draw 20-somethings to this hard-rockin' hot spot. Nothing disguises the fact that this building was once a warehouse.... *Tel 504/522-WOLF. www.thehowlinwolf.com. 828 S. Peters St. MC, V. Doors open at 9pm, shows start at 10pm. Call ahead for show prices.*

See Map 18 on p. 198.

Jazz Parlor at Storyville (p. 208) FRENCH QUARTER Smack on Bourbon Street, this joyous and boisterous club is (appropriately) one of the entrepreneurial group Bourbon Street Entertainment's four brain children. Playing on the notoriety of the city's long-ago red-light district, the club features lots of splashy red-and-gold murals, red velvet curtains—and, of course, live jazz, jazz, jazz.... *Tel 504/410-1000. 125 Bourbon St. AE, DISC, MC, V. Daily 5pm–closing. No cover.*

See Map 19 on p. 211.

Jimmy Buffett's Margaritaville (p. 209) FRENCH QUARTER Paradise for Parrotheads (Buffett buffs), New Orleans's answer to Key West is a barnlike place in the lower Quarter, where the decor runs toward pictures of Jimmy Buffett, who makes an occasional appearance.... *Tel 504/592-2565. www.margaritavillecafe.com. 1104 Decatur St. Noon–midnight; music 3pm–midnight. No cover.*

See Map 19 on p. 211.

Jimmy's Club (p. 206) UPTOWN Once an uptown version of Preservation Hall, Jimmy's is now an all-DJ dance club/bar aimed at the 21-to-30 set. Hip-hop, techno, and pop are on the sound system. There's a comfy VIP area, an excellent bar, and a 2,000-square-foot patio.... *Tel 504/861-8200. 8200 Willow St. No credit cards. 10pm–closing. Cover varies.*

See Map 20 on p. 212.

Krazy Korner (p. 208) FRENCH QUARTER As loud as they come, this tiny hole-in-the-wall is a slosh with tourists shakin', rattlin', and rollin' on a dance floor not much bigger than a phone booth. Red-hot mamas belt out blues to beat the band.... *Tel 504/524-3157. www.krazykorner.com. 640 Bourbon St. Mon–Wed 3pm–closing, Thurs–Sun 1pm–closing. AE, DC, DISC, MC, V. No cover.*

See Map 19 on p. 211.

Lafitte's Blacksmith Shop (p. 204) FRENCH QUARTER An institute of higher imbibing, Lafitte's—not to be confused with Café Lafitte in Exile—is a dark, grungy bar in a ramshackle cottage that's been here since 1772. It is bandied about that this was once the blacksmith shop of brothers Jean and Pierre Lafitte, and a front for their freebooting endeavors. Locals have been singing along at the piano bar for ages.... *Tel 504/522-9377. 941 Bourbon St. AE, DISC, MC, V. Mon–Thurs 11am–closing, Fri–Sun 10am–closing. No cover.*

See Map 19 on p. 211.

Loft 523 **(p. 205)** CBD Hip bar in an even hipper hotel. It's dark and industrial, with a private room called the Grotto. A place to see and be seen—if you have night-vision goggles, that is.... *Tel 504/ 200-6523. 523 Gravier St. Open Tues–Sat, 5pm–closing. AE, DC, DISC, MC, V.*

See Map 18 on p. 198.

Maison Bourbon **(p. 208)** FRENCH QUARTER When the jazzmen are on the bandstand, the doors are flung wide, and you can hang out on Bourbon Street and listen to Jamil Sharif, Dwayne Burns, and Jamie Wight laying out hot licks. This is a tiny bar with not much in the way of decoration, beyond a few tables loaded with tourists, a long and busy bar, and the raised bandstand at the rear facing the street.... *Tel 504/522-8818. 641 Bourbon St. No credit cards. Sun–Wed 2:15pm–12:15am, Thurs–Sun 3:15pm–1:15am. 1-drink minimum per person per set.*

See Map 19 on p. 211.

Mango Mango **(p. 205)** FRENCH QUARTER Home of the locals' favorite daiquiri, this tropical hangout will make you forget you're on the mainland. Greenery and bamboo are the backdrop against which the regulars sip—what else?—mango daiquiris. With three locations in the Quarter, there must be somethin' in the drinks.... *Tel 504/525–8108; 400 Bourbon St. Tel 504/566-1113; 201 Bourbon St. Tel 504/586–0787; 333 Bourbon St. No credit cards. Daily 11 am–closing. No cover.*

See Map 19 on p. 211.

Maple Leaf Bar **(p. 207)** UPTOWN A pressed-tin roof hovers over this madly popular place, where hordes of mostly young locals in cutoffs and tank tops shout and gyrate on a long, skinny dance floor. The Tuesday night ReBirth Brass Band gig often rages 'til dawn.... *Tel 504/866-9359, 504/866-LEAF. 8316 Oak St. AE, DC, DISC, MC, V. Daily 3pm–closing. Call ahead for show prices.*

See Map 20 on p. 212.

Mermaid Lounge **(p. 206)** WAREHOUSE/ARTS DISTRICT A local favorite, the Mermaid is a rollicking spot whose walls are decorated with artworks, and where live music ranges from New Orleans funk to blaring brass bands.... *Tel 504/524-4747. www. mermaidlounge.com. 1100 Constance St. No credit cards. Daily 8:30pm–closing. Cover varies; call ahead.*

See Map 18 on p. 198.

Michaul's Live Cajun Music Restaurant **(p. 208)** WAREHOUSE/ ARTS DISTRICT Real-live Cajun bands loosen things up in this dance hall, where a whole lot of two-stepping gets done and instructors offer free dance lessons. The music and dancing are much better than the food.... *Tel 504/522-5517. www.michauls.com. 840 St. Charles Ave. AE, DC, DISC, MC, V. Mon–Thurs 6:30pm–closing, Fri–Sat 7pm–closing. No cover.*

See Map 18 on p. 198.

Mid-City Bowling Lanes & Sports Palace (p. 208) MID-CITY A bowling alley with a twist. And a turn. And a whirl. The home of the locally famous Rock 'n' Bowl is well worth the climb up those stairs, and the accents are all New Orleans. The place is so popular it literally overflowed, and now there's a Rock 'n' Bowl Café with big-screen TVs to watch sporting events (and you can avoid those formidable stairs).... *Tel 504/482-3133. www.rocknbowl.com. 4133 S. Carrollton Ave. AE, DISC, MC, V. Daily 10am–closing. Cover varies; call ahead.*

See Map 20 on p. 212.

The Mint (p. 210) FAUBOURG MARIGNY Outside the Quarter, the area's only lesbian bar has been around since the 1970s (formerly known as Charlene's, then Kim's 940). There are three bars: The main one is open 24 hours, the Martini Bar serves 'em up between 4pm and 1am, and the Balcony Bar is open weekends from 4pm to 1am. There's also dancing and games like darts and pool.... *Tel 504/944-4888. 940 Elysian Fields Ave. No cover.*

See Map 18 on p. 199.

Molly's (p. 207) FRENCH QUARTER For reasons known to no one, the local media have made Molly's their bar of choice for years. Come to this divey old spot to talk politics with the crusty people who cover them.... *Tel 504/525-5169. 1107 Decatur St. Open daily 10am–6am. No cover.*

See Map 19 on p. 211.

Mother-in-Law Ernie K-Doe (p. 204) ST. CLAUDE The late, self-proclaimed Emperor of the World opened his namesake club in 1994 as a place for other Crescent City "living legends" to come drink and play. The place is a shiny shrine to the man who penned the 1961 number-one hit, "Mother-in-Law." His gracious widow Antoinette holds down the fort and keeps his memory alive.... *Tel 504/947-1078. www.k-doe.com. 1500 N. Claiborne Ave. No credit cards. Daily 5pm–closing. No cover.*

See Map 18 on p. 198.

Mulate's (p. 208) WAREHOUSE/ARTS DISTRICT A rustic place with a lot of cypress, Mulate's is a spinoff of a madly popular Cajun dance hall in Breaux Bridge, deep in the heart of Cajun country to the west of New Orleans. The 400-seat cafe turns out pretty good Cajun food. Not the place for a quiet tête-à-tête.... *Tel 504/522-1492. www.mulates.com. 201 Julia St. AE, DC, DISC, MC, V. Sun–Thurs 11am–10pm, Fri–Sat 11am-11pm. No cover.*

See Map 18 on p. 198.

Napoleon House (p. 205) FRENCH QUARTER The music is canned and classical, but this ancient sepia-colored bar is revered by Orleanians. The building dates from 1797 and shows its age. Sip a Pimm's Cup by candlelight here to cap off the night.... *Tel 504/524-9752. www.napoleonhouse.com. 500 Chartres St. AE, DC, DISC, MC, V. Sun–Mon 11am–6:30pm, Tues–Sat 11pm–closing. No cover.*

See Map 19 on p. 211.

O'Flaherty's Irish Channel Pub (p. 207) FRENCH QUARTER A tavern "Where the Celtic Folk Meet," the Irish Channel was the brain child of two true sons of Erin—Danny and Patrick O'Flaherty. A lot goes on here: nightly music by the Celtic Folk, bagpipe and jig lessons, and the occasional concert by visiting icons like Tommy Makem and Paddy Reilly.... *Tel 504/529-1317. www.oflahertysirishpub.com. 508 Toulouse St. AE, DC, DISC, MC, V. Daily noon–closing. Covers vary; call ahead.*

See Map 19 on p. 211.

Oz (p. 210) FRENCH QUARTER Gay men—mostly young—gather to dance together and swoon over the Thursday night Drag Queen Bingo and Calendar Boy revues. Otherwise, Oz is a cruisin', boozin', dancin' kind of place.... *Tel 504/593-9491. www.oznew orleans.com. 800 Bourbon St. No credit cards. Daily 24 hours. Cover on Fri and Sat $5–$10.*

See Map 19 on p. 211.

Palm Court Jazz Cafe (p. 205) FRENCH QUARTER A very New Orleans place, with tile floors, cafe curtains, and a noise level befitting Bourbon Street, the Palm Court showcases many of the Preservation Hall and traditional jazz greats, plus things like chairs and white-clothed tables that you don't get at the Hall itself.... *Tel 504/525-0200. www.palmcourtjazzcafe.com. 1204 Decatur St. AE, DC, DISC, MC, V. Dinner at 7pm, music 8–11pm. Closed Mon and Tues. Cover at tables $5 per person.*

See Map 19 on p. 211.

Pat O'Brien's (p. 208) FRENCH QUARTER Going strong since the 1930s, Pat's mixed up the very first Hurricane, the now-ubiquitous beverage made of rum, a mix, and fruit juices. There's a raucous piano bar to the right of the entrance and a splendid courtyard in the rear, plus a restaurant bearing the same moniker with an entrance on Bourbon St.... *Tel 504/525-4823. www.patobriens.com. 718 St. Peter St. AE, DC, DISC, MC, V. Open Sun–Thurs 11am–3am, Fri–Sat 10am–4am. No cover.*

See Map 19 on p. 211.

Phoenix Bar (p. 210) FAUBOURG MARIGNY An enduring gay bar, the Phoenix is the headquarters of several annual events, including the Mr. Louisiana Leather Contest and annual far-ranging block parties held during Mardi Gras and Southern Decadence weekend—elsewhere called Labor Day weekend.... *Tel 504/945-9264. www.phoenixbar.com. 941 Elysian Fields. No credit cards. Daily 24 hours. No cover.*

See Map 18 on p. 198.

Praline Connection Gospel & Blues Hall (p. 209) WAREHOUSE/ ARTS DISTRICT Not hard to spot—what with the outside walls splashed with jazzy paintings—the cavernous 9,000-square-foot hall is big enough to hold the facades of a couple of houses and still have room for the 50-foot bar. That's the gospel truth. Soul food is served along with the music.... *Tel 504/523-3973. www. pralineconnection.com. 907 S. Peters St. AE, DC, DISC, MC, V. Mon–Sat 11am–3pm; Sun brunch 11am–1am and 2–4pm. Daily lunch $10, Sun brunch $26.*

See Map 18 on p. 198.

Preservation Hall (p. 203) FRENCH QUARTER The definition of grunge (and creature discomfort), the Hall is the place to hunker down and hear the world's best traditional jazz. Get in line by about 7pm for the 8pm open or you may have to hunker down while standing up.... *Tel 504/523-8939, 888/946-JAZZ. 726 St. Peter St. Daily 8pm–midnight. Cover $5.*

See Map 19 on p. 211.

R-Bar (p. 207) FAUBOURG MARIGNY The red and black R is situated under the Royal Street Inn and attracts some of the city's freer spirits. It's a favorite stop along the route for the Society of St. Anne Marching Parade on Mardi Gras Day.... *Tel 504/948-7499, 800/449-5535. www.royalstreetinn.com. 1431 Royal St. AE, DISC, MC, V. Sun–Thurs 3pm–5am, Fri–Sat 3pm–6am. No cover.*

See Map 18 on p. 198.

Rawhide (p. 210) FRENCH QUARTER Gays of the leather and Levi's persuasion dance to the early '80s and the likes of Annie Lennox. It's boisterous, raw, and not for the faint of heart.... *Tel 504/525-8106. www.rawhide2010.com. 740 Burgundy St. No credit cards. Daily 24 hours. No cover.*

See Map 19 on p. 211.

St. Joe's Bar (p. 207) UPTOWN A surprisingly stylish neighborhood bar with a red lantern-lit patio that can make an otherwise run-of-the-mill summer night seem exotic and fun. A pool table and a friendly crowd round out the reasons to go.... *Tel 504/899-3744. 5535 Magazine St.. AE, DC, DISC, MC, V. Mon–Sat 5pm–closing, Sun 8pm–closing. No cover.*

See Map 20 on p. 212.

Saturn Bar (p. 206) BYWATER Way down yonder in Yat Country, a working-class neighborhood below the Quarter, lower even than Faubourg Marigny, this fabled New Orleans bar saluted its Golden Anniversary in 1997. The decor is of the plastic-and-vinyl discipline, with accents of neon and tinsel, and the devoted neighborhood crowd pretty much defines not just funk but "New Orleans funk...." *Tel 504/949-7532. 3067 St. Claude Ave. No credit cards. Daily 4pm–closing. No cover.*

See Map 18 on p. 198.

Sazerac Bar (p. 209) CBD A sleek hangout for the suits, the Fairmont's bar is small and intimate. The house drink, not surprisingly, is the Sazerac, touted as the world's first cocktail. Great place for a romantic rendezvous.... *Tel 504/529-7111. www.sazerac.com. Fairmont Hotel, 123 Baronne St. AE, DC, DISC, MC, V. Daily 10am–midnight. No cover.*

See Map 18 on p. 198.

735 Nightclub and Bar (p. 210) FRENCH QUARTER Billing itself as New Orleans's only true nightclub, 735 does pound the house 7 nights (and mornings) a week. People come here to dance and sweat their butts off. Thursday is '80s Night, Sunday is House Night, and Friday and Saturday feature local DJs. Oh, and just in case you're interested, they also tout Thursday as their "#1 hook-up night".... *Tel 504/581-6748. www.club735.com. 735 Bourbon St. No credit cards. Daily noon–closing. Cover charge Fri and Sat, $5.*

See Map 19 on p. 211.

Snug Harbor (p. 209) FAUBOURG MARIGNY Locals flock to this rambling and rustic two-story place, where modern jazz icons like Ellis Marsalis hold forth. Pretty good burgers and seafood gumbo are served in the restaurant.... *Tel 504/949-0696. www.snugjazz.com. 626 Frenchmen St. AE, DC, DISC, MC, V. Daily 5pm–closing. Shows at 9pm and 11pm, seats for dinner until 10:45pm on weekdays, 11:45pm on weekends. Cover varies for shows.*

See Map 18 on p. 198.

The Spotted Cat (p. 208) FAUBOURG MARIGNY This tiny little lounge in the Marigny hosts at least three accomplished jazz groups a night, every night.... *Tel 504/943-3887. 623 Frenchman St. AE, DISC, MC, V. Mon–Thurs 2pm–3am, Fri–Sun noon–4am. No cover.*

See Map 18 on p. 198.

Steamboat *Natchez* (p. 208) FRENCH QUARTER Tourists get carried away by this big white stern-wheeler, which does evening excursions featuring banjo-thumping traditional jazz and Dixie and a lavish buffet of local specialties. A tame evening for the kids.... *Tel 504/586-8777, 800/233-BOAT. www.steamboatnatchez.com. Toulouse St. Wharf. AE, DC, DISC, MC, V. Boards at 6pm at Toulouse St. Wharf, cruise 7–9pm. Closed for major holidays. Admission with dinner $51 adults, without dinner $30 adults.*

See Map 19 on p. 211.

360 (p. 206) CBD A great place to get an overview of the city and the river while relaxing on plush sofas, this revolving cocktail lounge/nightclub sits on the 33rd floor of the World Trade Center at the foot of Canal Street. On a clear day you can see about 30 miles—but good luck with the New Orleans haze.... *Tel 504/522-9795. 2 Canal St., World Trade Center. AE, DISC, MC, V.*

Sun–Thurs noon–closing, Fri and Sat until 4am. $10 minimum after 10pm.

See Map 18 on p. 198.

Tipitina's (p. 204) UPTOWN The venerable Tipitina's had its back against the wall after the House of Blues marched into town and staked out the Quarter. Tips bounced back, not only air-conditioning the Napoleon Street venue (now called Tipitina's Uptown), but opening two additional locations. Tipitina's Big Room in the Warehouse District is usually for private parties. But Tip's French Quarter is raging and open 6 nights a week.... *Tel 504/895-8477. www.tipitinas.com. Tipitina's Uptown, 501 Napoleon Ave.; Tipitina's Big Room, 310 Howard Ave.; and Tipitina's French Quarter, 233 Decatur St. No credit cards behind bar; no D, DC for merchandise. Tues 8:30pm–closing, Wed–Sun 9pm–closing, closed Mon. Box office open 11am–6pm. Cover varies, call ahead.*

See Map 18 on p. 198.
See Map 19 on p. 211.
See Map 20 on p. 212.

Tony Moran's Absinthe House (p. 205) FRENCH QUARTER A historic building—it dates from 1805—houses the seedy Old Absinthe House bar, whose very seediness seems to appeal to an older crowd of dedicated drinkers.... *Tel 504/523-3181. www.oldabsinthehouse.com 240 Bourbon St. AE, DC, DISC, MC, V. Sun–Thurs 9am–2am, Fri–Sat 9am–4am. No cover.*

See Map 19 on p. 211.

Tropical Isle Bourbon (p. 208) FRENCH QUARTER The house drink is called the Hand Grenade, but by itself the rock and pop packs a wallop. This is a hard-drinking dive with two floors, a balcony overlooking Bourbon, and a lineup of local bands.... *Tel 504/529-4109. www.tropicalisle.com. 721 Bourbon St. AE, DISC, MC, V. Daily noon–closing. No cover.*

See Map 19 on p. 211.

Tropical Isle Toulouse (p. 208) FRENCH QUARTER The Bourbon Street branch was a spinoff from this late-night den. The sounds and sensibilities are about the same in each place, though this locale is big on island music. Very loud, very late. Tropical Itch is the specialty cocktail.... *Tel 504/525-1689. www.tropicalisle.com. 738 Toulouse St. AE, DISC, MC, V. Daily noon–closing. No cover.*

See Map 19 on p. 211.

TwiRoPa (p. 205) LOWER GARDEN DISTRICT This big and fabulous club—formerly a twine, rope, and paper warehouse—is industrial and extremely hip for this down-home city. Because of a lot of nasty construction, it's not easy to find, and its environs resemble downtown Tikrit. But if you can find it, you will not be disappointed: Eight bars and six dance floors will see to that.... *Tel 504/587-3777. www.twiropa.com. 1544 Tchoupitoulas St. AE, DC, DISC, MC, V. Daily 10pm–closing. Cover $5–$10.*

See Map 18 on p. 198.

Utopia FRENCH QUARTER Live blues blares out of this 500-seat covered courtyard. In a departure from local tradition, the dance floor is actually big enough for dancing.... *Tel 504/523-3800. www.bourbonstr.com. 227 Bourbon St. AE, DISC, MC, V. Mon–Thurs 4pm–closing, Fri 2pm–closing, Sat--Sun noon–closing. Cover varies; call ahead.*

See Map 19 on p. 211.

Vaughan's Lounge (p. 205) BYWATER By agreement with the neighbors, this place is just a bar 6 nights a week. But on Thursdays it literally cooks: Local trumpet great Kermit Ruffins plays with his band the Barbecue Swingers, and between sets, he cooks up barbecue and dishes it out to his fans.... *Tel 504/947-5562. 800 Lesseps St. No credit cards. Mon–Fri 11am–closing, Sat–Sun, noon–closing. Cover on Thurs $10.*

See Map 18 on p. 198.

Vic's Kangaroo Cafe (p. 209) WAREHOUSE/ARTS DISTRICT This long, skinny cafe also lines out good gutbucket blues from a jazz jukebox. A short menu showcases burgers, sandwiches, and pizza. There's also a decent selection of Down Under wines.... *Tel 504/524-GDAY. 636 Tchoupitoulas St. AE, DISC, MC, V. 11pm–closing. No cover.*

See Map 18 on p. 198.

Victorian Lounge (p. 205) UPTOWN The dark, romantic Victorian Lounge seduces loads of locals with its wood-burning fireplace, clubby velvet-upholstered chairs, and pressed-tin ceiling. Live and sultry modern jazz Tuesdays, Wednesdays, and Fridays.... *Tel 504/899-9308. Columns Hotel, 3811 St. Charles Ave. MC, V. Mon–Thurs 3pm–midnight, Fri 3pm–2am, Sun 10am–midnight. No cover.*

See Map 20 on p. 212.

ENTERTA

INMENT

Map 21: New Orleans Entertainment

Information
Ferry Service to Algiers Point
Riverwalk streetcar route/stops
St. Charles streetcar route/stops
Canal streetcar route/stops
Vieux Carre loop route/stops

Big Daddy's **11**
Contemporary Art Center **7**
le chat noir **8**
Le Petit Theatre du Vieux Carré **12**
Mahalia Jackson Theatre of Performing Arts **6**
New Orleans Arena **2**
Orpheum Theatre **4**
Saenger Theatre **5**
Southern Repertory Theater **10**
Superdrome **3**
True Brew **9**
Zephyr Stadium **1**

ENTERTAINMENT

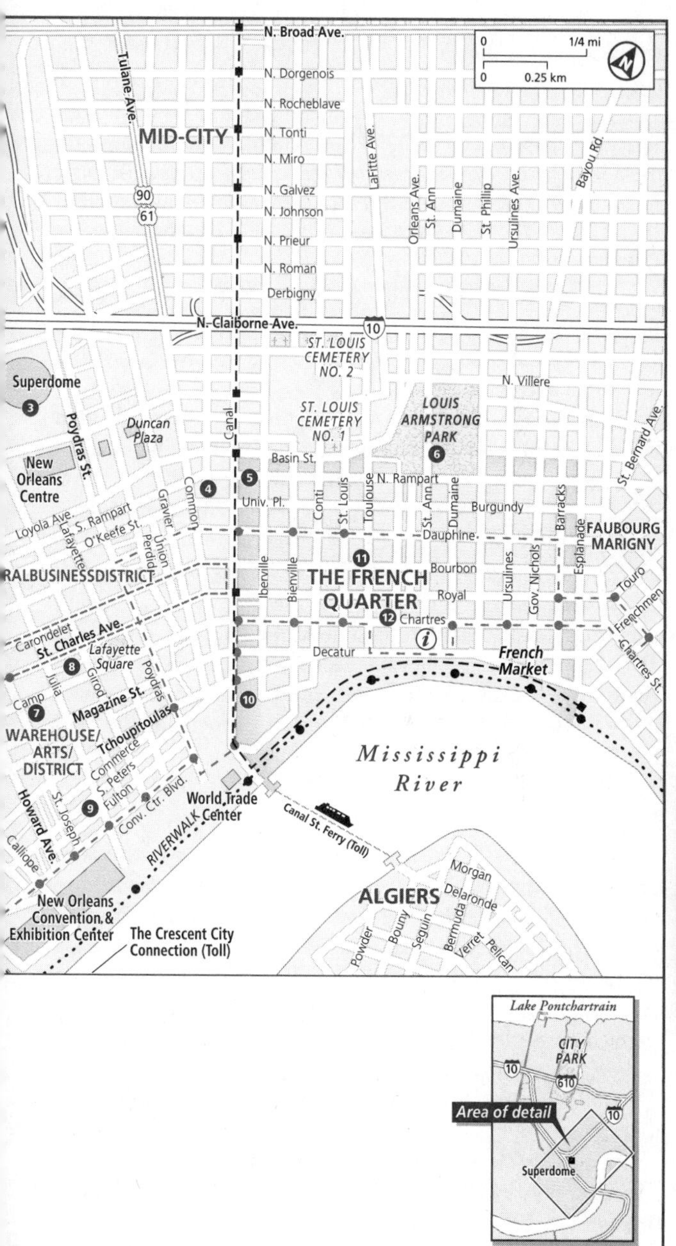

ENTERTAINMENT

Basic Stuff

Used to be, the local artsy crowd would wring their collective hands, deploring the fact that New Orleans was not New York. They loved New Orleans—wouldn't live anywhere else on the planet, to be sure—but still, they suffered from a bit of an inferiority complex. Okay, so New York is not very big on Mardi Gras, and Jazz Fest can certainly hold its own against New York's JVC Jazz Festival. But after that...? Eventually they stopped wringing their hands, got themselves together, and created what they like to refer to as the "SoHo of the South"—the Warehouse/Arts District. The centerpiece of that artsy district, the Contemporary Arts Center (CAC), is the shrine in which all local alternative artists worship. It's still not New York, but hey, is that such a bad thing?

Otherwise, the big scenes in New Orleans are played out in music clubs and restaurants. The city has no big-time theater, except for road shows that play the Saenger Performing Arts Center. Locally, there is only one professional Actors Equity company, the Southern Repertory Theatre, and it focuses on new works, primarily by Southern playwrights. Major concerts are booked into the Superdome or the newish New Orleans Arena next door. Other top-name acts come into the Kiefer UNO Lakefront Arena, but they don't necessarily have any local flavor—you're likely to catch the same shows in Cleveland or Salt Lake City. Check out the Nightlife chapter for the stuff that really makes New Orleans swing.

Sources

Frankly, if you're still in the planning stages of your trip to New Orleans, don't worry about scoping out the culture scene beforehand—you'll be able to get tickets easily enough once you're in town. (The one exception to this is Jazz Fest—see p. 10.) Pick up "Lagniappe," the ***Times-Picayune***'s weekend entertainment tabloid, which comes out with the paper every Friday. It gives a pretty trustworthy rundown on what's doing around town in theaters, art galleries, music clubs, and so forth.

Gambit, a free weekly paper available at newsstands and bookstores, also has listings of current events, though it's not as knowledgeable on the theater scene as it is on the music clubs.

Most hotels have copies lying around of ***This Week in New Orleans*** and ***Where,*** both of them free (and totally uncritical) magazines with calendars of events, feature articles, shopping news, and such.

Getting Tickets

The only really tough tickets in town are for the occasional major pop concerts, like Cher or Britney Spears. Tickets for events at the **Louisiana Superdome, New Orleans Arena, Kiefer UNO Lakefront Arena,** and **Saenger Performing Arts Center** are sold through **Ticketmaster** (credit card charge line tel 504/522–5555 or 800/488–5252). The other local theaters, however, are all small enough that any seat gives a decent view. The administrative offices of the city's opera, ballet, and symphony are staffed, usually weekdays from 9am until 5pm, if you need to call for information, but theater box offices are only open during the run of a show. Tickets for community-theater productions are in the $8 to $15 range; opera tickets are $30 to $80; ballet, concerts, and road shows can range anywhere from $15 to $100. Tickets for Saints or Hornets games start at $30, and for New Orleans Brass hockey games $6.

The Lowdown

The play's the thing... New Orleans has only one Equity theater company: **Southern Repertory Theatre,** which puts on a season of plays by known and unknown Southern playwrights in its plush and intimate 150-seat theater on the third level of the Canal Place mall. The quality of its productions can be pretty uneven; a few of their past productions, including their all-black version of Tennessee Williams's *The Rose Tattoo* some years ago, were roundly panned. More recently, however, the production of *Dyna Washington* got rave reviews—interesting, since the director, Tammye Myrick, had to fill in last minute for the lead.

They've also turned out a couple of other decent performances, such as Ernest Gaines's *A Lesson Before Dying,* and *Lady Day,* a show about the life of Billie Holiday. Southern Rep mounted the longest-running original comedy in New Orleans theater history, *...And the Ball And All,* written by Ricky Graham and starring Becky Allen, two local theater legends. The very funny play is about the fictitious all-female Carnival krewe, The Krewe of Terpsichore, and if it reprises when you're in town, do go see it. Also, look for theater listings that include the name David Cuthbert, another very talented local writer/composer who's conveniently the *Times-Picayune* theater critic. A play that featured all three—Graham, Allen, and Cuthbert—would most definitely be worth a special trip to New Orleans. Try to find out what the *Times-Picayune*'s critic has to say about whatever's on the marquee when you get to town.

The Southern Rep's theater is the occasional venue for co-productions with local producers, so don't expect everything that plays in this mall-top theater to fit the Southern Rep's criteria. If you're looking for the avant-garde, look first to the **Contemporary Arts Center (CAC).** The CAC got off the ground in 1976, after a local corporation donated a warehouse for use by a group of struggling alternative artists. The large two-story erstwhile warehouse, its exterior painted dark red, evokes an airy feeling of freedom, with its 10,000 square feet of space and big windows that let in the sunlight. The center has grown as it's been renovated, and now absolutely adores itself for its outrageousness, its outlandishness, and its ability to shock the socks off uptown Orleanians with various nudities and obscenities. But self-involved as it may be, it does attract some notable talent. In 1995, Edward Albee directed the regional premiere of his play *Fragments,* using only local actors.

The CAC has also featured the likes of Cassandra Wilson singing (what else?) jazz. Up until very recently, the prestigious theater in New Orleans, locally speaking, was **Le Petit Théâtre du Vieux Carré.** Claiming to be the oldest continuously operating community theater in the country, Le Petit used to do solid top-quality productions of mainstream plays and musicals—the CAC crowd thought these were far too staid and conservative, but they were still quite professionally done. But in the last several years, Le Petit productions have not been nearly as polished, and their ticket subscriptions have been dropping off. It's almost worth the price of a theater ticket, though, just to see the building—a charmingly restored 18th-century building on Jackson Square, built around a courtyard. In a corner of the building, **Teddy's Corner** presents well-attended children's plays.

True Brew is a funky little coffeehouse in the Warehouse/Arts District where some very good plays, usually one-acts by local playwrights, are performed. Orleanians adore True Brew—it has the flavor of Greenwich Village in the 1960s—and the arts crowd likes to hang out here even if there's no play on the boards at the moment.

Classical sounds... Emeril's restaurant, to name just one popular eatery, gets better local support than does classical music around here. New Orleans's only symphony orchestra is the **Louisiana Philharmonic Orchestra (LPO),** whose season runs September through May. The Classics Concerts include works by the standard classical composers—Mendelssohn, Prokofiev, Tchaikovsky, and the gang; audiences dress more casually for the Beethoven in Blue Jeans series, which mixes Beethoven with 20th-century artists like Copland, Bernstein, and Gershwin. In December, Handel's *Messiah* and a holiday concert series are always performed. The LPO also shows off its chamber music skills at least once a year in Roussell Hall at Loyola University. Playing in the ornate old Orpheum Theatre (129 University Place), the LPO is a fine orchestra, which ends up playing the same standards year after year because it can't count on a more adventurous audience. It is for the most part made up of dedicated musicians from the defunct **New Orleans Symphony,** which struggled for years and finally went belly-up in 1991. The maestro currently wielding the baton in front of the LPO is Klaus Peter Seibel of the Frankfurt and Dresden Operas.

Learn the Lingo

You'll never be far away from the term **second line.** *The most basic definition refers to the second line of people behind the coffin in a jazz funeral. The first line is the brass band, the second line is comprised of the mourners. On the way to the burial, the bands play low dirges and the mourners actually mourn. But once the body is interred and the procession leaves the cemetery, the mood transforms to one of jubilation as the departed's loved ones celebrate his rise into heaven. "Down by the Riverside" "I'll Fly Away," and even "Bourbon Street Parade" are songs commonly played while the second-liners do their thing. These days, the term second line extends to a variety of situations: People yucking and chucking behind brass bands in a Mardi Gras parade can be "second-lining." Or if the mood strikes patrons in a jazz club or under one of the tents at Jazz Fest, they can grab their decorated umbrellas (a common accessory that you pump up and down while you dance) or their white kerchiefs (to be twirled overhead), and boogie around the room or tent usually in conga-line fashion. In almost any situation, the song "When the Saints Go Marching In" will spark a spontaneous second line in this town.*

Grand ole opera... Opera was first performed in this country in New Orleans in 1796—the French opera *Sylvain* was the production. A permanent opera company was established here in 1813, and the city's present company, the **New Orleans Opera Association,** was formed in the 1940s. From 1859 until 1919, the French Opera House at the corner of Toulouse and Bourbon streets in the Quarter was the scene of lavish operas and balls. But despite the Orleanian love of opera, the opera house was not rebuilt after fire destroyed it, and its lot sat vacant until the 1960s, when a hotel was built there (at 541 Bourbon St.). These days, celebrity conductors and national and international opera stars perform with the New Orleans Opera Association in four annual productions (though there are eight total performances), running October through May. It ain't the Met, but the operas are handsomely mounted and fairly well attended by locals. They take place in the **Mahalia Jackson Theatre of the Performing Arts,** with its red plush seats and lovely sparkling crystal chandeliers. It's one of two performance spaces in the city's Cultural Center in Armstrong Park, which includes the Municipal Auditorium. The auditorium had been converted first to a casino and then to a venue for the New Orleans Brass ice hockey team, but now it's back in cultural commission as a host for concerts and Jazz Fest.

Men in tights... As is the case with the symphony, New Orleans does not have what you would call a good track record in terms of The Dance. The **New Orleans Ballet Association** is essentially a producer—or "dance presenter," as it is defined by the National Endowment for the Arts—bringing to town guest companies, both classical and modern, such as the Royal Winnipeg Ballet and the Chicago Dance Theater. It also promotes the New Orleans Ballet Ensemble, a multi-ethnic troupe of nonprofessional dancers performing in school outreach programs—a worthy community program but not much of a dance asset for visitors. The association evolved—or should we say devolved—from the New Orleans City Ballet which, from 1983 until 1991, did split seasons with the Cincinnati City Ballet, with the two cities sharing artists and repertoire. Ballet and other dance performances take place in the **Mahalia Jackson Theatre of the Performing Arts** in

Armstrong Park between September and June. If you love dance, it's worth checking the papers once you hit town to see whether a notable national company is performing during your stay; you can pretty well depend on tickets being available. For a taste of something not wholly "classical," you may want to investigate where **N.O.Madic Tribal Belly Dance Co.** is performing, or find out about participating in one of the classes they teach throughout the city.

Life is a cabaret... There are "cabarets" galore on Bourbon Street, if the term is quite loosely applied to the sundry topless, bottomless, and burlesque establishments. The longest-running and best known of them all is **Big Daddy's.** More respectable, and well across Canal Street from the Bourbon Street hustle, **le chat noir** is a chic venue for cabarets and revues. Adjacent to the Board of Trade building, the somewhat pretentiously lower-case black cat theater has mounted, among other things, *Soireé Edith Piaf,* locally produced Broadway and Off-Broadway hits like *Cabaret,* and some pretty hilarious comedy shows.

The big game... Well, how 'bout dem Saints? as dey say locally. The beleaguered **New Orleans Saints** of the National Football League play their home games on Sunday—and on the occasional Monday night—in the almost overpoweringly big Louisiana Superdome. Saints fans tend to be wildly demonstrative, especially so when the team is losing, as it does all too often. But passionate as these fans are, there aren't so many of them that they sell out the Dome (it's a pretty big place, after all); tickets are usually available. But, hey, they did make Game One of the playoffs in 2000, right? Regardless of their skills on the field, the Saints' halftime is a colorful event, with Dixieland and marching bands putting on a gaudy, high-spirited show. Home games of the **Tulane Green Wave** are played on Saturday during the season in the Dome, which is also home to the Sugar Bowl, one of the oldest of the college bowl games, played either on New Year's Eve or New Year's Day. Around Sugar Bowl time, the French Quarter is mobbed with shrieking, not altogether sober college kids, and nobody sobers up or becomes any more subdued inside the Dome. The Super Bowl, played in New Orleans more than in any other city, usually pops up here every 4 years.

The late January date causes the Super Bowl to more or less merge with the Sugar Bowl and then Mardi Gras (Carnival season begins annually on Jan 6, Twelfth Night), so the city at that time is awash with celebs, NFL, and media types.

If you're a baseball fan, you might enjoy watching the **New Orleans Zephyrs Baseball Club** play ball at **Zephyrs Stadium** in Metairie (admission charged). The AAA club, affiliated with the Houston Astros, manages to hold its own somewhere in the middle of the American Association's won/lost rankings. Think small-town Americana and you've captured the ambience. The way major-league baseball's going these days, there's something appealing and refreshing about an AAA game.

Ever since the New Orleans Jazz fled the city and became the Utah Jazz, loyal B-ball aficionados have fought to acquire another professional basketball team. In 2002, the Charlotte **Hornets** answered their prayers. The Hornets play in the **New Orleans Arena,** which opened in late 1999 with a price tag of $84 million in the side yard of the Superdome. The glitzy arena was constructed with the "if you build it, they will come" mentality. "They" are here.

The Index

Please see Map 21 on p. 228 for all Entertainment listings.

Big Daddy's (p. 235) FRENCH QUARTER The longest-running of Bourbon Street's raunchy burlesque clubs.... *Tel 504/581-7167. 522 Bourbon St. Daily 3pm–4am. AE, DC, DISC, MC, V. No cover.*

Contemporary Arts Center (p. 232) WAREHOUSE/ARTS DISTRICT The hottest spot in town for experimental and avant-garde theater, the CAC has two spaces at its Warehouse District headquarters. Both mount plays of regional playwrights, as well as traveling shows, national and international.... *Tel 504/528-3805, box office 504/528-3800. www.cacno.org. 900 Camp St. Gallery hours Tues–Sun 11am–5pm; show times vary. AE, MC, V. Tickets $5–$25; student and member discounts.*

Kiefer UNO Lakefront Arena (p. 231) LAKEFRONT A rather soulless 10,000-seat auditorium on the east campus of the University of New Orleans. During his 1987 visit, Pope John Paul II celebrated a huge outdoor Mass in a specially constructed gazebo on the grounds.... *Tel 504/280-7171, box office 504/280-7222. www.arena.uno.edu. 6801 Franklin Ave. at Lakeshore Dr. AE, MC, V. Call ahead for show prices and times.*

le chat noir (p. 235) CBD This determinedly lower-case theater, adjacent to the Board of Trade, presents sophisticated programs, such as the "New York–style cabaret" *A Cocktail Party in the Ladies Lounge,* which ran in early 2000. They feature some of the best in local music, comedy, and cabaret, plus locally produced Broadway and off-Broadway shows.... *Tel 504/581-5812. www.cabaretlechatnoir.com. 715 St. Charles Ave. Open 6 days, closed 1 rotating day per week. Show times vary. AE, MC, V. Tickets $10–$35.*

Le Petit Théâtre du Vieux Carré (p. 232) FRENCH QUARTER One of the nation's oldest continuously operating community theaters, Le Petit features musicals, plays, and productions for children in a historic building on Jackson Square in the French

Quarter. Children's shows are presented weekends in Teddy's Corner, in the same building as Le Petit during the season.... *Tel 504/522-2081 or 504/522-9958. www.lepetittheatre.com. 616 St. Peter St. Season Sept–June. Fri–Sun; show times vary. AE, DISC, MC, V. Ticket prices vary.*

Louisiana Philharmonic Orchestra (p. 233) CBD Classics and pops are performed in the Beaux Arts Orpheum Theatre in the CBD.... *Tel 504/523-6530. www.lpomusic.com. 305 Barrone St., Suite 600. Season Sept–May. Show times and days vary. AE, DISC, MC, V. Tickets $11–$52.*

Louisiana Superdome (p. 231) CBD The seats in the Dome, the largest facility of its kind, can be shuffled around like a deck of cards to accommodate everything from football games (the New Orleans Saints, Tulane Green Wave, New Orleans VooDoo) to rock concerts.... *Tel 504/587-3663. www.superdome.com. 1500 Sugar Bowl Dr. Football season Aug–Dec. AE, MC, V. Saints tickets start at $30.*

Mahalia Jackson Theatre of the Performing Arts (p. 234) FRENCH QUARTER The New Orleans opera and visiting ballet companies perform in the sophisticated theater, with red plush seats, crystal chandeliers, and warm wood paneling. It's on the fringe of the French Quarter, in Armstrong Park.... *Tel 504/565-7470. 801 N. Rampart St. Accepted credit cards vary per show. Tickets $15–$75.*

New Orleans Arena (p. 231) CBD Toward the golden goal of acquiring a professional basketball team, this 20,000-seat arena was constructed and opened in 1999. Now proud home to the Hornets (acquired from Charlotte in 2002) as well as Tom Benson's Arena Football team the VooDoo, this mini-Dome also hosts excellent big-name rock and pop concerts.... *Tel 504/587-3663, 800/756-7074. www.neworleansarena.com. 1501 Girod St. Call ahead for game/performance times. AE, MC, V. Ticket prices vary.*

New Orleans Ballet Association (p. 234) FRENCH QUARTER Classical ballets are performed by visiting companies in the Mahalia Jackson Theatre for the Performing Arts.... *Box office tel 504/565-7470. Performances at 801 N. Rampart St. Ballet office tel 504/522-0996. www.nobadance.com. 305 Baronne St., Suite 700. Season Sept–May. AE, DISC, MC, V. Tickets $26–$75.*

New Orleans Hornets (p. 236) CBD New Orleans hasn't had a pro basketball team since the long-ago days of the New Orleans Jazz. Now the Hornets, acquired from Charlotte in 2002, are here to stay and locals could not be happier.... *Tel 504/587-3663, 800/756-7074. www.hornets.com. 1501 Girod St. Call ahead for game times. AE, MC, V. Single game tickets $7–$216.*

New Orleans Opera Association (p. 234) FRENCH QUARTER Opera—grand and comic—is performed at the Mahalia Jackson Theatre for the Performing Arts.... *Box office tel 504/565-7470. Performances at 801 N. Rampart St. Opera office tel 504/529-2278, 800/881-4459. www.neworleansopera.org. 305 Baronne St., Suite 500. Season Oct–April. AE, MC, V. Ticket prices $30–$100.*

New Orleans Saints (p. 235) CBC The Crescent City entry in the National Football League plays home games on Sunday afternoons, and occasionally on Monday nights, in the Louisiana Superdome (see above). The hapless Saints have a knack for breaking their fans' hearts, either with downright abysmal seasons, or with strong starts leading to lackluster finishes.... *Ticket office tel 504/731-1700. www.neworleanssaints.com. 1500 Poydras St. Season Aug–Dec. AE, MC, V. Tickets $60–$150.*

New Orleans Zephyrs Baseball Club (p. 236) METAIRIE A triple-A club affiliated with the Houston Astros, the Zephyrs play home games in their own 10,000-seat stadium in Metairie (see below).... *Tel 504/734-5155. www.zephyrsbaseball.com. 6000 Airline Hwy. Season April–Sept. AE, DISC, MC, V. Tickets $5–$9.50.*

N.O.Madic Tribal Belly Dance Co. (p. 235) For a break from the two-step, check out this American tribal-style belly-dance troupe. You'll find them shaking their bellies (and more) at several venues throughout the city, including Cafe Brasil, the Dragon's Den, and the Contemporary Arts Center.... *Tel 504/914-5666. www.nomadictribal.com for upcoming performances.*

Orpheum Theatre (p. 233) CBD An ornate, acoustically fine, 1,700-seat theater with a Beaux Arts facade, this auditorium was built in 1918. These days it's home to the Louisiana Philharmonic Orchestra.... *Tel 504/524-3285. www.orpheumneworleans.com. 129 University Place. Show times vary. AE, MC, V. Tickets $25–$65.*

Roussell Hall (p. 233) UPTOWN The Louisiana Philharmonic occasionally performs in this recital hall on the campus of Loyola University. For information, contact the LPO administrative office (see above). They host other eclectic international music and dance performances throughout the year, and the New Orleans International Piano Competition in the summer.... *Tel 504/865-3492. www.music.loyno.edu. 6363 St. Charles Ave. Show times vary. MC, V. Tickets $5–$20; student discounts.*

Saenger Performing Arts Center (p. 231) FRENCH QUARTER Where the big acts play. Touring companies of Broadway shows and top-name nightclub acts perform in this 2,800-seat Italian Renaissance theater built in the 1920s and dramatically decorated with statuary and ersatz stars in a midnight-blue sky.... *Tel 504/525-1052. www.saengertheatre.com. 143 N. Rampart St. Show times vary. MC, V. Ticket prices vary.*

Southern Repertory Theatre (p. 231) FRENCH QUARTER The city's only Equity theater troupe performs plays by Southern playwrights, the known and the unknown, in a plush 150-seat theater on the third level of the Canal Place mall.... *Tel 504/522-6545. www.southernrep.com. 333 Canal St. Season Sept–June. MC, V. Tickets $23; student and senior discounts.*

True Brew (p. 232) WAREHOUSE/ARTS DISTRICT Some of the city's most popular plays have been—and are—performed in this very casual coffeehouse in a renovated warehouse, in (naturally) the Warehouse District.... *Tel 504/524-8441, box office tel 504/524-8440. 200 Julia St. MC, V. Tickets $26.*

Tulane Green Wave (p. 235) CBD On Saturday afternoons in the fall, Tulane University's football team plays home games in the Superdome. Some home games of the Green Wave basketball club are played in the New Orleans Arena.... *Tel 504/865-5506 (sports information line), 504/861-WAVE. www.tulanegreenwave.com. 1520 Sugar Bowl Dr. AE, MC, V. Football tickets $20–$30, basketball $10–$18.*

Zephyrs Stadium (p. 236) METAIRIE Where the Zephyrs play AAA baseball.... *Tel 504/734-5155. www.zephyrsbaseball.com. 6000 Airline Hwy. Season April–Sept. AE, DISC, MC, V. Tickets $5–$9.50.*

HOTLINES & OTHER BASICS

Airports... Soaring 4 feet above sea level, **Louis Armstrong International Airport** (tel 504/464-3547; www.flymsy.com) is in Kenner, a small town about 15 miles west of downtown New Orleans. All domestic airlines drop in, as well as several international carriers. **Airport Shuttle** (tel 504/522-3500, 866/596-2699; www.bigeasy.com) operates minivans from and to the airport; one-way fare is $13 per person, $26 round-trip. At the airport, you just walk out of the terminal and board one. Your hotel will make the (necessary) reservations for your return to the airport. If you call **United Cab Company** (tel 504/522-9771, 800/323-3303; www.united cabs.com) and reserve in advance, a United cab will pick you up at the airport; give them your name and arrival particulars (flight date, time, airline). There is no additional fee above the regular fare from the airport: $28 for up to two people. For more than a pair, the fare is $12 per person. Four or more is $8 to $10 per person. Or you could always head to the taxi stand and grab a cab just outside of baggage claim. The wait is hardly ever that long.

Babysitters... Both **Accent Child Care** (tel 504/524-1227; www.accentoca.com) and **Dependable Kid Care** (tel 504/486-4001, 800/862-5806; www.dependablekidcare.com) offer in-hotel sitters and, if you like, they'll take the kids out on specially designed kiddie-type tours while you're knocking back Sazeracs somewhere.

Buses... **Greyhound Bus,** 1001 Loyola Ave. (tel 800/231-2222) shares Union Passenger Terminal with Amtrak. City buses and streetcars are operated by the Regional Transit Authority. Call the 24-hour **RideLine** (tel 504/248-3900) for information about routes. Fare on the buses and the St. Charles Streetcar is $1.25; the Riverfront Streetcar costs $1.50. The **St. Charles Streetcar** rumbles up St. Charles Avenue from the CBD past Audubon Park and Tulane and Loyola universities; at the river's bend, where St. Charles Avenue dead-ends, it hangs a right on Carrollton Avenue and runs on to Palmer Park. The **Riverfront Streetcar** runs parallel with the river—though not exactly on the river's bank—from Esplanade Avenue on the lower border of the French Quarter, past the French Market, Jax Brewery, Riverwalk, and the Ernest N. Morial Convention Center in the Warehouse District. A **VisiTour pass** gives you unlimited rides on city buses and streetcars, at $5 for 1 day, $12 for 3 days. They're sold in hotels, shopping centers, and visitor information booths.

Car rentals... All of the major car rental companies have outlets at the airport and downtown: **Avis,** 2024 Canal St. (tel 504/523-4317, 800/331-1212; after 5pm, emergency contact at airport tel 504/464-9511; www.avis.com); **Budget,** 4841 Veterans Memorial Blvd. or 1245 Airline Dr. (tel 504/565-5617, 800/527-0700; airport contact tel 504/465-8740; www.budget.com); **Dollar,** 230 Loyola Ave. (tel 504/524-1800, 800/800-4000; airport contact tel 504/467-2286; www.dollar.com); and **Hertz,** 901 Convention Center Blvd. (tel 504/568-1645, 800/654-3131; airport contact tel 504/465-1202; www.hertz.com).

Convention center... One of these years, expansion of the **Ernest N. Morial Convention Center,** 900 Convention Center Blvd., CBD (tel 504/582-3000; www.mccno.com) will have to stop because they'll simply run out of land.

The Convention Center has several zillion square feet of "contiguous space," and the expansion continues. It's one of the largest such facilities in the country, and with New Orleans being a favorite party place, conventions are booked through 2007. The Sunday night before Fat Tuesday, Bacchus has its big bash in the center, replete with marching bands and floats. Giant floats (and very exuberant float riders) lumber round and round the floors amidst a shrieking throng of some 2,000. The boys of Bacchus save up their best beads to heave at their families and friends. Sorry, it's a members-only event.

Learn the Lingo

In any normal city, the strip running down the center of a boulevard is called a median. In New Orleans, a median is called the **neutral ground.** *The term harks back to when the city was divided between Creoles and Americans. Creoles took it as real tacky when the Americans came to town, and they gave the "barbarians" a royal snubbing. The Americans began building their homes on the upriver side of a broad dirt strip that bordered the French town. Fistfights frequently broke out between the French and the Americans, and the dirt strip became a sort of DMZ—a neutral ground—between them. The drainage canal that was to be built on the strip never happened, and now Canal Street runs over it—a wide street with city buses and streetcars wheezing through the "neutral ground." A sidewalk is a* **banquette,** *a French word that dates from colonial days. However, it's pronounced here to rhyme with "blanket."*

Dentists... For referrals, contact the **New Orleans Dental Association,** 2121 N. Causeway Blvd., Suite 153, Metairie (tel 504/834-6449).

Doctors... All of the major hospitals have referral services for specialists, or you can contact the **Tulane University Professional/Physicians Referral Group** (tel 504/588-5800) or **Touro Infirmary** (tel 504/897-7777).

Driving around... Interstate 10 is the major east–west artery through town; I-55 runs north–south, connecting with I-10 west of town. U.S. 90 (aka the Old Spanish Trail) loops through town, and I-12 runs east–west on the north shore of Lake Pontchartrain. I-59 is a north–south artery that connects with I-10 east of the city. Don't look for a French Quarter exit off I-10; it's called Vieux Carré, and it's exit

235A. Exit at Poydras Street to reach the Central Business District (CBD). Outside of the CBD and the French Quarter, New Orleans has a real problem with street signs—they're hard to spot, let alone read. And Orleanians are notoriously whimsical lane-switchers. One more note: If you're driving around town during Mardi Gras and innocently block a parade route, you'll be fined $100. Now you've been warned.

Gay and lesbian resources... There is a **Lesbian and Gay Community Center** at 2114 Decatur St., Faubourg Marigny (tel 504/945-1103; www.lgccno.net). Hours are Monday through Friday 2 to 8pm, Saturday and Sunday noon to 6pm. ***Ambush*** and ***Impact Gulf South Gay News*** chronicle the area's news and events from a gay perspective.

Medical emergencies... Dial 911 for emergency assistance. Hospitals with 24-hour emergency rooms are **Tulane University Medical Center,** 1415 Tulane Ave., CBD (tel 504/588-5711); **Touro Infirmary,** 1401 Foucher St., Uptown (tel 504/897-8250); and the **Medical Center of Louisiana,** 1532 Tulane Ave., CBD (tel 504/903-2311), which everyone locally calls Charity Hospital. The hotline of the **No/Aids Task Force** in New Orleans (tel 504/821-6050) and statewide (tel 800/99-AIDS9 or 800/992-4379, TDD 877/566–9448; www.noaidstaskforce.org) is staffed Monday through Friday from 10am to 8pm and Saturday from 9am to 4pm. Drop-in testing is available without an appointment at the Task Force office, 2601 Tulane Ave., Suite 500, Mid-City (tel 504/821-2601), Monday, Wednesday, and Friday between 5:30 and 7pm.

Festivals & Special Events

JANUARY: The **Sugar Bowl Classic** is played in the Louisiana Superdome at 1500 Sugar Bowl Dr., New Orleans, LA 70112, on either New Year's Eve or New Year's Day (it can vary from year to year), with attendant basketball tournament, sailing, tennis, swimming, and flag football championship games (tel 504/525-8573). **Carnival season** begins annually on January 6.

FEBRUARY–MARCH: **Mardi Gras** takes place in February or March, depending upon the date of Easter. Fat Tuesday, the final day of the Carnival season, falls 40 days before

Easter Sunday, not counting Sundays. On **Lundi Gras,** the Monday before Mardi Gras, the city throws a free masked ball on Spanish Plaza, with live music, fireworks, and big crowds (for Mardi Gras and Lundi Gras information, contact the **New Orleans Metropolitan Convention & Visitors Bureau:** tel 504/566-5011; 1520 Sugar Bowl Dr., New Orleans, LA 70112; www.neworleanscvb.com). Other March events whose dates can fluctuate are the **New Orleans Writers' Conference** and the **Tennessee Williams New Orleans Literary Festival** (for both: tel 504/581-1144; www.tennesseewilliams.net). There are always at least two **St. Patrick's Day parades,** one in the Irish channel—a working-class neighborhood near the Garden District—and another in the French Quarter (contact Molly's at the Market; tel 504/525-5169; 1107 Decatur St., New Orleans, LA 70116; www.mollysatthemarket.net). **St. Joseph's Day** is March 19, but the related Italian-American parade and celebration falls on the second Saturday of the month (American Italian Renaissance Foundation; tel 504/522-7294; 1608 S. Salcedo St., New Orleans, LA 70125). The **Black Heritage Festival** honors contributions of African Americans, with festivities at Armstrong Park, the New Orleans Museum of Art, and the Louisiana State Museum (Black Heritage Foundation; tel 504/827-0112; 4535 S. Prieur St., New Orleans, LA 70125). The **HP Classic**—a PGA event with a multimillion-dollar purse (which increases each year) and live television coverage—is played annually at the English Turn Country Club (tel 504/831-4653; 110 Veterans Blvd., Suite 170, Metairie, LA 70005).

APRIL: Held the second weekend in April, the **French Quarter Festival** is a blast covering several blocks, including Jackson Square and the French Market (tel 504/522-5730; 400 N. Peters St., Suite 205, New Orleans, LA 70130; www.fqfi.org). **Spring Fiesta** kicks off the Friday following Easter, with a parade through the Quarter featuring horse-drawn carriages, belles, and bands; the 5-day festival includes tours of private historic homes and courtyards all aglow with candles (tel 504/581-1367; 826 St. Ann St., New Orleans, LA 70116). About 20,000 runners take part in April's **Crescent City Classic,** a 10,000-meter race from Jackson Square to Audubon Park, with plenty of attendant hoopla and hype (tel 504/861-8686; P.O. Box 13587, New

Orleans, LA 70185; www.ccc10k.com). The dust has scarcely settled before it's time for the **New Orleans Jazz & Heritage Festival,** the second biggest event after Mardi Gras. Dates fluctuate, since it zings from the last weekend in April until the first weekend in May (tel 504/522-4786; 1205 N. Rampart St., New Orleans, LA 70116; www.nojazzfest.com).

MAY: The **Greek Festival** is a charmer, played out at the Hellenic Cultural Center and the Greek Orthodox church near City Park. Greek music, dancing, and food, of course, are featured (Holy Trinity Cathedral; tel 504/282-0259, 1200 Robert E. Lee Blvd., New Orleans, LA 70122; www.greekfestnola.com).

JUNE: June brings the **Great French Market Tomato Festival** (tel 504/522-2621; French Market Corporation, 1008 N. Peters St., New Orleans, LA 70116; www.frenchmarket.org); and **The Reggae Riddums Festival** in City Park (Orpus Entertainment Corporation and International Arts Foundation; tel 504/367-1313; P.O. Box 6156, New Orleans, LA 70174; www.internationalartsfestival.com).

JULY: **Go 4th on the River** is the big Independence Day blowout on the Mississippi, with enough fireworks to rattle the Ole Man right out of his sluggishness (tel 504/528-9994; 610 S. Peters St., Suite 301, New Orleans, LA 70130). Also this month is the **Essence Music Festival,** starring 3 days of empowerment seminars and 3 nights of concerts at the Superdome.

AUGUST: In August we sweat.

SEPTEMBER: The next to-do is the **Swamp Festival** at the Audubon Zoo—a 4-day event celebrating Louisiana bayou country with Cajun music, food, and crafts (Audubon Institute; tel 800/744-7394; 6500 Magazine St., New Orleans, LA 70118).

OCTOBER: The **New Orleans Film & Video Festival** is a film buffs' bash at Canal Place, the Prytania Theatre, and the Contemporary Arts Center, with local premieres and such (tel 504/523-3818; 843 Carondelet St., New Orleans, LA 70130; www.neworleansfilmfest.com). Halloween is celebrated in grand style in this city—we Orleanians love to don costumes.

NOVEMBER: The annual **Bayou Classic** at the Superdome pits Grambling State University against Southern University in an end-of-the-season grudge match (Louisiana Superdome Ticket Office: tel 504/587-3822; P.O. Box 50488, New Orleans, LA 70150). Thanksgiving is the beginning of the **thoroughbred racing season** at the Fair Grounds (tel 504/944-5515; 1751 Gentilly Blvd., New Orleans, LA 70119; www.fgno.com). The day after Thanksgiving, **Celebration in the Oaks** begins, when millions of lights illuminate 1,500-acre City Park—and millions of people, it seems, line their cars up to drive through the park (tel 504/483-9415; 1 Palm Dr., New Orleans, LA 70124; www.neworleanscitypark.com). The lights are lit until the first week in January.

DECEMBER: Papa Noel parades into town ushering in **A New Orleans Christmas** (French Quarter Festivals: tel 504/522-5730; 400 N. Peters St., Suite 205, New Orleans, LA 70130; www.fqfi.org) and discounted hotel rates. The celebration lasts the whole month, with historic houses dolled up in 19th-century style, food demonstrations (surprise!), bonfires on the river, and many restaurants featuring Reveillon menus. (It was the Creole custom to have lavish dinners—called Reveillons—after Midnight Mass on Christmas Eve.) **New Year's Eve** is celebrated loudly, with booming, sizzling fireworks rousing the Ole Man again. And then danged if it ain't **New Year's Day,** and the whole thing starts all over again.

Newspapers... The only daily paper is the ***Times-Picayune,*** which carries local, national, and international news. The paper is owned by the Newhouse publishing conglomerate, but publisher Ashton Phelps is a New Orleanian. In the Quarter, **Matassa's Market** at 1001 Dauphine St. (tel 504/412-8700) and **Sidney's Wine Cellar** at 917 Decatur St. (tel 504/524-6872) carry the *New York Times.* Local monthlies like ***Aqui New Orleans*** (a Spanish-language paper) and ***Ambush Magazine*** and ***Impact Gulf South Gay News*** (both of which are gay- and lesbian-oriented) can be found around town, though pretty sporadically. Check in with **Tower Records,** 408 N. Peters St. (tel 504/529-8897). ***Gambit*** is a free weekly paper covering local news and happenings, with especially knowledgeable music listings; and ***Offbeat*** is a free monthly magazine with news and reviews of the music scene, available in bookstores, on newsstands, and in some hotels and music clubs.

Opening and closing times... Normal business hours are weekdays from 9am until 5pm. Banks are open from 9am until 3 or 4pm on weekdays. Banks are closed on New Orleans's two indigenous holidays, November 1 (All Saints Day) and Mardi Gras (Fat Tuesday). On Fat Tuesday, all offices close as well.

Parking... It makes the hair turn white just to contemplate parking in the French Quarter. The French Quarter is a very small residential area—a small town that everyone wants to visit. Quarter residents are issued parking permits—those who have cars, that is; a slew of them don't and never leave the Quarter anyway. It is not necessary to have a permit in order to park in the Quarter, but parking places are very scarce, and nobody—nobody—understands the signs. Parking in the considerably less-congested CBD and other parts of the city is much less of a hassle. But you must always beware of the tow-truck drivers (a term that strikes terror in the hearts of Orleanians). A government blue ribbon panel should do a study to ascertain what it is that makes these people relish their work so much. They move at lightning speed—locals have been seen flinging themselves across the hoods of their cars to prevent them from being towed away. Towed cars are taken, swiftly, to the **Claiborne Auto Pound** at 400 N. Claiborne Ave. (tel 504/565-7450). Precious few hotels in town offer free parking. However, be of good cheer: **Standard Parking** at 201 St. Charles Ave., Suite 4208 (tel 504/524-2919; www.standardparking.com) has more than 40 locations in the CBD and the Quarter. In the Quarter, there is secured indoor parking at **Standard Parking,** 911 Iberville St. (tel 504/522-5389); and at 528 Chartres St. (tel 504/523-2731). There are large open pay lots at the **Jax Brewery** (Decatur St. between Toulouse and St. Louis sts.) and behind the **French Market** (between Dumaine and Toulouse sts.). Outside the Quarter, **Central Parking Systems,** 365 Canal St., Suite 2330, Box 29 (tel 504/525-5476) operates garages at Poydras Plaza, 1301 Girod St., CBD (tel 504/524-5474) and at the New Orleans Centre, 1400 Denison St., CBD (tel 504/525-1451). **Standard Parking**

operates a garage at the LLE Tower, 909 Poydras St., CBD (tel 504/584-5065). And there is a huge (5,000-vehicle) indoor garage at the **Louisiana Superdome,** 1550 Sugar Bowl Dr., CBD (tel 504/587-3663).

Pharmacies... A pharmacy open 24 hours is **Walgreens,** 4400 S. Claiborne Ave. (tel 504/891-0976). Other Walgreens operate daily at 900 Canal St. (tel 504/568-9544), 3311 Canal St. (tel 504/822-8073), and 3057 Gentilly Blvd. (tel 504/282-2621). There's also a **Rite-Aid** in the Quarter at 3401 St. Charles Ave. (tel 504/896-4575).

Post offices... The **main office** of the U.S. Postal Service is at 701 Loyola Ave. (tel 504/589-1706). There is a branch in the French Quarter at 1022 Iberville St. (tel 504/525-4896). In the heart of the Quarter, the **French Quarter Postal Emporium,** 1000 Bourbon St. (tel 504/525-6651) is a private mail service that sells stamps and offers most services Uncle Sam provides, at a slightly higher price. They'll also wrap packages for shipping; sell you postcards, maps, and envelopes; and let you use their photocopying and fax machines—for a fee, of course.

Radio stations... For lots of talk, tune to **WSMB 1350 AM.** National Public Radio is on **WWNO 89.9 FM,** which also has late-night jazz. **WWOZ 90.7 FM** is the community radio station, with lots of jazz and news of musical happenings. Oldies are on **WTKL 90.5 FM,** country is on **WNOE 101.1 FM,** and rock and gospel are on **WYLD 940 AM.**

Restrooms... Downtown, there are clean public restrooms in the malls (Jax Brewery, Millhouse, Canal Place, New Orleans Centre, and Riverwalk). There are also public restrooms (note the absence of the adjective "clean") in the 900 and 1200 blocks of the French Market and at St. Louis Street in Woldenberg Riverfront Park. In City Park, there are facilities in the casino building, at 1 Dreyfous Ave. (where you pick up your City Park fishing permits and rent pedal boats), and in Audubon Park, at the tennis courts (Henry Clay and Tchoupitoulas sts.). Now, about Mardi Gras: The city's public facilities are perfectly adequate at all

> **Getting to Know the NOPD**
> *In 1993, a tourist staying in a CBD hotel got in her rental car, struck off down Canal Street, and made an illegal left turn–something that's all too easy to do on a street where turning left is a minor art form. She was arrested and taken to Central Lockup, where she was fingerprinted, strip-searched, deloused, and tossed in the clink. She was forced to spend the night there before frantic out-of-town relatives could spring her. Okay, besides making an illegal turn, this "criminal" was also driving without a license. Still, the poor woman will probably never recover from the ordeal.* ***The New Orleans Police Department*** *defended themselves, however, by saying she was treated no differently from any other persons who likewise break the law. That's a relief, isn't it? All of which is an introduction to the NOPD. Their work is dangerous and difficult, which is probably why they get extra pissed off for the minor, irritating infractions common with tourists. With these they seem to vie with local tow-truck drivers and meter maids in their zeal. Knowing this, it's wise to exercise extreme caution: Don't speed, don't drive without a license, do not drive while drinking, and obey all traffic signs. Or else.*

other times, except on Fat Tuesday. On Fat Tuesday, you have a million or so beer-swilling people milling around Downtown. The city sets up portable toilets in the CBD and in the Quarter, but not nearly enough of them. In self-defense, local hoteliers and restaurateurs—who are accustomed to anything during Mardi Gras—post signs proclaiming "Restrooms for customers only."

Smoking... If you're a nonsmoker, you'll be pleased to note that New Orleans has a lot of the same restrictions that apply in other cities. If you're a smoker, you'll be happy to know they have not banned it from bars and restaurants—yet. Smoking is prohibited in all public buildings, doctors' offices, hospitals, theater lobbies, the Superdome (except for the corridors, and they will probably become "smoke-free" as well), streetcars, and buses. Most taxicabs also post NO SMOKING signs.

Taxes... Combined local and state sales tax comes to 9%. Hotels are worse: The hotel tax is 11%, but the city imposes an additional $1 to $3 per room per night, depending on how many rooms are in the property. The bigger the hotel, the bigger the bite. This little fundraiser for the city coffers takes a lot of visitors by surprise. The state offers some relief for visitors from out of the country in its **Louisiana Tax-Free Shopping program (LTFS;** tel 504/568-5323; www.lousianataxfree.com). International visitors can get a sales tax refund by following the bouncing ball thusly: Buy stuff in a store that displays the LTFS insignia and obtain a voucher with your sales receipt. Just before your departure from the city, present the voucher and receipt at the LTFS refund office at the airport, along with your passport and round-trip airline ticket of less than 90 days' duration. Refunds of up to $500 will be made in cash on the spot. Refunds in excess of that will be mailed to your home address.

Taxis and limos... The most ubiquitous taxi company is **United Cab Company** (tel 504/522-9771). If you can't get through to United, call **Checker-Yellow Cabs** (tel 504/ 943-2411). Many local cabs accept plastic (though Checker doesn't); ask in advance for a car that accepts the cards you're carrying. Don't be startled by the local cabdrivers' custom—usually—of leaping out to open the back door. In-town fare starts at $2.50, plus 20 cents for each one-third of a mile or 40 seconds, plus $1 for each additional passenger—in other words, if there are two of you, the fare jumps to $3.50 first crack out of the box. For traveling in style, call **London Livery** (tel 504/586-0700, 800/284-0660), **A Touch of Class** (tel 504/522-7565), or **Signature Livery** (tel 504/523-5466; www.signaturelivery.com).

Tipping... New Orleans is not typically American, except in the tipping department. If you can find an airport skycap, tip a buck per bag. Cabdrivers get about 10% of the fare. Tip 15% to 20% in restaurants, and leave $2 to $3 per night for the hotel maid.

Trains... Amtrak trains arrive and depart at **Union Passenger Terminal,** 1001 Loyola Ave., CBD (tel 800/872-7245; www.amtrak.com).

Travelers with disabilities... Somewhat surprisingly, since the city has only recently roused itself from its 19th-century slumber, there are a number of advocacy groups for people with disabilities. Some of the more active are the **Advocacy Center for the Elderly and Disabled,** 225 Baronne St., Suite 2112 (tel 504/522-2337, 800/960-7705, voice or TDD); and the **Easter Seal Society of Louisiana for Children and Adults with Disabilities,** 305 Baronne

St., 4th floor (tel 504/523-7325 voice or TDD, or 800/ 695-SEAL). Travelers with hearing disabilities may contact the **Louisiana Commission for the Deaf,** 8225 Florida Blvd., Baton Rouge, LA 70806 (tel 800/256-1523 voice, 800/543-2099 TDD). Or make a call using the **Louisiana Relay Service** (tel 800/947–5277 voice, 504/ 525-3323 TT, 800/846-5277 TDD). Both www.access-able.com and www.cripworld.com provide excellent online resources.

TV channels... The local CBS affiliate is **WWL-TV,** channel 4; NBC is **WDSU-TV,** channel 6; ABC is **WGNO-TV,** channel 26; Fox is **WVUE-TV,** channel 8, and PBS is **WYES-TV,** channel 12. On Fat Tuesday, local anchors on channels 4, 6, and 8 usually provide live coverage decked out in costumes and beads.

Visitor information... For information before you take off, contact the **New Orleans Metropolitan Convention and Visitors Bureau,** 2020 St. Charles Ave., 70130 (tel 504/ 566-5011, 800/672-6124; www.nawlins.com). Other good websites are www.neworleans.com, www.nola.com, and www.bestofneworleans.com. After you've hit town, head for the bureau's **New Orleans Welcome Center** on Jackson Square, 529 St. Ann St. (tel 504/568-5661). The **Folklife Center of the Jean Lafitte National Historical Park,** 419 Decatur St., French Quarter (tel 504/589-2636) has information about the French Quarter, as well as about the parks at **Chalmette Battlefield** and **Barataria** (see the Diversions chapter).

GENERAL INDEX

Accommodations

Restaurants

Notes

Notes

Notes

Notes

Notes

Notes

Suzy Gershman's Born to Shop Guides

The Ultimate Guide for People Who Love Good Value!

Check out the complete list of Born to Shop Guides:

- France
- Italy
- Hong Kong, Shanghai & Beijing
- London
- New York
- Paris

Frommer's

Frommer's® Complete Travel Guides

Alaska
Alaska Cruises & Ports of Call
American Southwest
Amsterdam
Argentina & Chile
Arizona
Atlanta
Australia
Austria
Bahamas
Barcelona, Madrid & Seville
Beijing
Belgium, Holland & Luxembourg
Bermuda
Boston
Brazil
British Columbia & the Canadian Rockies
Brussels & Bruges
Budapest & the Best of Hungary
Calgary
California
Canada
Cancún, Cozumel & the Yucatán
Cape Cod, Nantucket & Martha's Vineyard
Caribbean
Caribbean Ports of Call
Carolinas & Georgia
Chicago
China
Colorado
Costa Rica
Cruises & Ports of Call
Cuba
Denmark
Denver, Boulder & Colorado Springs
England
Europe
Europe by Rail
European Cruises & Ports of Call
Florence, Tuscany & Umbria
Florida
France
Germany
Great Britain
Greece
Greek Islands
Halifax
Hawaii
Hong Kong
Honolulu, Waikiki & Oahu
India
Ireland
Italy
Jamaica
Japan
Kauai
Las Vegas
London
Los Angeles
Maryland & Delaware
Maui
Mexico
Montana & Wyoming
Montréal & Québec City
Munich & the Bavarian Alps
Nashville & Memphis
New England
Newfoundland & Labrador
New Mexico
New Orleans
New York City
New York State
New Zealand
Northern Italy
Norway
Nova Scotia, New Brunswick & Prince Edward Island
Oregon
Ottawa
Paris
Peru
Philadelphia & the Amish Country
Portugal
Prague & the Best of the Czech Republic
Provence & the Riviera
Puerto Rico
Rome
San Antonio & Austin
San Diego
San Francisco
Santa Fe, Taos & Albuquerque
Scandinavia
Scotland
Seattle
Shanghai
Sicily
Singapore & Malaysia
South Africa
South America
South Florida
South Pacific
Southeast Asia
Spain
Sweden
Switzerland
Texas
Thailand
Tokyo
Toronto
Turkey
USA
Utah
Vancouver & Victoria
Vermont, New Hampshire & Maine
Vienna & the Danube Valley
Virgin Islands
Virginia
Walt Disney World® & Orlando
Washington, D.C.
Washington State

Frommer's® Dollar-a-Day Guides

Australia from $50 a Day
California from $70 a Day
England from $75 a Day
Europe from $85 a Day
Florida from $70 a Day
Hawaii from $80 a Day
Ireland from $80 a Day
Italy from $70 a Day
London from $90 a Day
New York City from $90 a Day
Paris from $90 a Day
San Francisco from $70 a Day
Washington, D.C. from $80 a Day
Portable London from $90 a Day
Portable New York City from $90 a Day
Portable Paris from $90 a Day

Frommer's® Portable Guides

Acapulco, Ixtapa & Zihuatanejo
Amsterdam
Aruba
Australia's Great Barrier Reef
Bahamas
Berlin
Big Island of Hawaii
Boston
California Wine Country
Cancún
Cayman Islands
Charleston
Chicago
Disneyland®
Dominican Republic
Dublin
Florence
Frankfurt
Hong Kong
Las Vegas
Las Vegas for Non-Gamblers
London
Los Angeles
Los Cabos & Baja
Maine Coast
Maui
Miami
Nantucket & Martha's Vineyard
New Orleans
New York City
Paris
Phoenix & Scottsdale
Portland
Puerto Rico
Puerto Vallarta, Manzanillo & Guadalajara
Rio de Janeiro
San Diego
San Francisco
Savannah
Vancouver
Vancouver Island
Venice
Virgin Islands
Washington, D.C.
Whistler

Frommer's® National Park Guides

Algonquin Provincial Park
Banff & Jasper
Family Vacations in the National Parks
Grand Canyon
National Parks of the American West
Rocky Mountain
Yellowstone & Grand Teton
Yosemite & Sequoia/Kings Canyon
Zion & Bryce Canyon

Frommer's® Memorable Walks

Chicago
London
New York
Paris
San Francisco

Frommer's® With Kids Guides

Chicago
Las Vegas
New York City
Ottawa
San Francisco
Toronto
Vancouver
Walt Disney World® & Orlando
Washington, D.C.

Suzy Gershman's Born to Shop Guides

Born to Shop: France
Born to Shop: Hong Kong, Shanghai & Beijing
Born to Shop: Italy
Born to Shop: London
Born to Shop: New York
Born to Shop: Paris

Frommer's® Irreverent Guides

Amsterdam
Boston
Chicago
Las Vegas
London
Los Angeles
Manhattan
New Orleans
Paris
Rome
San Francisco
Seattle & Portland
Vancouver
Walt Disney World®
Washington, D.C.

Frommer's® Best-Loved Driving Tours

Austria
Britain
California
France
Germany
Ireland
Italy
New England
Northern Italy
Scotland
Spain
Tuscany & Umbria

The Unofficial Guides®

Beyond Disney
California with Kids
Central Italy
Chicago
Cruises
Disneyland®
England
Florida
Florida with Kids
Inside Disney
Hawaii
Las Vegas
London
Maui
Mexico's Best Beach Resorts
Mini Las Vegas
Mini Mickey
New Orleans
New York City
Paris
San Francisco
Skiing & Snowboarding in the West
South Florida including Miami & the Keys
Walt Disney World®
Walt Disney World® for Grown-ups
Walt Disney World® with Kids
Washington, D.C.

Special-Interest Titles

Athens Past & Present
Cities Ranked & Rated
Frommer's Best Day Trips from London
Frommer's Best RV & Tent Campgrounds in the U.S.A.
Frommer's Caribbean Hideaways
Frommer's China: The 50 Most Memorable Trips
Frommer's Exploring America by RV
Frommer's Gay & Lesbian Europe
Frommer's NYC Free & Dirt Cheap
Frommer's Road Atlas Europe
Frommer's Road Atlas France
Frommer's Road Atlas Ireland
Frommer's Wonderful Weekends from New York City
The New York Times' Guide to Unforgettable Weekends
Retirement Places Rated
Rome Past & Present